1968

ON THE EDGE OF WORLD REVOLUTION

Philipp Gassert and
Martin Klimke (eds.)

FOREWORD BY DIMITRIOS ROUSSOPOULOS

Montréal • New York • Chicago • London

Copyright ©2018 Black Rose Books

No part of this book may be reproduced or transmitted in any form, by any means electronic or mechanical including photocopying and recording, or by any information storage or retrieval system – without written permission from the publisher, or, in the case of photocopying or other reprographic copying, a license from the Canadian Copyright Licensing Agency, Access Copyright, with the exception of brief passages quoted by a reviewer in a newspaper or magazine.

Black Rose Books No. SS392

Library and Archives Canada Cataloguing in Publication

    1968 : on the edge of world revolution / edited by Philipp Gassert and Martin Klimke.

Issued in print and electronic formats.
ISBN 978-1-55164-647-3 (hardcover).—ISBN 978-1-55164-645-9 (softcover).—ISBN 978-1-55164-649-7 (PDF)

    1. Nineteen sixty-eight, A.D. 2. History, Modern—1945-1989. 3. Radicalism—History—20th century. 4. Insurgency—History—20th century. 5. Political violence—History—20th century. I. Gassert, Philipp, editor II. Klimke, Martin, editor III. Title: Nineteen sixty-eight.

D848.A193 2018   909.82'6   C2018-901282-X
                                                                         C2018-901283-8

Cover Design: A.J,.Specht

C.P. 35788 Succ. Léo Pariseau
Montréal, QC H2X 0A4
CANADA
www.blackrosebooks.com

ORDERING INFORMATION:

USA/INTERNATIONAL	CANADA	UK/EUROPE
University of Chicago Press Chicago Distribution Center 11030 South Langley Avenue Chicago IL 60628	University of Toronto Press 5201 Dufferin Street Toronto, ON M3H 5T8	Central Books Freshwater Road Dagenham RM8 1RX
(800) 621-2736 (USA) (773) 702-7000 (International) orders@press.uchicago.edu	1-800-565-9523 utpbooks@utpress.utoronto.ca	+44 (0) 20 852 8800 contactus@centralbooks.com

Black Rose Books is the publishing project of Cercle Noir et Rouge

TABLE OF CONTENTS

vii	**Foreword** Dimitrios Roussopoulos
5	**Introduction: 1968 from Revolt to Research** Philipp Gassert and Martin Klimke

THE AMERICAS

27	**Argentina: The Signs and Images of "Revolutionary War"** Hugo Vezzetti
33	**Bolivia: Che Guevara in Global History** Carlos Soria-Galvarro
39	**Canada: 1968 and the New Left** Dimitrios Roussopoulos
47	**Colombia: The "Cataluña Movement"** Santiago Castro-Gomez
51	**Mexico: The Power of Memory** Sergio Raúl Arroyo
57	**Peru: The Beginning of a New World** Oscar Ugarteche
63	**USA: Unending 1968** Todd Gitlin
67	**Venezuela: A Sociological Laboratory** Félix Allueva

ASIA & AUSTRALIA

73   **Australia: A Nation of Lotus-Eaters**
Hugh Mackay

79   **China: The Process of Decolonization in the Case of Hong Kong**
Oscar Ho Hing-kay

83   **India: Outsiders in Two Worlds**
Kiran Nagarkar

89   **Japan: "1968"–History of a Decade**
Claudia Derichs

95   **Pakistan: The Year of Change**
Ghazi Salahuddin

99   **Thailand: The "October Movement" and the Transformation to Democracy**
Kittisak Prokati

AFRICA & THE MIDDLE EAST

105   **Egypt: From Romanticism to Realism**
Ibrahim Farghali

111   **Israel: 1968 and the "'67 Generation"**
Gilad Margalit

119   **Lebanon: Of Things that Remain Unsaid**
Rachid al-Daif

125   **Palestinian Territories: Discovering Freedom in a Refugee Camp**
Hassan Khadr

129   **Senegal: May 1968, Africa's Revolt**
Andy Stafford

137   **South Africa: Where Were We Looking in 1968?**
          John Daniel and Peter Vale

147   **Syria: The Children of the Six-Day War**
          Mouaffaq Nyrabia

EASTERN EUROPE

155   **Czechoslovakia: Lines of Tanks in Prague**
          Petruîka Šustrová

159   **East Germany: "Solidarity with Red Prague"**
          Philipp Gassert and Elisabeth Piller

163   **Hungary: The Year of Disillusionment**
          László Márton

167   **Poland: The March Events of 1968**
          Jerzy Eisler

171   **Russia: The Philosophy of the Long-Haired Rebellion**
          Victor Yerofeyev

175   **Turkey: The Lost Generation**
          Zafer Şenocak

181   **Yugoslavia: "Down with the Red Bourgeoisie!"**
          Želimir Žilnik

WESTERN EUROPE

191   **Belgium: The End Started in 1968**
          Paul Goossens

195   **Denmark: Protest and Pragmatism**
          Thomas Ekman Jørgensen

199	**France: A Journey to Freedom** Mohammad Bennis	
205	**Great Britain: "No Place for a Street Fighting Man"** Hans Kundnani	
209	**Greece: The Other Side of 1968** Petros Markaris	
213	**Ireland: Breaking the Shackles** Nell McCafferty	
219	**Italy: "We Demand the Impossible"** Giuseppe Carlo Marino	
225	**Netherlands: The Second Liberation** Roel van Duijn	
231	**Norway: A Political Awakening** Dag Solstad	
235	**Sweden: What Happened to 1968?** Svante Weyler	
239	**West Germany: A Return from Cultural Nostalgia to Political Analysis** Claus Leggewie	
247	**EPILOGUE: ONE, TWO, THREE, MANY 1968s? A PANEL DISCUSSION** Norman Birnbaum, Patty Lee Parmalee, and Tom Hayden	
265	**ACKNOWLEDGMENTS**	
266	**PHOTO CREDITS**	

FOREWORD

Dimitrios Roussopoulos

No previous social and political upheaval matches the scope of 1968. If one examines the revolutions of 1789, 1793, 1848, 1871, 1905, 1917 and 1936, and the many other revolutions that have taken place in Asia or Central and Latin America since then, none matches 1968—and where and how this wild fire spread across the world in only a year. The book in hand is seminal in this regard. The year 1968 still requires further research; however this book is a worthy beginning. It is also one of the few that covers the entirety of 1968. There is an old Greek proverb that should be kept in mind by readers, 'when the finger points to the sun, the idiot looks at the finger.'

Early in 1968, Murray Bookchin found himself in Paris, where he met and discussed with a whole range of left-wing intellectuals and activists, 'what is happening, where are radical politics today, what is likely to happen?' He encountered nothing but gloom and hopelessness.[1] By March of that same year, the whole city was on the move.

It bears underlining that nobody foresaw 1968. True, those of us who were working on trying to build the foundations of a new society during that decade—bringing together thousands of youth across several countries into the new left—had high expectations. But what happened in 1968 burst upon the world without warning.

We know that 1848 witnessed extraordinary revolutions: in that year the old imperial power and absolutism throughout Europe was shaken to its foundations. The advocates of the new social values were defeated for the main part, but their ideas and actions left a permanent imprint upon the development of that continent and the world. The revolutions of 1848 were part of the political and social consequences of a profound industrial revolution slowly and forcefully being born.

In 1968, all modern industrial societies, whether capitalist, socialist or social democratic, underwent upheavals under the advance of an onrushing revolutionary technology, with the most complex social and political problems arising from it. This jarred the international political and economic systems, in particular those which had grown up around industrial states. In over twenty-five countries, youth-led rebellions had left a mark on the social order in 1968. The war in Vietnam, the student revolts and general strikes, the threatened collapse of the Western monetary system, the transformation in Czechoslovakia and the Soviet invasion, the wars and civil wars in Africa and the Middle East, the manned flight around the moon, China's 'cultural revolution', the murders of Martin Luther King and U.S. presidential candidate Robert Kennedy, suggest a struggle between revolution and counter-revolution.

What is significant is that the upheavals that took place in 1968 had a momentum of their own, and that the degree to which individuals appeared as inspiring or controlling them in a significant way is more often than not an illusion. What is needed is a new set of insights or theory of dual consciousness, which can account for abrupt and unexpected ruptures and shifts. Social consciousness shows uneven and combined developments as does history. What made students and other youth, a social group that had been integrated into society, turn into society's most radical force? To be sure, a new subjectivity evolved throughout the sixties, which had a pronounced cultural dimension. No revolution can occur before maturity, and maturity is the phase in which the forces of material circumstances that shape much of history have brought about a decisive development in consciousness. We know that a very large part of a modern capitalist economy and social life (market or state capitalism) is generally given over to the production of consciousness. One only need be reminded of the ideological power of mass entertainment in its various forms, and of consumerism and the drive to money-making security. And yet the 1968 revolt took place among these same strata. Recall a June 1968 cry by a young person, "I was an imbecile. I believed that I alone could rebel and that this was first and foremost an individual act."[2][3]

In North America, which is often the cutting edge of new waves of social grassroots action, the year 1968 had witnessed an extraordinary upsurge in Mexico, the U.S. and Quebec. The major segments of these societies were students, Afro-Americans and Franco-Quebecers. As well as a number of ethnic and radical groups, the wave included certain sections of the new and industrial working class. There were more strikes in 1967 and 1968 than in any year since 1947.

College and university students led protests across the continent on an unprecedented scale, joined for the first time by a significant number of high school (secondary school) students. This development heralded new areas for radical organizing, because high schoolers and their decisions determined not only the tempo of future insurgency on campuses but also the nature of the future labour force. In October 1968, for example, of greater importance than the 55 terrorist bombings by the FLQ in Quebec was the general strike of more than 50,000 students in the technical and junior colleges, which in some cases lasted up to six weeks. This wave of school occupations was an advance in the forms of direct action used and it inspired the class conscious of the working population (winning nominal trade union support) and among university students who had previously been unengaged.

Fortune magazine (the preferred periodical of the corporate elite) reported during this period that approximately 40% of American college students showed a "lack of concern about making money" and tended to "embrace positions that are dissident and extreme." This magazine hired an opinion research firm to conduct a survey of people in the 18 to 24 age bracket in October, only to discover that about 750,000 students "identify with the new left". Further, it was revealed that such radical notions were affecting the thinking and behaviour of the rest of the student population.[4]

The English left-of-center newspaper, the *Guardian*, noted in a Viewpoint piece that "The great strength of the new left has come from the ability to change course when the demands of political struggle indicate change. We view the present transition in that light. One great weakness of the new left, however, has often been the failure to implement theoretical developments in practice. We hope that the youth movement resolution will produce more than a new level of rhetoric."[4]

Part of the political earthquake of 1968 was the Soviet invasion of Czechoslovakia in August of that year. Three editors of the Montreal-based new left quarterly journal, *Our Generation*, attended the new left congress of the German SDS in Frankfurt, after which we went to Prague. Lucia Kowaluk, Jogues Girard and myself met a large number of personalities in Prague who were attempting everywhere to instill a spirit of reconstruction, a new sense of purpose, a feeling of experimenting with new forms of "democratizing the socialist revolution", and about which there was open debate. We left Prague four hours before the Warsaw Pact troops crossed the border to crush what was being advanced, with great hope. In fact we did not know about the invasion until our train arrived in Ljubljana, in then-Yugoslavia, for two meetings. The first meeting was of the international council of the International Confederation of Disarmament and Peace (founded at Oxford University it grouped together the non-aligned—that is independent of both Moscow and Washington, peace movements of the 1960s)—and later with the German SDS, a second meeting bringing together for the first time activists in the SDS of the U.S., the new left S.U.P.A.[Student Union for Peace Action] in Canada, and a range of new left activists from Britain, Germany and other European countries. It was one of the first face-to-face meetings of the new generation of young radicals, a rare experience in a pre-internet era. The main means of contact between the new radicals—about what was happening in various parts of the world was through travel, the telephone, photo-journalism and television reporting of major events.

What 1968 showed in Paris and much of France, was, after all a logical evolution of events which had already occurred in Berlin and New York. *The Observer*, newspaper in Britain, in its May 19, 1968 issues summed it up thus:

"This is revolution. What is happening in the Sorbonne and the Free University of Berlin, in France, West Germany, Italy and (embryonically) in Britain, is not a mere generational conflict. Nor is it just a fight for university reform—not any more. It is a total onslaught on modern society...This particular rising will probably fall. Its roots are too shallow, the State, its enemy, too massive. But it has already stormed places thought impregnable...

> "The enemy is the 'bureaucratic State – east and west. It is the society organized for efficiency at the expense of liberty, the system which 'offers the people consumer goods and calls them freedom'. It is the system which adapts education—so it seems—to the mass production of docile technocrats. It is the party system posing as true democracy, repression masked as tolerance."[5]

Or, in conclusion, consider the insightful words of the celebrated playwright Arthur Miller:

> "From Moscow to Warsaw to Prague to Paris to Rio to Berkeley and New York, there is a deep and boiling rebellion against institutions and institutionalized feeling. Be it a government, a university, a moral code or a way of life, the institution as king is naked now. The mere fact that it exists is no longer

proof of its value. In the past four years the war in Vietnam has become an institution, an institution with high private, sacred ceremonies of death and sacrifice, and all the sanctifications of a holy crusade…" 5

Let us celebrate 1968, and dig deeper into its history. The deep desire for radical social change is still there, under the surface. The institutions of top-down power are more naked than ever. An experience fed consciousness will surface again among both young and older as, for example, during the massive student strike of 2012 in Quebec. In the meantime let us work at posing alternatives to what is, to our fellows, meet with them, face to face, because the enduring lesson of the 60s is that community is [in] a process of construction.

ENDNOTES

1. Murray Bookchin and Dimitri Roussopoulos in conversation, Montreal, 1969.
2. L'Evenement, (Paris), June 1968
3. See the studies of Kenneth Keniston, *The Uncommitted–alienated youth in American society*, 1965, Harcourt, Brace & World, New York and *Young Radicals–notes on committed youth*, 1968, Harcourt, Brace & World, New York.
4. Our Generation, Vol.6, No.3 , January 1969
5. Our Generation, Vol. 6, Nos.1 & 2, July 1968

INTRODUCTION

1968 FROM REVOLT TO RESEARCH

Philipp Gassert and Martin Klimke

In May 1968, after the occupation of the main building at the Sorbonne had been ended by French police, the young Franco-German student leader, Daniel Cohn-Bendit, stood trial in a court in Paris. When the judge kept demanding his name, he finally identified himself as "Kuroń-Modzelewski," using the names of two well-known Polish dissidents of the 1960s (who would later become the founding fathers of the 1980s Polish oppositional movement *Solidarność*).[1]

By 1968, Jacek Kuroń's and Karol Modzelewski's 1964 "Open Letter to the Party," in which they had criticized Poland's stale postwar communism, was widely circulated among Western students. As the 1968 preface to the English edition suggested,

> the worldwide wave of protests, rallies, marches, sit-ins, and battles with the police have brought consternation to the capitalist establishment of the West and the bureaucratic establishment of the deformed workers' states of the East; they have brought hope and inspiration to truly revolutionary socialist forces everywhere.[2]

Even though Western European students knew little about the nature and causes of events in Eastern Europe (not to mention the so-called Third World), they readily imagined themselves as part of the same global fight against capitalist exploitation and communist repression, against colonial rule and imperialist domination. After all, 1968 saw the eruption of protests all over the globe, which stretched—it has become a cliché—from Berkeley to Berlin, from Bangkok to Buenos Aires, and from Cairo to Cape Town.[3]

While protests played out primarily on national stages, the rebellious young people of 1968 sincerely believed that they were involved in a struggle against established orders (and world orders) worldwide.[4] The student (and sometimes worker) unrest in almost every country around the globe, along with major challenges to superpower hegemony, further reinforced their vision. These uprisings and challenges included Chairman Mao's reigning in of the "Cultural Revolution" turned terrorist nightmare in China, the North Vietnamese Tet Offensive, and the Prague Spring.[5]

During the late 1960s, political unrest, thus, was by no means limited to the advanced capitalist societies of the West. It had an immediate impact on the political culture of the socialist Eastern countries, as well. Furthermore, there were long-term repercussions in the Middle East, Africa, Asia, and Latin America. With respect to Eastern Europe, only Czechoslovakia, Poland, and Yugoslavia saw major disruptions. Yet East Germany, Hungary, Russia, the Ukraine, and others were indirectly affected by the Prague Spring. After the tanks had quashed hopes of reform in Prague, dissident movements received a new start.[6]

In the Middle East, the Six-Day War of 1967, as an event, greatly overshadowed the less dramatic social transformation of societies. Yet here, too, some of the essential '60s reforms, such as experimenting with new forms of cultural, intellectual, and political expression, took place. In Syria, students took the streets raising questions about sexuality. In the Palestinian Territories, paternal authority was in decline. In Israel, one year after the military triumph of 1967, no one staged protest demonstrations, yet beneath the surface, the seeds of an intellectual, anti-militarist, and pacifist critique had been sown.[7]

As the individual chapters in this book demonstrate, protesters and activists were aware of what was going on across borders and across oceans. They were inspired by "Tet" and the "French May." They were outraged by the attempted assassination of Rudi Dutschke in Berlin and the Soviet invasion. While the motives for protests varied from country to country, people readily imagined themselves as part of a global community of protest.

This global nexus of protesters in various countries did not escape the attention of established political forces across the globe. In West Germany, Federal Chancellor Kurt Georg Kiesinger summarily labeled student unrest an American revolutionary export.[8] On the American side, the executive secretary of the US State Department's Inter-Agency Youth Committee, Robert Cross, described the youth of the 1960s as the "first truly international generation." For Cross, this was not the result of well-established, organizational infrastructure but from "a great cross-fertilization, a very rapid and effective student grape-vine" that developed when students with similar political and philosophical problems looked to peers in other countries to solve them. As Cross summed it up, "What happens in New York is known overnight in

Paris and Manila. The speeches of Rudi Dutschke are in the hands of Mark Rudd faster than you can seem to get your mail delivered."[9]

The globalism of 1968 captured more than just *contemporary* imaginations. Forty years on, "1968"—the preferred shorthand for the social and cultural transformations of the "Sixties" in most of continental Europe—has become a powerful myth. "1968" lingers on in memory all over Europe, in Asia, and in the Americas. In the culture wars of our time, it has grown so powerful that politicians like French President Nicolas Sarkozy or his Mexican counterpart Felipe Calderón have used it to stake out political territory.[10] Forty years later, this imagined "global '68" still stirs up raw and powerful emotions.

Such intense retrospective interest calls for an explanation. While, by now, most scholars in Europe and North America acknowledge that "1968"—the actual events as well as the imagined connection—had a global quality (which was not a common view only ten to fifteen years ago), few have attempted to present the events of that "crucial decade" in a country-by-country survey. Barely more attention has been given to answering the riddle of why "1968" still strikes a chord in people's imaginations.

This book hopes to fill this gap by presenting voices on "1968" from more than three dozen countries. It grew out of a digital project by the Goethe-Institut in 2008 to commemorate the fortieth anniversary (broadly conceived) of the events of the late 1960s and early 1970s and out of a series of events held at the Goethe-Institut and the German Historical Institute in Washington, DC.[11] The perspectives represented here are necessarily subjective and occasionally contradictory and provocative, yet both their analytical and at times emotional elements aptly illustrate the plethora of approaches to "1968" in today's memorial culture. Although this volume cannot do justice to the complexity of the questions involved, we hope that the following contributions from a variety of intellectuals, historians, artists, and activists can provide impulses for further discussion and research on the imagined global revolution around 1968. To this end, we asked contributors to reflect personally on the events and their legacies in their respective countries, as well as to provide a short survey of those events.

The making of 1968 as memory and history

Why is it that "1968" is still so viciously contested in contemporary memory? And how does historiography come into the picture? In his masterful survey of the 1960s, Gerry DeGroot observed, "After the decade died, it rose again as religion."[12] This is true. In 2007, the "1968" memory train went into overdrive. The number of conferences, books, and lecture series devoted to "1968" has been without parallel. One historian even spoke of a "publicistic orgy" that has swept Europe.[13] All over the continent, the memory of "1968" has gone far beyond the level of personal anecdote and public acknowledgment, coming to signify something larger.

While this critical mid-century decade "refuses to go away" and while stories of "1968" still allow contemporary actors to stake out political claims, the 1960s are ever more an object of historical inquiry. By this we mean that "1968" is now being studied with the methods of the historical sciences. Historians, many born long after the 1960s, or, in any case, too young to remember this "crucial decade," have started to dig into the archives. They increasingly analyze the events of the late 1960s within the decade's long-term contexts, such as the breakthrough to consumer society,[14] the struggles for Third World liberation,[15] the temporary ebbing of the Cold War,[16] and the emergence of new cultural and political formations in Western countries that have been labeled "postmodernity" or "postindustrial society."[17]

At first glance, this simultaneous politicization and historicization of "1968" may strike observers as a paradox: Does writing the 1960s into history not mean that they lose their contemporary usefulness?[18] This perspective, however, overlooks historiography's perpetual (and not disinterested) role in the process of translating events into bits and pieces of cultural memory. As Jan Assmann and others have argued, memories of specific historical events often gain in their potential to generate controversy before being absorbed into a new consensus.[19] Historical master narratives are generated by preceding controversy. "Historicization" and "mythologization" are not necessarily opposed to each other. Rather, they may be two sides of the same coin.[20]

A survey of the current literature thus may help us to understand why memories of "1968" linger and how they are constructed. By providing a brief overview of current research that focuses primarily on the transatlantic dimension, we also hope to demonstrate to non-specialist audiences how history as a discipline helps to shape cultural memory. Although historians face stiff competition from other, often more visible sources of influence (such as media outlets, politicians, and contemporary eyewitnesses), their contribution is critical.

At the current crossroads in 1960s scholarship, we see five broad avenues professional historians have taken since "historicization" started in earnest about ten years ago.[21]

First: Social context. There is an emerging consensus that the movements of the 1960s need to be studied as part and parcel of the great postwar transformations. The precise relationship between protest activities—especially during the late 1960s, when youth unrest exploded all across the globe—and the profound social and cultural transformations that started as far back as in the late 1940s and 1950s, is still hotly debated, however.

Second: Global revolt. Starting in the second half of the 1990s, research has paid increasing attention to the transnational/global/international networks of "1968." Although contemporaries often took the interconnectedness of events for granted, few empirical studies have looked at specific processes of transnational cooperation and identification.

Third: Regional response. While the globalism of '68 has been en vogue in recent scholarship, more and more local studies have been published, too. Regional approaches are a sensible tool for understanding how '60s protests impacted the social and cultural fabric of societies. They give us insight into how the general trends of the 1960s were created or negotiated at the grass-roots level. They also help to integrate different viewpoints into a history of the 1960s.

Fourth: The establishment. Historians increasingly acknowledge that the interaction of established, i.e., institutionally entrenched, actors and "anti-establishment" forces shaped the events of the '60s protest movements. Both American and European historians frequently discuss the extent to which the dynamics between the two sides affected outcomes.

Fifth: The cultural turn. By now, cultural history has entered the historiographical mainstream. This means that the historical study of the '60s, as in other areas of historical investigation, abounds with works on cultural artifacts such as symbolic forms, rituals, performative staging, and the representations of protest in the media or in a variety of other locations. This research also pays greater attention to how "1968" is retrospectively constructed.

In the following survey, we will first look at each of these five major areas of investigation and then conclude with a few thoughts on why

"1968" has acquired such an important role in Western and global memory.

1968 in social context

A large number of historians decry the sensationalist treatment of the dramatic events of "1968" in public and its use for contemporary political positioning, arguing instead that the events desperately need to be understood within their long-term contexts. On the events in Germany, for example, Axel Schildt emphasizes that "1968" came on the heels of a dynamic modernization of German society that had been well under way since the late 1950s.[22] The New Left's rise to a mass phenomenon was more a symptom than a cause of change.[23]

In the American scholarly literature, this long-term perspective has been established for some time. It helps that the label "1968" is not very common in the English language. When used, it refers rather to the actual events of that year, in "which the dream died" (as the journalist Jules Witcover once put it).[24] In the American case, 1968 recalls the murders of Robert F. Kennedy and Martin Luther King Jr., the violent explosions in inner-city ghettos, and the confrontations during the "siege of Chicago." It is less about "Sex, Drugs, and Rock 'n' Roll." Debates about the 1960s rather than 1968 in America automatically evoke long-term views.[25]

Thus, what matters is not so much the overused label "1968," but the social transformations associated with the long 1960s that "1968" often stands for in continental Europe. Because "1968" evokes specific events, the history of the 1960s has often been turned into an abbreviated one that regards protest as a catalyst rather than a symptom of change. With regard to Eastern Europe, this narrow view of "1968" does not make much sense because there was not much protest activity outside Poland, the ČCSR, and (non-aligned) Yugoslavia in this particular year. Therefore, scholars of Warsaw Pact countries see "1968" more in the context of the long-term undermining of Soviet rule leading up to the events of the late 1980s.[26]

In Britain, Arthur Marwick's *Sixties* brought the history of "everyday" experiences back into the study of this era. Calling the postwar transformations a "cultural revolution," by which he meant a change in the habits and lifestyles of millions of people (and not just a small cultural and intellectual avant-garde), Marwick portrayed the emerging counterculture as being enabled by larger societal transformations rather than being the catalyst of change. More recently, Gerry DeGroot also made a conscious effort to ground the 1960s more thoroughly in the postwar period. His "kaleidoscopic history" of the decade starts with the end of World War II and broadens the subject by including both liberal and conservative actors, including Tom Hayden and the (conservative) Young Americans for Freedom, Robert F. Kennedy and Ronald Reagan, and the Rolling Stones as well as the Monkees.

In Germany, numerous monographs with long-term approaches have been published in the last ten years. Detlef Siegfried's study of the youth culture of the "long 1960s,"[27] Christina von Hodenberg's work on the emergence of the "critical paradigm" in journalism,[28] recent collections on the West German churches[29] and on how Germans "dealt with the Nazi Past"[30] all analyze the late 1960s as a time when long-term trends coalesced into a short-lived upsurge in protests.

Global 1968

A second area that has seen spectacular growth in scholarship is "Global 1968," a perspective that focuses on the emerging networks of protest worldwide, as well as the real and imagined cooperation among anti-establishment forces across national borders. A steady stream of publications has flowed on this theme since the 1990s. Yet few monographs have been devoted to the specifics of interaction.[31]

Nowadays, the conventional wisdom seems to be that "in the beginning there was America."[32] Even surveys that focus on Germany—like those of Norbert Frei and Wolfgang Kraushaar—open with descriptions of the rise and fall of the Californian-American counterculture.[33] They tell a story of humble beginnings among Beat Poets, the germinating Civil Rights Movement, the rise of the Free Speech Movement in Berkeley, the Haight-Ashbury "Summer of Love," and so on. After pausing at the great summit of Woodstock, such accounts then continue with the dystopian aspects of the protest culture, with the Manson murders and the nightmare of Altamont. This often serves as a boiler plate for developments elsewhere; for example, in Germany, where "1968" has been described as a descent from the February 1968 Vietnam Congress into RAF terrorism.[34]

Never has there been so much historical expertise on the various "1968s." Apart from the essays published in this volume, there are now studies available in English and German on many countries, including but not limited to Denmark, France, the Netherlands,

Northern Ireland, Sweden, Yugoslavia, etc.[35] The "French May" has been covered in hundreds of books, articles, and monographs. The long Italian "hot summer" has received an equal amount of attention.[36] Several collected volumes present varied and often problem-oriented approaches on various aspects of 1968, and many of them offer cross-cultural comparisons. With these individual country studies, we are now in a much better position to understand what the specifics of each "1968" were and how they resembled each other.[37]

Comparison needs to be informed by an understanding of interactions and mutual observation. For some time, social movement research has been interested in the question of the extent to which the success of individual movements hinges on transnational connections.[38] Diachronic comparison with earlier European revolutions suggests that movements in one national context can be jump-started by events across the border (as was the case with the French February revolution of 1848).[39]

Also, certain nonconformist networks like the Situationist International, first founded in France, with allies in Belgium, Denmark, Germany, Great Britian, and the Netherlands, have been the focus of research for a while now.[40] Similar to the American Beat poets, these networks helped to pave the way for the larger New Left revolt in the late 1960s. That the New Left in itself was an international phenomenon is almost a truism. Its networks were often grounded in the old Left, which had a transnational character, too.[41] Moreover, after the Hungarian crackdown in 1956, "consensus liberals" in various European and North American countries shared a disenchantment with Soviet communism.

For the German-American case, the basic research has been done. It demonstrates how important these interactions were for the development of movement tactics.[42] Similar studies are emerging in the Eastern European and Latin American context.[43] Historians are looking at the global interconnectedness of the Prague Spring.[44] Others explore the role that revolutionary imports played in South America and how these ideas were then reimported into the European context.[45] Although histories of the "Paris May" and "Prague 1968" are abundant, both places could serve as a global history case study. Historians could use Paris and Prague not only to understand how representations of events in one place influence actors abroad, but also which specific interactional mechanisms were at play. This would help to explain why certain events have gained canonic status in memories of 1968, whereas others have been forgotten.

Local 1968

While research on "1968" has gone global, increasing attention has been devoted to how protests played out in local contexts. This is particularly true for research on the United States and West Germany, but also for other European countries. Up to the 1990s, movement historians focused on the "epicenters of protest" such as the US West Coast, New York, Berlin, Frankfurt, Paris, Tokyo, or Mexico City. Such a centralist perspective may have made sense for launching research in this field because it was these central locations where events started or where they gained the attention of wider audiences. Yet local studies now provide a necessary complement to this view, revealing a much more nuanced and multi-faceted story.

Local studies are one good way to get a grasp of the social and cultural impact of protest movements. Movements faced similar challenges in different local areas. But they also had to deal with specific circumstances. While movements were often focused on global issues—such as the war in Vietnam or the postcolonial struggles in Africa and Latin America—the long-term consequences can best be understood if we look at specific communities. One study focusing on Philadelphia, for example, shows how the emerging New Left had to negotiate older traditions, the specific Quaker heritage of this city, as well as the often conflicting agendas of mostly white students and the sizeable civil rights movement there. This multi-perspectivity has certainly complicated the picture.[46]

Thus, it is at the local level that movement and establishment perspectives can most easily be examined together. A recent study on the German university town of Heidelberg, for example, looks at how the local student movement emerged slowly, months after events in Berlin had already reached their climax. Nevertheless, once the movement did emerge, the US military presence and the local government's willingness to take a stand against the students contributed to events stretching out for years.[47] This case suggests that different chronologies are required for various locations. In other countries, too, research with a local focus has often been centered on particular universities.[48]

As we can see, such local studies contribute to a more varied image of the '60s. In United States scholarship, historians have always looked beyond the campus revolt. As one monograph on Lawrence, Kansas, shows, the metaphorical "Sixties" were populated not only by the usual suspects, such as campus radicals, demonstrators against the war in Vietnam, intellectual dissenters, members of the civil rights movement, feminists, and radical groups like the Black Panthers and the Weathermen, but that conservatives also got into the game. Not unsuccessful in fending off quite a few challenges, conservatives also managed to change the rules.

That the "personal is political," for example, was once a Leftist sentence of faith. Yet conservatives were not afraid to follow the example of an originally Leftist counterculture. They also inaugurated processes of what the historian Rusty Monhollon has called the personalization of politics. While some made the political personal through their participations in the protest movements, others reacted with opposing political agendas driven by similar forms of protest. This all played itself out on the local level, where many critical decisions were made. In the end these small local changes added up to an overall transformation of culture and society.[49]

Bringing the establishment back in

From local studies, the crucial importance of the "other" side is quite evident. In addition to placing "1968" more firmly in the long postwar period and its transnational context, therefore, historians have increasingly begun to look at how protest was shaped by the interaction between movements and established actors.[50] In political science, students of social movements now see activists' ability to draw support from establishment actors as the single most crucial element for their success.[51] For example, as we know from South America, liberation theology, which became a powerful source of inspiration for activists during the 1970s and 1980s, had a firm grounding in the Catholic establishment of the 1960s.[52]

In fact, one less developed area of research seems to be the relationship between the churches and protest movements. In Germany, discussion has often centered on the question of whether its protests were culturally grounded in a Protestant milieu.[53] In Italy and Belgium, the Catholic Church played an active role as a target, stage, or commentator of protest.[54] In the United States, the link between protest movements and non-conformist religious groups such as the Quakers has a long tradition.[55] Obviously, the civil rights movement came out of established black churches.

In most of Europe, the labor movement, represented by the labor unions, was another established force that should not be overlooked. Unions and workers were a contributing and sometimes driving factor in the events that were unfolding during the late 1960s.[56] The German demonstrations against the so-called emergency laws were pushed by well-established labor unions such IG Metall.[57]

The relationship between activists and established political figures, likewise, is increasingly scrutinized. From research on West Germany's student movement, we now know that many politicians were sympathetic to it, even though they quite adamantly criticized violent excesses.[58] Götz Aly, although sensationalizing (and superficial) in drawing parallels between the student movement of the late '60s and the National Socialist seizure of power in 1933, provided some remarkable insight into the discussions within the chancellor's office in Bonn. Chancellor Kiesinger and some of his advisers perceived the students as helpful in broadening democratic attitudes in Germany.[59] Martin Klimke's research on discussions within the White House demonstrates that agencies such as the CIA were quite perceptive in their analysis of worldwide student unrest.[60]

Anyone who wishes to understand the long-term consequences of the '60s would be well advised to look at how the cultural revolutions of the 1960s were absorbed by established actors, within institutions like political parties and especially universities.[61] The impact on academia became a very contentious issue during the 1980s in the US, when the '60s counterculture was blamed for a "closing of the American mind." The argument could be made, however, that new academic paradigms and fads coming out of the 1960s, such as ethnic and women's studies, post-colonialism, and the much broader cultural studies, have further strengthened the cultural influence of the United States abroad.[62] For most European countries, though, we know very little about how the reform impulses worked themselves out within the university system.[63]

A particularly interesting point is how the originally New Leftist impulses of "1968" were picked up by activists on the other side of the political spectrum.[64] In the US, grass-roots organizations that resisted liberal reforms, such as busing or the Equal Rights Amendment, successfully acquired tactics from the '60s movement. Similarly, the youth organization of the (conservative) Christian Democratic Union (CDU) in Germany hoped to learn from the New Left. Furthermore, conservative evangelical Christians were quite willing to adopt countercultural methods.[65]

With more and more studies now devoted to understanding how established actors reacted to the unrest in the streets, we move beyond simple oppositions. In many cases, reform-oriented politicians of a liberal or conservative persuasion perceived the student movement as helpful to their efforts to reform universities. Of course, one could ask whether the break-up of the grand alliance of conservative and liberal reformers, which occurred in the late 1960s, is one little-noticed "cost" of 1968. On the other hand, it becomes clear by looking at both sides, established forces as well as protest movements, that historians should avoid replicating contemporary divisions of "us vs. them." Rather, we should move beyond such clichés by looking at how both sides interacted with and perceived each other.

1968 as cultural history

The recent fortieth anniversary of "1968" was the first one since cultural history approaches have become mainstream in the last two decades. While the "cultural turn," which started in France in the 1970s, has been underway for a while, it took some time before its impact began to be felt among contemporary historians. However, "1968" research is one point of entry for this "constructivist" paradigm into the once heavily guarded traditionalist quarters of contemporary history.

One promising new area of research is media and communications of the protest movements. Obviously, protest hinges on specific forms of expression. This new research paradigm—most prominently advanced by Joachim Scharloth[66]—focuses on the ways protest has been generated, historically, by means of specific communication strategies. Scholars in this paradigm now ask how social order and "identities" are shaped by public and highly visible actions, such as street marches, demonstrations, happenings, street theater, mock tribunals, or panels. It seems that activists consciously try to challenge, subvert, and redefine established social rituals, as the opening example of this essay demonstrated, when Daniel Cohn-Bendit refused to play according to the rules in a court of law.

The new cultural history of 1968 is not the domain of historians alone. To a large extent, it has become an interdisciplinary endeavor, as the contributions to some of the more recent collections demonstrate. Furthermore, media scholars like Kathrin Fahlenbrach and Dorothee Liehr underscore the fact that the movements of 1968 gained their public notoriety in part because the 1960s marked a period in which the media stood at a critical juncture.[67] This is especially true for continental Europe, where the media became more visual during the 1960s. In the US, however, these developments had set in half a decade earlier, whereas many societies outside the old "Western core" communicated mostly via radio and print.[68]

Research on the cultural history of "1968" in the narrower sense of the term has also exploded. In the West German case, we now have studies on hitherto virtually unkown areas such as graffiti,[69] counter-publics,[70] street theater,[71] performativity,[72] body and sexual politics,[73] emotions and lifestyle,[74] the anti-ritual performances in court cases,[75] and literary and musical avant-gardes.[76] Scholars also address how performances of a critical nature later slipped into terrorism and murder.[77] Music, especially, has become a major area of research currently teeming with activities.[78]

These new cultural studies approaches to the '60s, with their attention to the sources and detail and with their pronounced unwillingness to enter into debates about who lost or won, seem to be returning some of the original flavor of the era to the collective memories of the events. While most of the debates of the 1980s and 1990s centered on questions of the impact of "1968," or the dichotomy of its success or failure, it now seems to be less necessary to frame the issues in such a fashion.

This brings us to our last and concluding question, which cannot be answered here in a satifisfactory manner, because the issues involved still demand years of research: How is "1968" being remembered—and what has been forgotten during the past forty years? Historians now hotly debate this issue.[79]

With respect to France, Kristin Ross has described "May's Afterlife" as one of an emerging consensus of "1968" as a cultural revolution that was undone in the 1980s and 1990s.[80] Nonetheless, every strike or large-scale protest in France thereafter has instantly been measured against 1968. However, Eddy Fougier, writing on the occasion of the fortieth anniversary, observed that the usefulness of 1968 as a stand-in for contemporary conflicts has been played out. Quoting Marc-Olivier Padis, he asserts that "It has become impossible to play an imaginary civil war with respect to May 1968. May 1968 has become a part of history."[81]

For Germany, Albrecht von Lucke recently traced how "1968," starting in the late 1970s, was increasingly seen as the project of a generation.

This happened in part during the "lead years," when the former protagonists of the West German student movement wanted to distance themselves from RAF terrorism, on the one hand, and show what the original liberating impulses of "1968" had been, on the other. Not unlike neighboring France, Germany's consensus on 1968 was greatest during the late 1980s, when, on the twentieth anniversary, "everybody seemed to love 1968."[82] While it remains unpublished, Elizabeth Peifer's dissertation, "1968 in German Political Culture, 1967-1993: From Experience to Myth,"[83] offers further insight into this process of "working through 1968" up to the early 1990s.

As the proliferation of photo books on "1968" shows, the memories of "1968" are often transmitted by visual icons—which lend themselves to crass commercialization.[84] In this respect, the historicization of the "visual 1968" has barely begun. Many recent photo books repeat the stereotypical visual confrontations of the late 1960s and early 1970s. They barely ask how these images were constructed and how they became "key texts" of 1968. Furthermore, these illustrated volumes often center on one country, with "global" 1968 receiving only a token presence. In part, these difficulties come with the genre, because copyright issues limit images' use even more than written text.

It remains to be seen whether "1968," despite national idiosyncracies, can serve as a reference point in transnational memory. In a unified Europe, where an active search for common symbols is underway, "1968" could be one historical marker that Europeans from both East and West could relate to, if they so desired. Establishing a line, albeit tentative, to the pivotal year 1989, Europeans could frame "1968" as an event in which struggles for freedom brought people to the streets in Eastern and Western countries—as an event thus symbolizing European unity. But will they so desire? And will "global 1968" be able to play a similar role worldwide? We cannot yet tell whether people in Mexico, Japan, Egypt, and Europe are prepared to envision "1968," broadly conceived, as part of one global, historical whole. It seems many historians themselves may not (yet) be prepared to make this case.

In his address at the University of Cape Town in South Africa on June 6, 1966, Robert F. Kennedy painted a grim picture of the state of the world: "There is discrimination in New York, the racial inequality of apartheid in South Africa, and serfdom in the mountains of Peru. People starve to death in the streets of India; a former Prime Minister is summarily executed in the Congo; intellectuals go to jail in Russia; and thousands are slaughtered in Indonesia; wealth is lavished on armaments everywhere in the world." Yet, he argued, "as I talk to young people around the world I am impressed not by the diversity but by the closeness of their goals, their desires, and their concerns and their hope for the future."

For Kennedy, the young generation across the globe represented "the only true international community" that was able to transcend "obsolete dogmas and outworn slogans" and "a present that is already dying." In his view, "this world demands the qualities of youth: not a time of life but a state of mind, a temper of the will, a quality of imagination, a predominance of courage over timidity, of the appetite for adventure over the life of ease." Hence, amidst revolutionary transformations worldwide, Kennedy called on the young to take the lead, admitting that "you, and your young compatriots everywhere have had thrust upon you a greater burden of responsibility than any generation that has ever lived."[85] If and how the young generation rose to this challenge and what the legacies of this turbulent time were will no doubt continue to occupy the minds of historians for some time to come.

Philipp Gassert, a former Deputy Director of the GHI, is currently a Professor of Transatlantic History at the University of Augsburg. He specializes in contemporary European and international history. Among his many publications is *1968: The World Transformed* (1998), which he co-edited with Carole Fink and Detlef Junker.

Martin Klimke is a Research Fellow at the German Historical Institute in Washington, DC, whose research focuses on the transnational dimensions, as well as the political and cultural history, of the protest movements of the 1960s and '70s. His most recent book is *The Other Alliance: Student Protest in West Germany and the United States in the Global Sixties* (2010).

ENDNOTES

[1] Jerzy Eisler, "March 1968 in Poland," in *1968: The World Transformed*, ed. Carole Fink, Philipp Gassert, Detlef Junker (New York, 1998), 243.

[2] George Lavan Weissman, ed., *Revolutionary Marxist Students in Poland Speak Out (1964-1968)* (New York, 1968), 2.

[3] Surveys of global "1968" include George Katsiaficas, *The Imagination of the New Left: A Global Analysis of 1968* (Boston, 1987); David Caute, *The Year of the Barricades: A Journey through 1968* (New York, 1988); Etienne Francois, ed., *1968 - Ein europäisches Jahr?* (Leipzig, 1997); Gerard J. DeGroot, ed., *Student Protest: The Sixties and After* (London, 1998); Wolfgang Kraushaar, "Die erste globale Rebellion," in idem, *1968 als Mythos, Chiffre und Zäsur* (Hamburg, 2000), 19-52; Geneviève Dreyfus-Armand et al., *Les années 68: Le temps de la contestation* (Brussels, 2001); Jeremi Suri, *Power and Protest: Global Revolution and the Rise of Détente* (Cambridge, 2003); Gerd-Rainer Horn, *The Spirit of '68: Rebellion in Western Europe and North America, 1956-1976* (Oxford, 2007); Martin Klimke and Joachim Scharloth, eds., *1968 in Europe: A History of Protest and Activism,*

1956-1977 (New York, 2008); Norbert Frei, *1968: Jugendrevolte und globaler Protest* (Munich, 2008); Ingrid Gilcher-Holtey, *1968: eine Zeitreise* (Frankfurt, 1998); Jens Kastner and David Mayer, eds., *Weltwende 1968? Ein Jahr aus globalgeschichtlicher Perspektive* (Vienna, 2008); Karen Dubinsky et al., eds., *New World Coming: The Sixties and the Shaping of Global Consciousness* (Toronto, 2009); Angelika Ebbinghaus, Max Henninger, and Marcel van der Linden, eds., *1968—Ein Blick auf die Protestbewegung 40 Jahre danach aus globaler Perspektive* (Leipzig, 2009). See also the contributions in the forum "The International 1968, Part I & Part II," *American Historical Review* 114, No. 1 (February 2009): 42-135, and No. 2 (April 2009): 329-404.

[4] Ronald Fraser, *1968: A Student Generation in Revolt* (New York, 1988); Martin Klimke, *The Other Alliance: Student Protest in West Germany and the United States in the Global Sixties* (Princeton, 2009).

[5] Suri, *Power and Protest*; Fink et al., eds., *1968: The World Transformed*.

[6] See the contributions on Hungary and East Germany in this volume. On the latter, see also Timothy S. Brown, "'1968' East and West: Divided Germany as a Case Study in Transnational History," *American Historical Review* 114 (Feb. 2009): 69–96.

[7] See the contribution on Israel in this volume.

[8] Philipp Gassert, *Kurt Georg Kiesinger, 1904-1988: Kanzler zwischen den Zeiten* (Munich, 2005), 628.

[9] President of the SDS chapter at Columbia University, Mark Rudd gained national notoriety as a leader and spokesperson during the student strike and occupation of campus buildings in April 1968. See Klimke, *The Other Alliance*, 236.

[10] Kastner and Mayer, eds., *Weltwende*, 9.

[11] The digital project by the Goethe-Institut can be found at http://www.goethe.de/1968. The series "Revolution is in the Streets: The Sixties from an International Perspective," including film screenings, lectures, and a panel discussion, took place May 5-21, 2008. This volume also stands in the context of a workshop, "1968: 40 Years Later," which occurred at Vassar College, Poughkeepsie, NY, on April 12, 2008, and an international conference, "1968 in Japan, Germany, and the USA: Political Protest and Cultural Change," which was held at the Japanese-German Center in Berlin on March 4-6, 2009, and was co-sponsored by the GHI.

[12] Gerard J. DeGroot, *The Sixties Unplugged: A Kaleidoscopic History of a Disorderly Decade* (Cambridge, MA, 2008), 449.

[13] Timothy Garton Ash, "This Tale of Two Revolutions and Two Anniversaries May Yet Have a Twist," *The Guardian*, May 8, 2008.

[14] Axel Schildt and Detlef Siegfried, eds., *Between Marx and Coca-Cola* (New York, 2006); Detlef Siegfried, *Time Is on My Side. Konsum und Politik in der westdeutschen Jugendkultur der 60er Jahre* (Göttingen, 2006).

[15] See, for example, Victoria Langland, "Birth Control Pills and Molotov Cocktails: Reading Sex and Revolution in 1968 Brazil," in *In from the Cold: Latin America's New Encounter with the Cold War*, ed. Gilbert M. Joseph and Daniela Spenser (Durham, 2008), 308-49; "The Sixties: Glimpses from Latin America and Beyond," *ReVista, Harvard Review of Latin America* (Winter 2009); Samantha M. R. Christiansen and Zachary A. Scarlett, eds., *1968 and the Global South* (New York, forthcoming).

[16] See Fink et al., *1968: The World Transformed*; see also Lawrence S. Wittner, *Resisting the Bomb: A History of the World Nuclear Disarmament Movement, 1954-1970* (Stanford, 1997).

[17] Daniel Bell, *The Coming of Post-Industrial Society: A Venture in Social Forecasting* (New York, 1973); Ronald Inglehart, *The Silent Revolution: Changing Values and Political Styles Among Western Publics* (Princeton, 1977); on the historiography of the 1970s as an age of societal and cultural transformation, see Ansel Doering-Manteuffel and Lutz Raphael, *Nach dem Boom: Perspektiven auf die Zeitgeschichte seit 1970* (Göttingen, 2008).

[18] This is the point most commonly made, for example, in David Farber, ed., *The Sixties: From Memory to History* (Chapel Hill, 1994); Ingrid Gilcher-Holtey, ed., *1968. Vom Ereignis zum Gegenstand der Geschichtswissenschaft* (Göttingen, 1998); Franz-Werner Kersing, "Entzauberung des Mythos? Ausgangsbedingungen und Tendenzen einer

gesellschaftsgeschichtlichen Standortbestimmung der westdeutschen '68er'-Bewegung," *Westfälische Forschungen* 48 (1998): 1-19; Felix Dirsch, "Kulturrevolution oder Studentenbewegung? Ansätze zur Historisierung der Ereignisse von '1968'," *Zeitschrift für Politik* 55 (2008): 5-32.

[19] The German *Historikerstreit* is a prime example of such a process.

[20] Jan Assmann, *Das kulturelle Gedächtnis. Schrift, Erinnerung und politische Identität in frühen Hochkulturen* (Munich, 1992), 76.

[21] See the titles of the two volumes edited by Gilcher-Holtey, *1968. Vom Ereignis zum Gegenstand der Geschichtswissenschaft,* and Farber, *The Sixties: From Memory to History.*

[22] See the preface in Axel Schildt, Detlef Siegfried, Karl Christian Lammers, eds., *Dynamische Zeiten. Die 60er Jahre in beiden deutschen Gesellschaften* (Hamburg, 2000).

[23] Coming from a different interpretative angle, Ulrich Herbert also characterizes "1968" as an excessive revolt in an increasingly liberal social environment; see Ulrich Herbert, ed. *Wandlungsprozesse in Westdeutschland. Belastung, Integration, Liberalisierung 1945-1980* (Göttingen, 2002).

[24] Jules Witcover, *The Year the Dream Died: Revisiting 1968 in America* (New York, 1997).

[25] Philipp Gassert, "Kein annus mirabilis: 1968 in den USA," *Auslandsinformationen* 24 (2008): 7-36.

[26] Eckard Jesse, "Das Jahr 1968 und die Bürgerbewegung in der DDR," *Forschungsjournal Neue Soziale Bewegungen* 21, No. 3 (2008): 87-95; Helmut Fehr, "Von 1968 bis 1989: Die Studentenproteste als Kristallisationspunkt für eine neue politische Generation in Ostmitteleuropa," *Forschungsjournal Neue Soziale Bewegungen* 21, No. 3 (2008): 96-105.

[27] Detlef Siegfried, *Time Is on My Side.*

[28] Christina von Hodenberg, *Konsens und Krise: Eine Geschichte der westdeutschen Medienöffentlichkeit 1945-1973* (Göttingen, 2006).

[29] Bernd Hey and Volkmar Wittmütz, *1968 und die Kirchen* (Bielefeld, 2008).

[30] Philipp Gassert and Alan Steinweis, eds. *Coping with the Nazi Past: West German Debates on Nazism and Generational Conflict, 1955-1975* (New York, 2006).

[31] Ingo Juchler, *Die Studentenbewegungen in den Vereinigten Staaten und der Bundesrepublik Deutschland der sechziger Jahre. Eine Untersuchung hinsichtlich ihrer Beeinflussung durch Befreiungsbewegungen und -theorien aus der Dritten Welt* (Berlin, 1996); Wolfgang Kraushaar, "Die transatlantische Protestkultur: Der zivile Ungehorsam als amerikanisches Exempel und bundesdeutsche Adaption," in *Westbindungen: Amerika in der Bundesrepublik,* ed. Heinz Bude and Bernd Greiner (Hamburg, 1999), 257-84; Claus Leggewie, "1968: A Transatlantic Event and its Consequences," in *The United States and Germany in the Era of the Cold War, 1945-1990,* ed. Detlef Junker (New York, 2001); Philipp Gassert, "Atlantic Alliances: Cross-Cultural Communication and the 1960s Student Revolution," in *Culture and International Relations,* ed. Jessica Gienow-Hecht and Frank Schumacher (New York, 2003), 134-56; Michael Schmidtke, *Der Aufbruch der jungen Intelligenz: die 68er Jahre in der Bundesrepublik und den USA* (Frankfurt, 2003).

[32] Frei, *1968: Jugendrevolte und globaler Protest,* 31.

[33] Ibid., and Wolfgang Kraushaar, *Achtundsechzig. Eine Bilanz* (Berlin, 2008).

[34] On the complicated relationship between the student movement and 1970s terrorism, which cannot be covered here, see the various contributions in Wolfgang Kraushaar, ed., *Die RAF und der linke Terrorismus,* 2 vols. (Hamburg, 2006).

[35] For the various European countries, see the contributions in Klimke and Scharloth, eds., *1968 in Europe;* as well as http://www.1968ineurope.com. See also Thomas Ekman Jørgensen, *Transformation and Crises: The Left and the Nation in Denmark and Sweden, 1956-1980* (New York, 2008); Boris Kanzleiter and Krunoslav Stojaković, *1968 in Jugoslawien: Studentenproteste und kulturelle Avantgarde zwischen 1960 und 1975: Gespräche und Dokumente* (Bonn, 2008).

[36] On France, see the overview of the literature by Eddy Fougier, "Mai 68 in Frankreich: 40 Jahre danach. Mythos und gegenwärtige Debatte," *Auslandsinformationen* 24, No. 7 (2008): 58-80. On Italy, see Jan Kurz and Marica Tolomelli, "Italy," in *1968 in Europe,* ed.

Klimke and Scharloth, 83-96; and Stuart Hilwig, *Italy and 1968: Youthful Unrest and Democratic Culture* (Basingstoke, 2009).

[37] See Horn, *The Spirit of '68*.

[38] Doug McAdam and Dieter Rucht, "The Cross-National Diffusion of Movement Ideas," *Annals of the American Association of Political and Social Science* 528 (July 1993): 56-74; Sidney Tarrow, *Power in Movement: Social Movements, Collective Action, and Politics* (Cambridge, 1994), 153-69; Charles Chatfield et al., eds., *Transnational Social Movements and Global Politics: Solidarity Beyond the State* (Syracuse, 1997); Margaret E. Keck and Kathryn Sikkink, *Activists Beyond Borders: Advocacy Networks in International Politics* (Ithaca, 1998); Donatella Della Porta, Hanspeter Kriesi, and Dieter Rucht, eds., *Social Movements in a Globalizing World* (New York, 1999); Ann Florini et al., eds., *The Third Force: The Rise of Transnational Civil Society* (Washington, DC, 2000); Jackie Smith and Hank Johnston, eds., *Globalization and Resistance: Transnational Dimensions of Social Movements* (Lanham, 2002); Joe Bandy and Jackie Smith, *Coalitions Across Borders: Transnational Protest and the Neoliberal Order* (Lanham, 2005).

[39] Charles Tilly, *European Revolutions, 1492-1992* (Oxford, 1993).

[40] Ingrid Gilcher-Holtey, *"Die Phantasie an die Macht:" Mai 68 in Frankreich* (Frankfurt, 1995); and Thomas Hecken, *Gegenkultur und Avantgarde 1950-1970: Situationisten, Beatniks, 68er* (Tübingen, 2006); Thomas Hecken and Agata Grzzenia, "Situationism," in *1968 in Europe*, ed. Klimke and Scharloth, 23-32.

[41] Geoff Eley, *Forging Democracy: The History of the Left in Europe, 1850-2000* (New York, 2002); see also Geoff Eley, "Telling Stories about Sixty-Eight: Troublemaking, Political Passions, and Enabling Democracy?" *German Studies Association Newsletter* 23, No. 2 (Winter 2008/09): 39-50.

[42] Belinda Davis, Martin Klimke, Carla MacDougall, and Wilfried Mausbach, eds., *Changing the World, Changing the Self: Political Protest and Collective Identities in 1960/70s West Germany and the United States* (New York, forthcoming).

[43] See, for example, Van Gosse, *Where the Boys Are: Cuba, Cold War America and the Making of a New Left* (New York, 1993); Jennifer B. Smith, *An International History of the Black Panther Party* (New York, 1999); Cynthia Young, *Soul Power: Culture, Radicalism and the Making of a U.S. Third World Left* (Durham, 2006); Quinn Slobodian, "Radical Empathy: The Third World and the New Left in 1960s West Germany," Ph.D. diss., New York University, 2008.

[44] Dieter Segert "Prag 1968," in *Weltwende*, ed. Kastner and Mayer, 114-29; Stefan Karner et al., eds., *Prager Frühling: Das internationale Krisenjahr 1968*, 2 vols. (Cologne, 2008).

[45] Martina Kaller-Dietrich, "Theologie der Befreiung: Medellín 1968," in *Weltwende*, ed. Kastner and Mayer, 68-82; David Mayer, "Vor den bleiernen Jahren der Diktaturen: 1968 in und aus Lateinamerika," in ibid., 153-58.

[46] Paul Lyons, *The People of this Generation: The Rise and Fall of the New Left in Philadelphia* (Philadelphia, 2003).

[47] Katja Nagel, *Die Provinz in Bewegung: Studentenunruhen in Heidelberg, 1967-1973* (Heidelberg, 2009); other local studies in Germany and Switzerland include Stefan Hemler, "Von Kurt Faltlhauser zu Rolf Pohle. Die Entwicklung der studentischen Unruhe an der Ludwig-Maximilians-Universität München in der zweiten Hälfte der sechziger Jahre," in *1968: 30 Jahre danach*, ed. Venanz Schubert (St. Ottilien, 1999), 209-42; Detlef Michelers, *Draufhauen, Draufhauen, Nachsetzen. Die Bremer Schülerbewegung, die Strassenbahndemonstrationen und ihre Folgen 1967/1968* (Bremen, 2002); Anna Christina Berlit, *Notstandskampagne und Roter Punkt: Die Studentenbewegung in Hannover 1967-1969* (Gütersloh, 2007); Angelika Linke and Joachim Scharloth, eds., *Der Züricher Sommer 1968. Zwischen Krawall, Utopie und Bürgersinn* (Zürich, 2008).

[48] Mary Ann Wynkoop, *Dissent in the Heartland: The Sixties at Indiana University* (Bloomington, 2002).

[49] Rusty L. Monhollon, *This is America?: The Sixties in Lawrence, Kansas* (New York, 2002), 6.

[50] For an earlier appeal "to bring the establishment in," see Philipp Gassert and Pavel A. Richter, eds., *1968 in West Germany: A Guide to Sources and Literature of the*

Extra-Parliamentarian Opposition, GHI Reference Guide No. 9 (Washington, DC, 1998), 15; Philipp Gassert, "Ein Wendepunkt der Nachkriegszeit? '1968' in der Jubiläumsliteratur zum Dreißigsten," *Historische Mitteilungen* 15 (2002): 286-96; Philipp Gassert, *Kurt Georg Kiesinger,* 615ff.; See also Kathrin Fahlenbrach, Martin Klimke, and Joachim Scharloth, eds., *The 'Establishment' Responds: Power and Protest During and After the Cold War* (forthcoming).

[51] Roger Karapin, *Protest Politics in Germany: Movements on the Left and the Right Since the 1960s* (University Park, 2007).

[52] Kaller-Dietrich, "Theologie der Befreiung," 79-80.

[53] Hey and Wittmütz, *1968 und die Kirchen;* Kraushaar, *Achtundsechzig,* 268. See also Michaela Karl, *Rudi Dutschke: Revolutionär ohne Revolution* (Frankfurt, 2003), 173-181; Jörg Herrmann, "'Unsere Söhne und Töchter': Protestantismus und RAF-Terrorismus in den 1970er Jahren," in *Die RAF und der linke Terrorismus,* ed. Kraushaar, 1:644-56; Pascal Eitler, *"Gott ist tot – Gott ist rot": Max Horkheimer und die Politisierung der Religion um 1968* (Frankfurt, 2009).

[54] Hilwig, *Italy and 1968;* Louis Vos, "Belgium," in *1968 in Europe,* ed. Klimke and Scharloth, 153-62.

[55] For the role of religion, see also Douglas Rossinow, *The Politics of Authenticity: Liberalism, Christianity, and the New Left in America* (New York, 1998).

[56] Bernd Gehrke and Gerd-Rainer Horn, eds., *1968 und die Arbeiter: Studien zum "proletarischen Mai" in Europa* (Hamburg, 2007); Knud Andresen, "Die bundesdeutsche Lehrlingsbewegung von 1968 bis 1972. Konturen eines vernachlässigten Phänomens," in *Alte Linke – Neue Linke? Die sozialen Kämpfe der 1968er Jahre in der Diskussion,* ed. Peter Birke, Bernd Hüttner, Gottfried Oy (Berlin, 2009), 87-102.

[57] Michael Schneider, *Demokratie in Gefahr? Der Konflikt um die Notstandsgesetze: Sozialdemokratie, Gewerkschaften und intellektueller Protest, 1958-1968* (Bonn, 1986).

[58] The question of violence and the connection of 1960s' protest movements to terrorism—especially in the case of West Germany, Italy, Japan, and the US—also has, and continues to be, one of the major points of contention when historians evaluate the legacy of "1968." For the German case, see, for example, Wolfgang Kraushaar, "Rudi Dutschke und der bewaffnete Kampf," in *Rudi Dutschke, Andreas Baader und die RAF,* by Wolfgang Kraushaar, Jan Philipp Reemtsma, and Karin Wieland (Hamburg, 2005), 28-31; Dorothea Hauser, "Terrorism," in *1968 in Europe,* ed. Klimke and Scharloth, 269-80; Ingrid Gilcher-Holtey, "Transformation by Subversion? The New Left and the Question of Violence," in *Changing the World, Changing the Self,* ed. Davis et al., 155-70.

[59] Götz Aly, *Unser Kampf, 1968: Ein irritierter Blick zurück* (Frankfurt, 2008), 88.

[60] Klimke, *Other Alliance,* 195-235.

[61] See, for example, Maud Bracke, *Which Socialism? Whose Détente?: West European Communism and the Czechoslovak Crisis, 1968* (New York/Budapest, 2007); Kimmo Rentola, "The Soviet Communist Party and 1968: A Case Study," in *New World Coming,* ed. Dubinsky et al., 56-67.

[62] Winfried Fluck, "Inside and Outside: What Kind of Knowledge Do We Need? A Response to the Presidential Address," *American Quarterly* 59, No. 1 (2007): 23-32.

[63] For some preliminary reflection with regard to West Germany, see Wolf-Dieter Narr, "'68': Protestierender Abglanz der Ordinarienuniversität – Konkrete Utopie demokratischer Universität. Bleibende Ambivalenzen," *Forschungsjournal Neue Soziale Bewegungen* 21, No. 3 (2008): 57-66.

[64] This comprehensive view has most often been neglected. Exceptions are Rebecca Klatch, *A Generation Divided: The New Left, the New Right, and the 1960s* (Berkeley, 1999); Lisa McGirr, *Suburban Warriors: The Origins of the New American Right* (Princeton, 2001); Hartmuth Becker, Felix Dirsch, and Stefan Winckler, eds., *Die 68er und ihre Gegner: Der Widerstand gegen die Kulturrevolution* (Graz, 2003).

[65] John G. Turner, *Bill Bright and Campus Crusade for Christ: The Renewal of Evangelicalism in Postwar America* (Chapel Hill, 2008).

[66] Joachim Scharloth, "Ritualkritik und Rituale des Protest. Die Entdeckung des Performativen in der Studentenbewegung der 1960er Jahre," in *1968. Handbuch zur*

Kultur- und Mediengeschichte der Studentenbewegung, ed. Martin Klimke and Joachim Scharloth (Stuttgart, 2007), 75-87; Joachim Scharloth, *1968. Eine Kommunikationsgeschichte* (Munich, forthcoming).

[67] Kathrin Fahlenbrach, *Protestinszenierungen. Visuelle Kommunikation und kollektive Identitäten in Protestbewegungen* (Wiesbaden, 2002); Dorothee Liehr, "Ereignisinszenierung im Medienformat: Proteststrategien und Öffentlichkeit – eine Typologie," in *1968. Handbuch,* ed. Klimke and Scharloth, 23-36.

[68] Philipp Gassert and Christina von Hodenberg, "Media: Government vs. Market," in *The United States and Germany, 1890-2000: Competition and Convergence,* ed. Kiran Klaus Patel and Christof Mauch (New York, forthcoming).

[69] Mererid P. Davies, "'Eiffe erobert die Welt': Graffiti und der umstrittene öffentliche Raum," in *1968. Handbuch,* ed. Klimke and Scharloth, 49-60.

[70] Dominik Lachenmeier, "Die Achtunsechziger-Bewegung zwischen etablierter und alternativer Öffentlichkeit," in *1968. Handbuch,* ed. Klimke and Scharloth, 61-72.

[71] Dorothea Kraus, *Theater-Proteste: zur Politisierung von Strasse und Bühne in den 1960er Jahren* (Frankfurt, 2007).

[72] Martin Klimke and Joachim Scharloth, "Utopia in Practice: The Discovery of Performativity in Sixties' Protest, Arts and Sciences," in "Historizing 1968 and the Long Sixties," ed. Ada Dialla, Vangelis Karamanolakis, Kostis Kornetis, *Historein* 8: forthcoming.

[73] Mererid P. Davies, "Bodily Issues: The West German Anti-Authoritarian Movement and the Semiotics of Dirt," in *Un-civilising Processes: Excess and Transgression in German Society and Culture,* ed. Mary Fulbrook, (Amsterdam, 2007), 225-53; Dagmar Herzog, *Sex After Fascism: Memory and Morality in Twentieth-Century Germany* (Princeton, 2005).

[74] Jakob Tanner, "Motions and Emotions," in *1968 in Europe,* ed. Klimke and Scharloth, 71-80; Sven Reichardt, "Authentizität und Gemeinschaftsbindung. Politik und Lebensstil im linksalternativen Milieu vom Ende der 1960er bis zum Anfang der 1980er Jahre," *Forschungsjournal Neue Soziale Bewegungen* 21, No. 3 (2008): 118-30.

[75] Joachim Scharloth, "Ritualkritik," 78-82.

[76] Roman Luckscheiter, *Der postmoderne Impuls: die Krise der Literatur um 1968 und ihre Überwindung,* Schriften zur Literaturwissenschaft 16 (Berlin, 2001); Beate Kutschke, *Musikkulturen in der Revolte. Studien zu Rock, Avantgarde und Klassik im Umfeld von "1968"* (Stuttgart, 2008); Robert Adlington, ed., *Sound Commitments: Avant-Garde Music and the Sixties* (New York, 2009).

[77] Thomas Hecken, *Avantgarde und Terrorismus: Rhetorik der Intensität und Programme der Revolte von den Futuristen bis zur RAF* (Bielefeld, 2006); Sara Hakemi, "Terrorismus und Avantgarde," in *Die RAF und der linke Terrorismus,* ed. Kraushaar, 1:604-19.

[78] Arnold Jacobshagen and Markus Leniger, eds., *Rebellische Musik. Gesellschaftlicher Protest und kultureller Wandel um 1968* (Cologne, 2007); Detlef Siegfried, *Sound der Revolte. Studien zur Kulturrevolution um 1968* (Weinheim, 2008).

[79] Ingo Cornils and Sarah Waters, eds., *Memories of 1968: International Perspectives* (Bern, forthcoming).

[80] Kristin Ross, *May '68 and Its Afterlives* (Chicago, 2002).

[81] Fougier, "Mai 68 in Frankreich," 79.

[82] Albrecht von Lucke, *68 oder neues Biedermeier: Der Kampf um die Deutungsmacht* (Berlin, 2008).

[83] University of North Carolina-Chapel Hill, 1997.

[84] For countless examples of this, see, for example, the blog of the exhibition "'So geht Revolution' – Werbung und Revolte," at http://home.bawue.de/~mauss/revo.html.

[85] Robert F. Kennedy, "Day of Affirmation Address (as delivered)," University of Cape Town, Cape Town, South Africa, June 6, 1966, in John F. Kennedy Presidential Library & Museum, Boston, MA.

THE AMERICAS

ARGENTINA: THE SIGNS AND IMAGES OF "REVOLUTIONARY WAR"

Hugo Vezzetti

In 1966, the Argentinian army called General Juan Carlos Onganía to lead the new government after the coup against elected President Arturo Illia. Under Onganía's rule, the violent civil conflict haunting the country increased. In 1969, there was severe unrest in the city of Córdoba, the "Córdobazo," an uprising that heralded the end of Onganía's presidency. In 1970, General Alejandro Agustín Lanusse seized power and opened the country to free elections, which were held in March 1973. Juan Domingo Perón, who had already been president of Argentina from 1946 to 1955, was re-elected after he returned from exile in 1973. After his death in 1974, his second wife Isabel occupied his office until she was deposed in a coup by officers under the leadership of General Jorge Videla in March 1976.

In the "Dirty War" of this new regime, a campaign of destruction began against left-wing workers, unionists, critical intellectuals, and journalists. Many students were also targeted. When their mothers protested on the central "Plaza de Mayo," demanding information on the fate of their children, they exposed themselves to mortal danger. According to official statistics, around 13,000 opponents of the regime were killed or disappeared without trace under the bloody military dictatorship. Human rights experts estimate that almost twice as many people were affected. It is only recently that the courts have started to work their way through this historical period.

In order to define the repercussions the French May had on the situation in Argentina, it is advisable to discard the simple notion of a "center versus the periphery." It was not a single event that spurred the spirit of rebellion spreading throughout Latin America but rather a variety of overlapping discourses. There was no *global 1968*, and all attempts to press this date into one political or historical framework, either during the events or afterwards, are untenable. In addition, looking at the 1960s in Argentina while concentrating on 1968 irremediably delays the achievements of an entire era. This date is too late to begin if one wants to understand all of the ideas, movements, and the politicization of issues that the great myth of the revolution contains.

The main components of this political and cultural construct had been present since the beginning of the decade: the struggle in the Third World, Algeria, Vietnam, and—above all—the revolution in Cuba. Revolutionaries were certain that the revolution would follow an irreversible historical course, first asserting itself in the peripheral countries. A student revolt could not shake this belief and could only be regarded with a mixture of astonishment and sympathy, if not mistrust, which the historical outcome soon justified: a movement led by the academic middle classes could not overthrow a consolidated capitalist state that—sustained by a working class that believed in reformism—formed part of the imperialistic domain.

This political interpretation, however, did not prevent left-wing intellectuals in Argentina—who derived their ideas primarily from French philosophers (from Jean-Paul Sartre to Louis Althusser)—from evoking images of the Paris barricades of 1871. It was only after the fact, however, that the impression of a homogeneity to all these rebellions, embodied in the image of Argentine-born revolutionary Che Guevara as an icon of all kinds of non-conformity, was constructed. Looking back from the present, where such struggles lie deep in the past, one tends to overemphasize the cultural and moral aspects of that time (anti-authoritarism, youth cultures, and anti-establishmentarianism). But in order to truly evaluate this period and save it from anachronisms, it is necessary to recall the conceptualization of the revolutionary war.

The founding of guerilla movements

The impulse for rebellion in Argentina actually did come from a different place. In 1959, the successful Cuban Revolution spread the strategy of "foquismo." That same year, the first attempt to create a rural guerrilla group took shape, the so-called Uturuncos. A second attempt in 1963, the EGP (Ejército Guerrillero del Pueblo [The People's Guerrilla Army]) ended tragically. Ricardo Masetti led the group and called himself Comandante Segundo [Second Commander] because the first commander was Che Guevara, who intended to take over the leadership of the group in the future. This year also saw the appearance of *Pasado y Presente* [Past and Present]. This communist magazine severed ties with the old Soviet Party in the name of a new generation that declared itself to be "the expression of a historical process characterized by a strong leaning toward a revolutionary break."

In 1966, after General Onganía's military coup, another magazine was founded, *Cristianismo y Revolución* (C&R [Christianity and

Revolution]). It gave voice to a radical position that combined the anti-imperialistic nationalism of Peronism, the Guevarism, and a new Christian messianism with explosive results. From this point of view, the struggle was no longer about stating that the revolution was "the new sign of our times" nor about announcing the Third World as "the world of the revolutionaries." More decisive was the insight that armed rebellion—following the example of the Colombian priest, liberation theologist, and guerilla fighter Camilo Torres—was "the only efficient and comprehensive means of expressing one's love for all."

The rhetoric of armed revolution

What happened in May 1968? *C&R*, the dominant magazine for the Peronist and Guevarist Left, did not mention the events in Paris even once. The French influence was focused on the work of Régis Debray, who was often cited and interviewed before and after his disastrous adventure in Bolivia. He was an intellectual who claimed that the gun should replace—and direct—the pen. The magazine's international coverage was dominated by expressions of solidarity with the struggling peoples in Africa, Asia, and Latin America (the first Conferencia Tricontinental had been held in Havana in 1966). Aside from Vietnam and the fighting in the Third World, above all in Latin America, the magazine only included international news about the "Black Power" Movement, which it regarded as representative of oppressed minorities in the United States, with any regularity. Che Guevara had been killed in Bolivia in 1967, and in Cuba, 1968 was proclaimed to be "the year of the heroic guerrilla." In Argentina, it seemed that the conditions for armed revolution were not at hand; the political and economic power of Onganía's dictatorship had stabilized.

Nonetheless, the situation changed decisively when the former Argentinian president Juan Perón turned to the rhetoric of armed revolution. In October 1967, prompted by Che's death, he stated that "He was one of us" and lamented the "irretrievable loss for peoples fighting for liberty." But the real shift occurred in May 1969, when the cycle of protest that ended in the Córdobazo (the brutal suppression of a citizen's revolt in the provincial capital of Córdoba) gave rise to the notion of popular insurrection, even in the cities. Although the first victims were students, the groups of mobilized workers later comprised a driving force in the movement and also suffered substantial loss of life.

The Peronist guerilla organization, Montoneros, came into being in May 1970, when it abducted and murdered General Pedro Aramburu. In September that same year, the ERP (Ejército Revolucionario del Pueblo [The People's Revolutionary Army]) was founded. What happened next is well known: the story ended just a few years later in a state-orchestrated massacre—the military takeover in March 1976—and in a new, incomparably brutal dictatorship that lasted until 1983.

Paris, Prague, Buenos Aires

I would like to turn again to the overlapping images of the barricades in Paris and Córdoba and to the complicated entanglement of encounters and evasions, of misunderstandings and small myths, that arise from them. Even though *C&R* did not mention the French May, it did cover another great European event in 1968—the Prague Spring, which the Soviet invasion stamped out. As is well known, Fidel Castro approved of this intervention, which astonished many people. Thus, he began to end the experiment to construct a socialism independent of the Soviet model. The lesson was clear: if civil society got involved in a way that exceeded the party's established boundaries, it led inexorably to the apostasy of liberalism and the demise of the revolution.

Argentinians in Cordoba stand before a street barricade on May 30, 1969.

The Cuban leader has adhered resolutely to this position for over forty years. *C&R*, the magazine of the Argentinian Guevaristas, fell in line with this position: the military intervention in Czechoslovakia was an unfortunate necessity that, though it revealed errors in the construction of a new society, was justifiable considering the risk of a socialist country falling to the imperialistic camp. Even if the "new man" of socialism did not (yet) exist, one could at least count on the international "solidarity" of Soviet troops. The magazine made no secret of its criticism of the Soviet parties, thus agreeing with the new Latin American and European Left. Furthermore, it held them responsible for "betraying" Che Guevara in Bolivia. Nevertheless, ideological differences concerning ideas and strategies in the Third World struggle died out when confronted with the larger, bipolar world of the Cold War. If Che had still been alive in 1968, would he have expressed a different idea?

The contradictory texture of an era

Finally then, with regard to the retrospective visions that seem to grow out of wishful thinking—as in the writings of Carlos Fuentes—and seek to align the French May with the Prague Spring and Latin American rebellions, one ought to first reconstruct the raw and contradictory texture of this historic era. So close to and yet so distant from the present, this era cannot be pressed into simple schemata nor invoked in embellished legends in line with the banal narratives on the epos of longing and imagination.

After all, in this history, on the Latin American side, there is a great deal of blood and a large number of dead. Out of respect for them—and for the truth—we must bear witness to and interpret this age in a responsible manner. We must continue to research, rethink, and retell the history of this period, which is still far from having revealed all of its enigmas.

Hugo Vezzetti teaches at the University of Buenos Aires and is a research scientist at CONICET (Consejo Nacional de Investigaciones Científicas y Técnicas). He took his degree in psychoanalysis and specializes in the history of culture and ideas.

BOLIVIA: CHE GUEVARA IN GLOBAL HISTORY

Carlos Soria-Galvarro

Otra vez siento bajo mis talones el costillar de
Rocinante, vuelvo al camino con mi adarga al brazo....

[Once again I feel beneath my heels the ribs of
Rocinante, I return to the road with my shield on my arm ....]

        Che Guevara, from a farewell letter to his parents (1965)

Historic personalities are such precisely because in some way or other they embody the spirit of an era and, therefore, transcend their time. Ernesto Guevara de la Serna, commonly known as "Che," is one of them. Born in Argentina, he wandered through several Latin American countries, reaching the peak of his fame in Cuba. His tragic death in Bolivia contributed to making him one of the most significant figures of the twentieth century.

Armed conflict between Che's guerrilla group and the Bolivian army began with the first ambush at the river Ñacahuasu on March 23, 1967. Che's troops numbered less than four dozen, including twenty-three Bolivians, sixteen Cubans, three Peruvians, and two born in Argentina (Tania, the only woman in the group, and Che himself). This list does not count two "visitors," four who withdrew for health reasons, and two deserters. Even so, from March to October, the balance seemed favorable to Che. His guerrilla group caused forty-nine casualties among the Bolivian troops, wounded about as many more, and took a number of prisoners. They acquired a substantial pile of weapons and provisions as booty. Furthermore, on July 6, they succeeded spectacularly in conquering the village of Samaipata on the road from Cochabamba to Santa Cruz, a vital thoroughfare between the west and east of Bolivia.

Surrounded by thousands of soldiers

Nevertheless, the activities of Che's group were isolated and sporadic from the beginning. Nobody even knew for sure whether Che was in charge. He had nothing but the diffuse sympathies of left-wing parties and potential allies like miners, who, simply for showing sympathy for the guerrillas, had been hit by a brutal preemptive strike on June 24 that has gone down in history as the "Massacre de San Juan." (The army took advantage of traditional festive bonfires marking the summer solstice, attacking peaceful mining camps by surprise at dawn and causing dozens of deaths.) Che's rearguard had been eliminated during an ambush on August 31, and on September 26, three hardened members of the advance guard fell. At the beginning of October, surrounded by thousands of soldiers, Che was in a desperate situation.

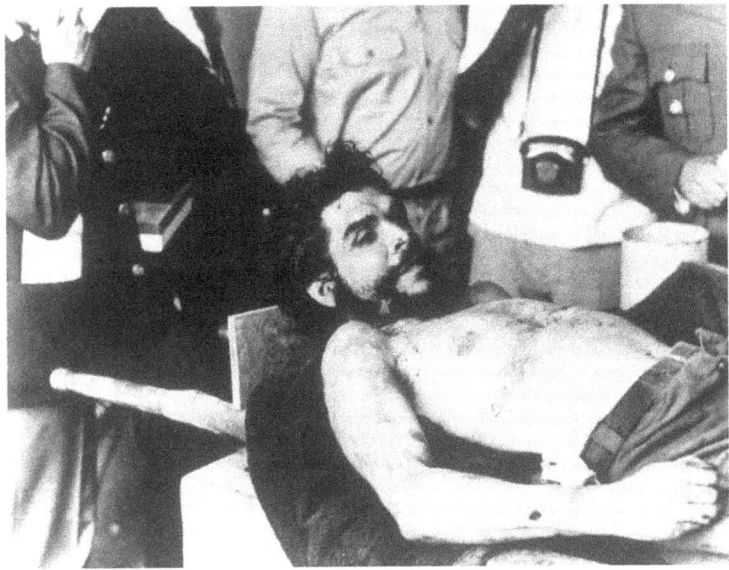

Che Guevara's lifeless body after his execution on October 9, 1967.

Under these conditions and with only seventeen men left, he was drawn into battle in the gorge of El Churo. On October 8, wounded in his right calf and without a functioning gun, Che was taken prisoner by a squadron of "ranger" soldiers who had recently been trained by US instructors. Together with Che was "Willy," a Bolivian miner named Simeón Cuba. The prisoners were led to the village of La Higuera and imprisoned in a small school where both were executed the next day by "orders from above."

A shock wave and radicalization

These events in Bolivia triggered a shock wave. As almost never before, the country was at the center of the world's attention. In Bolivia itself, broad swathes of society, above all the youth, grew more radical in their political convictions and started to fervently admire the romantic heroism of Che and his men, who had tried, from the heart of the continent, to alter the course of Latin American and world history. Even some sectors of the Bolivian military, without admitting it officially, let themselves be carried away by this tide. Between 1969 and 1971, the military pursued nationalizing policies and other measures regarded as patriotic and anti-imperialistic.

But Bolivia was not an island. So what events dominated the world stage at that time? First and foremost, Vietnam: a contest that debased the superpower to the north and proved once again that tremendous military and economic power are not enough to win a war. The conflict came from the previous decade, since the US had replaced the defeated French colonial troops. By the mid-1960s, the US intervention in the Asian southwest had grown enormous, swelling from 23,000 soldiers in 1964 to the dizzying figure of over half a million in 1968. The fighting front between Marines and Vietnamese guerrilla forces—and the merciless bombing of cities and towns in the north—began precisely at this time and did not stop until America was finally defeated in April 1975. All this occurred against the backdrop of the Cold War. The Soviet Union, the other superpower, supported Vietnam, like China, but without compromising the precarious atomic balance.

In his famous message to the Tricontinental Conference, which Che wrote in hiding in Cuba before leaving for Bolivia and which was read in April 1967, Che compared the solidarity of all progressive forces in the world with Vietnam to the audience cheers for gladiators in Rome. The message was unmistakable: "To create two, three, many Vietnams...." And this is exactly what he tried to achieve in Bolivia: consistency, however quixotic, between what he thought and what he did in terms of how he perceived himself.

Interwoven facts and figures

Then, in 1968, the French May occurred, with vast repercussions. Promoted by the students and, at its height, drawing in millions of workers, this movement was stamped by the creative daring of its intellectual proposal, which aimed to destroy the dominant concepts and frameworks. The storm of rebellion turned the crusty ideological and institutional bases—those of both the right and left—upside down. The slogans "Everything is possible," "Imagination to power," "Forbid the forbidden," along with portraits of old Marx, Lenin, Trotsky, Mao, Ho Chi Min, Fidel Castro, and Che Guevara, set the tune.

Subtle laces wove situations, events, and characters together. One focal point of the protests was the University of Nanterre, where students named the theater after Che Guevara, who had died in Bolivia months earlier. A university committee had passed repressive directives in support of Vietnam, sparking the uprising.

Spurred by these incidents and encouraged by the example of Cuba, armed movements began to spread through several Latin American countries, driven especially by the youth. A wave of readiness to make sacrifices engulfed the continent, and the military dictatorships supported by Washington reacted with destructive, genocidal policies. This included Hugo Banzer's dictatorship in Bolivia (1971–1978). What followed was the successive establishment of neoliberal political models. After the utopias of great change appeared to have been eradicated forever by violence, activists agitated for the only achievable programmatic goal, to attain democratic liberties once again.

Lasting popularity

Nevertheless, as we enter a new millennium under local, regional, and worldwide circumstances very different from those of the 1960s and 1970s, the winds of change are blowing once again. A new generation has taken the stage and, although its political proposals have their own stripe and do not repeat the misfortunes of the past, they are somehow related to the ideas of those years. Che has reappeared as a symbol in the background, as well. In Bolivia, the first indigenous president, Evo Morales Ayma, mentioned Che in his inaugural address on January 22, 2006, as one of his precursors. He hung a huge portrait of him in the government palace and paid his respects to him on the fortieth anniversary of his assassination.

Evo Morales Ayma, however, has probably never heard of the programmatic speech Che outlined in Ñacahuasu, which has remained almost unknown. In it, Che formulated this stirring slogan: "Democratization of the country with the active participation of principle ethnic groups in the big decisions of government." The speech demanded that the country cultivate endemic languages and incorporate them into its technological infrastructure, eradicate diseases that had long since been eradicated in other countries, allow workers and peasants to participate in planning both the uses of natural resources and the fertile land, and the development of the communications system "to turn Bolivia into a great, unified country rather than a fragmented giant in which the departments and provinces are strangers to each other."[1]

Che Guevara as a symbol of struggle

It is also quite possible that Che himself paid little attention to programmatic ideas for Bolivia, since he was principally concerned

---

[1] "Departments" refers here to the nine politico-administrative territorial units into which Bolivia is divided. They remain weakly integrated and regionally diverse up to today.

with a plan for the continent that was supposed to culminate in his return to Argentina as a guerrilla fighter. Later he was chiefly concerned with helping his bedraggled and famished troop survive. So what connects this project of armed struggle of 1967, which had no popular support, to the social movements of peasants and indigenous peoples fighting for democratic rights that finally won the elections at the end of 2005?

To find an answer, we must consider the following: the symbolic image of Che became an icon that always and everywhere accompanies the struggle of the poor, the outcast, and the excluded; also, the events in the 1960s and 1970s raised issues that have remained—revitalized humanism, visionary ecological ideas, radical democracy, unattained social equality, and longed for respect between nations and countries. And thus, *mutatis mutandis*, the old battle cries of liberty, fraternity, and equality, now freed of their exclusively liberal bonds, have today gained a new validity.

Carlos Soria-Galvarro is a Bolivian journalist and author. Among other books, he has published *El Che en Bolivia: Documentos y testimonios* [Che in Bolivia: Documents and Testimonies] (La Paz, 1992 and 2005).

CANADA: 1968 AND THE NEW LEFT

Dimitrios Roussopoulos

The seeds of the New Left in Canada were sown in the first nuclear disarmament movement born in November 1959 in Montreal. The Combined Universities Campaign for Nuclear Disarmament (CUCND), after organizing the first student demonstration in the country's capital city of Ottawa, spread rapidly from coast to coast in December; every university campus set up a chapter. At first, the campaign focused on preventing Canada from joining the nuclear club and acquiring nuclear weapons for a set of anti-aircraft missiles. Then, the CUCND went on to adopt a policy position favoring non-alignment. By 1963, however, despite its considerable influence and high level of activism, which melded with other organizations like the Canadian Campaign for Nuclear Disarmament and the Voice of Women, the movement failed: the Liberal Party of Canada, having won the elections, reversed its anti-nuclear stance and imported nuclear warheads for the Bomarc missiles—anti-aircraft missiles developed as a joint US-Canadian effort against the Soviet threat.

Bitterness among activists was widespread; cynicism among citizens in general was rampant. As a result, the CUCND transformed itself in 1964 into the Student Union for Peace Action (SUPA), the New Left of Canada, in Regina, Saskatchewan. The logic of the group's founding was as follows: the institutions of liberal democracy, being unable to reflect popular will, were flawed. Thus, it was necessary to start a movement that would articulate and promote participatory democracy and a non-violent revolutionary approach, bringing the powerless in civil society together to act in concert to effect much needed social change. Although Prime Minister Pierre Elliot Trudeau, a Montrealer, eventually removed all nuclear weapons from Canadian soil, by that time the youth movement had been radicalized by students undertaking grass-roots organizing projects across the country from 1964 to 1967. With an action program centered on the "primacy of peace," the movement ultimately aimed to create new, democratic, decision-making citizen institutions that would transform Canada on the international stage into a non-aligned country. Such Third Bloc countries were trying to shift the balance of power to reduce the tensions between the two superpowers and reverse the Cold War.

SUPA surpassed the CUCND in influence and image. Its impact on other youth organizations was legendary. As SUPA tried to root itself in the various communities where it planted its projects, however, its links with the campuses shriveled up. After internal disagreements erupted and political mistakes of various kinds occurred, fatigue brought an end to the organization by 1967.

Democracy, democracy, more democracy

Nonetheless, a new wave of New Left activism was not long in coming. During the fall of 1967, hundreds of students got involved in direct actions at the Universities of British Columbia, Toronto, and Waterloo over the presence in Canada of the US-based Dow Chemical Company, which manufactured the napalm used in Vietnam. The campuses of Memorial University in Newfoundland, Bishops University in Quebec, as well as Sir George Williams University and McGill University in Montreal, likewise, were rocked by campaigns to democratize education and give students more power.

In 1968, members of this new New Left movement declared that their direct actions involving civil disobedience were "acts of solidarity" with the poor in the ghettos and elsewhere. Invariably, they linked their demand for student power with their desire to make the university relevant to the need for social and political change in industrial/technological society. At McGill University, for example, a student uprising led to the occupation of the administration building. The community, including the UGEQ (the Quebec student union, which advocated student syndicalism), displayed its solidarity with the students and offered support. However, the revolt failed to achieve student power or social change: it ended with police heavy-handedness and student and faculty arrests.

Links within the North American New Left and beyond

As the CUCND-to-SUPA transition was taking place from 1964 to 1966, leading activists in the New Left of Canada and the US established many cross-border links. In time, links also developed with Mexican students when they began to agitate for social change, culminating in the pre-Olympic horror of the Tlatelolco massacre on October 2, 1968. That year North America witnessed an upsurge in extra-parliamentary political activity in all three countries primarily involving students, youths, blacks, and certain segments of the industrial working class. College students led protests across the continent on an unprecedented scale, and in Canada, they were joined by an increasing number of high school or secondary school students for the first time. Canada also witnessed more labor strikes in both 1967 and 1968 than in any year since 1947. By October 1968, direct actions taking place in schools proved more potent than the 55 terrorist bombings carried out by the Front de Liberation du Quebec (a leftist-nationalist organization). Strikes and school occupations marked an organizational advance in direct-action methods, inspiring the class-conscious population (it gained minimal trade union support, for example), but did not involve the student body at large.

A college culture had spread across the North American continent that *Fortune* magazine characterized as having a *"lack of concern"* about making money (original italics), with 40 percent of American college students embracing extreme and dissenting positions. In an opinion research survey, *Fortune* magazine in October 1968 reported that approximately 750,000 people aged 18-24 identified with the New Left. In this context, American, Mexican, and European examples of insurgency powerfully influenced the student and youth of Canada, who followed quickly on such models with their own actions.

The violent Mexican student uprising of July-October 1968 came to Canadians' notice not least from an article in the Montreal-based magazine *Our Generation* in its December 1968/January 1969 edition. Author Nardo Perello not only described the horrific events but also composed a section pointing out similarities to Canada. That such articles on Mexico (and others on Czechoslovakia) were published in this Canadian journal demonstrates that Canadians (and the world) were watching such events through the radical media.

I myself provided a link with events in Europe, and especially Czechoslovakia, when I went there in the summer of 1968, making lots of contacts along the way. In July, I left Montreal for Europe with two colleagues to attend the SDS convention in Frankfurt and went on to Prague for ten days. My train left Prague traveling south to Vienna and Ljubljana (Slovenia) on August 20, the very day that Warsaw Pact armies were crossing the northern border.

In Ljubljana, I attended a conference of the International Confederation for Disarmament and Peace (ICDP), a non-aligned umbrella of NGOs in many countries that the Canadian New Left had helped to create. It made the occupation a major priority, beginning early with an emergency session, in which it resolved to have leaflets written in a number of languages that would encourage nonviolent resistance to the invasion; it also sent three delegates to Prague immediately to distribute these and make contact with the opposition to the occupation. The ICDP also helped facilitate the first international meeting of leading New Left activists from several countries including the USA, Germany, the UK, Yugoslavia, and Canada. One action discussed was a German SDS march on and occupation of the Soviet Military Mission in Frankfurt to protest the invasion.

Meanwhile in Canada

These few notes on international links and meetings show that the Canadian New Left did not simply rely on traditional means of communication. The pipeline into Canada came through Montreal. This city was the hot zone and crossroads between the French-speaking world, Europe, and the movement. Montreal played a crucial role with its ample publications for reporting, analyzing, and evaluating what was going on and why. As close as we were to the American New Left, we were different from most of its members in our efforts to know what was happening elsewhere, and we often provided the information link between militants for them. Hence, when American draft-dodgers and military deserters began to cross the border, Montreal attracted a great many of them. With thousands of such refugees arriving in Canada, it was rumored around 1968 that US government spies numbered in the several hundreds in Montreal.

Despite these important functions for Montreal and the Canadian New Left, SUPA, the premier organization of the movement, disintegrated by 1967. A combination of factors led to its demise. First, even though its image, driven by its ambitious rhetoric, influenced most of the student and youth organizations in the country, SUPA was conventional in its strategy. There were also ongoing tensions and disagreements between the liberal-minded SUPA in Toronto, and its more radical leftist centers in Western Canada and Montreal. Furthermore, there were a number of issues that the movement failed to adequately address: there was a lack of understanding of the psychological burden of our colonial status, a lack of intellectual rigor in understanding the nature of liberal corporatism and neo-capitalism, an incapacity among those outside Montreal to openly sympathize with the Quebec's struggle for self-determination, as well as a fear of nonviolent direct action and civil disobedience.

However, it was not long after SUPA's demise that a series of New Left organizations sprang up on campuses to replace it in six of Canada's ten provinces. In the Pacific province of British Columbia, students organized the New Left Students for a Democratic University (SDU). A strike in October 1968 at Simon Fraser University got 114 arrested, with $26,000 in fines or two months in jail on their heads. In Alberta, an SDU was founded on the campus of the University of Alberta, and a radical secondary student movement emerged in Calgary in the spring of 1968; the spring and fall of 1969 also witnessed a series of militant actions and a lecture tour by Karl-Dietrich Wolff, head of the German SDS. Next door, in the underpopulated province of Saskatchewan, 1,000 students demonstrated in the early fall of 1968 over university democratization; this action in turn led to the formation of an SDU. In Winnipeg, Manitoba (population of 550,000 in 1968), an intense New Left militancy against Dow Chemical Co. and the Vietnam War took place and a Free University was established. In university-rich Ontario, the Toronto Student Movement (TSM) was founded in the summer of 1968, focusing primarily on the education system. Student groups emerged in five universities in a matter of weeks, and by the fall of 1968, the TSM was also supporting striking workers in various cities. These groups employed a full-range of actions from sit-ins and occupations to confrontations with reactionary public speakers. By December, thousands of secondary school students protested the extension of their school year. By early 1969, a new, major free university was founded, Rochdale College, and the first women's liberation group came onto the scene.

Two of the remaining provinces saw intense protest activities in specific cities—among the blacks in Halifax, Nova Scotia, and in the militant student and faculty organization Canadian Struggle for a Democratic Society in Fredericton, New Brunswick. Unfortunately, these activities were poorly reported—a weakness typical of Canada, which functioned more like a subcontinent than a unitary country according to Peter Warrian, the president of the Canadian Union of Students, in the May-June issue of *Our Generation* in 1968:

> In reality we are a colony of a neo-capitalist metropolises mostly centered in the United States. The consequence of this is that, at one and the same time, our economy serves the further development of an imperial metropolis and

generates the structural underdevelopment of various Canadian regions. If students and faculty ally to take over the whole or parts of the university, then its fundamental redirection must be part of the process. Concretely, this will mean a struggle for democratization, which is of necessity an anti-imperialist struggle.

Incidentally, it was in this same issue of *Our Generation* that John and Margaret Rowntree published the famous essay "Youth as Class" with comments by Edgar Z. Friedenberg and Marcel Rioux, which influenced the emergence of the Revolutionary Youth Movement in the US following the SDS.

But the 1968 protest wave was hottest in Montreal. The technical and junior colleges of Montreal experienced a general strike of 50,000 students that lasted six weeks. On October 22, 1968, 10,000 students and unemployed youths marched along Sherbrooke Street (between St. Urbain and Jeanne Mance) in downtown Montreal, in solidarity with all strikers, proceeding past the Ecole des Beaux Arts and flying the black flag of freedom, and past the Ecole Polytechnique flying the red flag of revolution.

More than 10,000 students marched in Montreal on Oct. 21, 1968, to protest the Quebec government's higher education policies.

These and many other actions formed part of a tableau illustrating an entire society awakening to the power of popular action. It was the theory and practice of student syndicalism first propagated in the mid-1960s that laid the groundwork for this student revolt in Montreal. While it was known in the rest of Canada through SUPA and in the US through the SDS, it was most deeply rooted in Quebec.

By 1969, this stream of student actions was shaping itself into a revolutionary youth movement. This movement, in turn, sought to expand into a broad extra-parliamentary opposition with a distinct New Left program and action strategy. The political bent of all of this was clearly a form of libertarian socialism, waiting to be fully born, predicated on a severe critique of parliamentary democracy.

All this New Left activism in and around 1968 helped transform Canadian universities. Reforms included electing students to university governing councils, establishing procedures for student evaluation of faculty, and allowing universities to cooperate directly with their neighboring communities. The notions of public participation and consultation that swept the country at that time profoundly affected the whole of the educational system and other public policy institutions.

The legacy of '68 and the '60s influenced the social movements that emerged in the 1970s. Although these single-issue movements were driven by "identity politics" and thus contributed to a fragmented view of social change, they nevertheless embodied many of the same organizational values, such as horizontal decision-making and developing a sense of community. What was missing was a sense of movement—common movement—across the board for the radical transformation of society from the bottom up.

The legacy of participatory democracy is best embedded to this day in the new urban movements that seek to create new cities. In Montreal, Toronto, Vancouver, and other large cities, a multi-issued approach focusing on community-organizing—with goals like developing participatory budgets, decentralizing urban governments in the direction of citizen councils, carrying on efforts toward gender equality, and balancing urban life with nature and the bio-region—exemplifies continuity with the previous generation. Equally significant is the goal of these urban movements to seek to connect with the World Social Forum as part of the worldwide anti-globalization movement and to network with people engaged in similar struggles across the planet. In such discourse, one hears echoes of the New Left ideas of the '60s throughout. The seeds have firmly taken root.

Dimitrios Roussopoulos is an editor, writer, and economist who has written widely on international politics, democracy, and social change. Among his recent publications is *Legacy of the New Left: The Sixties to Seattle* (2006).

COLOMBIA: THE "CATALUÑA MOVEMENT"

Santiago Castro-Gómez

The student movement of 1968 was the first movement that was able to set off critical self-reflection on the global system. Although the struggles of students in different parts of the world ran different courses, they all had something in common: they rejected the primacy of the economy over life.

The center of this social and cultural unrest inhered in the criticism of consumption, the rejection of achievement-oriented society, and the search for alternative lifestyles free from the encroachment of capital. The students' utopia was a world in which science and technology were used to reduce work hours to a minimum and to make it possible for all people to have equal access to resources and the fruits of collective labor. At the same time, they protested against the greed of imperialist powers, especially in Third World countries, and dreamed of nations living together in peace.

Students on strike

The reverberations of the French May of 1968 were also felt in Colombia, especially within the student movement of the 1970s. However, in contrast to comparable movements in Latin America, the Colombian student movement was relatively weak, never maturing into a united, political front. Even so, in 1971, during President Misael Pastrana Borrero's administration, the movement held a protest—perhaps the only one—that stirred the entire nation. Students of the Universidad del Valle in Cali went on strike because the Consejo Superior Universitario, the university's highest administrative board, refused to consider candidates for the position of rector that the students and professors had put forward. The strike had the support of all the country's student councils, mobilizing the students as never before.

Students at public universities, such as the Universidad Nacional in Bogotá, the Universidad de Antioquia, and the Universidad Industrial de Santander (UIS) in Bucaramanga, went on strike as well—even students at the private universities of Bogotá, like the Universidad de los Andes, Externado, and the Javeriana, supported them in this. Everywhere, students decried the "cultural infiltration" of North American imperialism, as well as the government's inability to reform an educational system whose higher levels they denounced as anti-democratic. At the same time, they lobbied for support of the workers' and peasants' struggles.

The "Cataluña Movement"

At the Jesuit Pontificia Universidad Javeriana in Bogotá, the students in the sociology department had already started organizing in 1970 to demand a more practical orientation in the curriculum from the university administration. In an open letter addressed to the dean of the sociology department, the students asked him to fire a professor of political sociology whose approach, they complained, was "too dogmatic," and who left no room for student opinion. This same year, the conflict between the student committee and the administration exploded in the strike known as the "Cataluña Movement," which was named for the building in which the students held their meetings.

Although the strike was triggered by a tuition hike, students' underlying dissatisfaction with and challenges to the structures of the university also played a fundamental role. They complained that there was no participation whatsoever by professors and students in institutional decisions—in fact, the university's bylaws were even written in Latin. In a letter addressed to the dean of the university, Father Alfonso Borrero, some of the sociology professors declared their support for the movement and demanded greater participation in academic questions and university administration.

The protests spurred other university departments to express their solidarity, which included organizing some "action days of reflection." Alarmed by the unprecedented situation, and in view of the momentum the protests gained in other universities across the country—not to mention the fear that spread in church circles because of the close relationship between Marxism and liberation theology—the Javeriana's administration promptly decided to close the departments of sociology and social work completely in 1971. At the Universidad de los Andes and at the Javeriana, several professors were dismissed, and at several public universities, there were severe confrontations between demonstrators and the police. Pressure from students grew so great that the Colombian secretary of education Luis Carlos Galán promised to review a reform plan for higher education that he had been presented with.

In the end, however, the protest had no concrete results. Rather, the government reacted with a decree that granted the secretary of education the power to close any and all institutions of secondary and higher education where strikes or activities that generally disturbed "the public order" occurred. On this basis, the Universidad de Antioquia, the UIS, and the Universidad Nacional de Bogotá were closed. The countless assemblies, protests, and demonstrations all over the country were unable to do anything about it, since the government imposed its will by force. This precipitated the gradual decline of the Colombian student movement so that, by the end of the decade, it left almost no traces in national memory.

Decline of the student movement

It is not hard to understand the reasons for this decline when one considers the various ideological tendencies competing to influence Colombian students: there were communists (through the Juventudes Comunistas [JUCO, the Communist Youth], Trotzkyists, Maoists, "Camilists" (admirers of liberation theologist and guerilla fighter Camilo Torres), nationalists (generally from the Right) and anarchists. One could argue that it was precisely this fierce ideological quarreling that prevented the student movement from finding a unified structure with which it could impact public discourse in the 1970s.

Demonstrators in the Colombian capital Bogotá march for freedom of the press in 1957 during the civil war (1948-1958) that racked the country.

There were various points of contention. Some guerrilla groups, like the ELN (Ejército de Liberación Nacional [National Liberation Army]) and EPL (Ejército Popular de Liberación [Popular Liberation Army]), recognized the student movement as an opportunity to recruit new supporters among the university youth. Yet groups opposed to armed struggle resisted this. On the other side, Trotzkyist and Maoist factions, especially the MOIR (Movimiento Obrero Independiente Revolucionario [Revolutionary and Independent

Workers' Movement]), accused the student movement of being "blind to reality" because real changes would not be effected by students (that is, the "intellectual sector") but by workers and peasants. In their view, the only reasonable political path for the movement was for students to join these sectors in their revolutionary fight. Still others preferred direct actions in street fighting, like burning cars and throwing stones, but the JUCO attributed the government's violent suppression of the movement precisely to these provocations. In the end, the student movement of the 1970s succumbed to this internal ideological trench warfare and the influence of leftist extremist trends.

Nevertheless, it must be emphasized that, although the Colombian student movement achieved only short-lived renown, it became one of the most important forces opposing the Frente Nacional [National Front]—the coalition of the liberal and conservative parties that governed the country from 1958-1974—in the 1970s. Moreover, it managed to generate, even at elite universities like the Universidad de los Andes and the Javeriana, a great deal of critical reflection among students, not only specifically about higher education but also about social conditions in general in the country. Colombian universities have never been the same.

Santiago Castro-Gómez is a Professor of Philosophy in the Instituto Pensar, Universidad Javeriana (Bogotá, Colombia).

MEXICO: THE POWER OF MEMORY

Sergio Raúl Arroyo

"A massacre turns a place into a garbage can." This quotation by the writer Juan García Ponce refers to the state crime that ended the Mexican student movement on October 2, 1968, resulting in a still unknown and controversial number of deaths. The movement, which began on July 23, 1968, consisted of a series of episodes that demonstrate just how great the demand for basic civil liberties had grown among a large sector of Mexican society, how mobilized that sector had become, and the intransigence of a government repelled by criticism, unfamiliar with the negotiations inherent to a democratic society. Indeed, the events of this student movement unveil Mexico as a nation whose democratic tradition was conceived as a mere technical formality that could be fulfilled by means of appearances when the Olympic Games brought it into the international spotlight.

The Mexican 1968 disclosed a grim state of affairs in a country where politics was a matter of caste. The students had a long list of demands: the release of political prisoners, the repeal of sections 145 and 145b of the Penal Code (which gave the government the power to imprison people meeting in groups of three or more if it believed they threatened public order), the decommissioning of the body of grenadiers, the punishment of the police chiefs responsible for acts of repression, and compensation for the families of those killed and injured in government violence. These demands represented a desire to truly dismantle the Mexican state's legal instruments and other means of oppression. "A massacre turns a place into a garbage can." Forty years ago, the Mexican government led us into the garbage can of history.

As with all totalitarian regimes in the twentieth century, the Mexican governments that followed the Mexican Revolution of 1910–1920 were driven by the desire to systematize the mastery of memory, to control it by any possible means and make it selective and abstract. The management of memory became part of the governmental program, and controlling the flow of information that was not for public use became routine and methodical. First, one had to silence all testimonials and experiences that broke out of the ideological cages of the post-revolutionary period; then one created a sort of vacuum around historical facts and played down all troubling circumstances until they were merely banal. Finally, one just had to wait until the remains of any particular testimonials or memories had grown so old and mute that they acquired the opacity that the dust of time spreads along its paths. In this way, the facts came to be diffuse and unprovable, as well as unrecognizable. After this "vaporizing" treatment, all that remained for history was a wink for the initiated, a vague reference in a chronology, nonexistence. Amid this political trickery, the press buried its head in the sand and reached out its hand.

A movement banished from history

Whoever scans the textbooks on Mexican history that are designed for Mexican schoolchildren will see that the student movement of 1968 is practically nonexistent. In the best case, it will appear in one or the other book as a spectral reference in a paragraph as confusing as it is short. For most Mexicans, this will be the only source of information on one of the most important chapters of twentieth-century Mexican history. In spite of all the political changes that have occurred in Mexican society since the 1980s—and especially since the transition to a new government in 2000—this indifferent attitude has persisted up to today. All the state education policies have shared the aim of transforming 1968 into something distant, into an event that grows ever further from the concrete reality in which we move.

It is possible to discern some of the reasons for this secrecy. The most obvious are political and ideological motives relating to the deep-rooted ties between the successive governments of the Partido Revolucionario Institucional [Institutional Revolutionary Party] that were in power from the 1920s to 2000. In the later part of this period, the history of the 1968 movement was repeatedly veiled, or the government expressed regret about the tragic outcome that was as simple as it was insincere. This was all part of a rhetorical strategy—a mere formula employed according to the state of things—for elections, publicity campaigns, appearances in congress, etc. None of it constituted any sort of real self-criticism that justly represented the facts of the massacre and dealt with those responsible for it. The country moved gradually from a state of induced amnesia to simulation, from simple guilt to culpable complicity.

Justice as a dead-end street

The administrations of the Partido Acción Nacional (PAN [Party of National Action]), which relieved the PRI of power in 2000 and was re-elected in 2006, have displayed an ambivalent attitude about the events of 1968. On the one hand, they have engaged in discussions about seeking justice in relation to them, and, on the other, they have seemed irritated by them. As for seeking justice, the government merely drafted a strategy for investigating the events that is no different, really, from any previous strategies. And now, even after several years, this has hardly progressed at all (that is, it has not been successful in prosecuting those responsible for the deaths). As for their irritation, the PAN—clearly a part of the "Mexican Right"—has no historical or ideological ties to 1968 that would enable it to identify with or exhibit interest in this student movement from over forty years ago. Thus, the party cannot move beyond an utterly unconvincing formal stance. Moreover, some economic and judicial powers are involved that have no interest in pursuing investigations.

In short, even the current government, which is trying hard to be politically correct (an apparent sign of the times) has not been able to legally clarify who was responsible for the murder of civilians by paramilitary forces in 1968, and especially for the mass murder at a rally on October 2 that year in Tlatlolco, north of Mexico City, and bring them to justice.

Mexican student buckling in pain at a demonstration in Mexico City, Sept. 22, 1968.

1968 as a key point of reference

The Universidad Autónoma de México (UNAM) construction of the "Memorial of 1968," which was opened in October 2007, marks an attempt to counteract the refusal to acknowledge these events and the apathy toward this topic that the government has exhibited over the years. The UNAM is interested in portraying 1968 as a key point of reference for understanding the last forty years of Mexican history. In this, the UNAM, which played a central role in the movement, is making use of its autonomy and academic authority. It has followed an ethical commitment to create a space that recalls the days of the student movement and promotes reflection on its legacy for the country's recent history.

The construction of this memorial brought up a fundamental problem that had nothing to do with the attitudes, fears, and interests of the incumbent powers. Rather, it concerned a political and conceptual question that the memorial team had to address. As the events were so recent, in historical terms, the team had to be sure that its view was not clouded, that it did not create an exhibition, without a critical perspective, that would only convince those who were already convinced.

Confronting memory

Commemorating the past cannot be done in a forced manner; it should not represent a voluntary revival of a dying ideology, nor should it be done as a sterile act to clear the country's conscience. It should render the events neither sacred nor banal. It should not succumb to nostalgia nor water down what happened in the sea of time and forgetfulness into which so many other events have disappeared. The UNAM's memorial attempts to confront its spectators with the peculiar power of memory while retaining the necessary distance from the dullness of predetermined value judgments. Aimed primarily at human nature, including its contradictions, it construes this power of memory as a creative experience.

The memorial and the museum do not merely echo another era but lay a path that turns the visitor to a description of and reflection on a world recalled by its eyewitnesses. This mixes reportage with mythology, as well as the individual and collective dimensions of history. In it, we find the phenomena that characterized this indelible moment: the leading role of the masses, the counterculture, the complaints against systematic political persecution, the impunity of those in power and the forces of repression, the tireless struggle for the rights of the minorities and, above all, the critical attitude that prompted a large part of society to put despotism in its place.

A source for political imagination

A basic principle in developing the project was to free the memorial from its necrological burden and transform it into something else: an exercise in memory. A great chorus that recalls the stations of the student movement attests to its internal political diversity but also reveals that it was inscribed in an ever more interdependent world, a world in which Prague, Paris, and many cities in the United States and Latin America appear to be part of a broad pattern of youth rebellions that shook the whole planet. They were processes of profound resistance that were repressed with the same fury in both capitalist and socialist regimes.

From a historiographic perspective, this documentation is the decisive center from which everything else emerges: cinema, oral history, literature, media, photography, and sociology are the stages for the theater of the world and of an unmanageable history that has long since begun to point in more than one direction. The commemoration of the student movement of 1968 in Mexico, therefore, must position itself beyond any uncritical triumphalism or fatalistic defeat. The critical importance of 1968 will not be found on the altars of official history, nor in screaming radicalism, nor in the silence of the graves. Rather, it is in the era's shaking off of fear, in its disturbingly direct and nonconformist language, that one can find sources to feed one's imagination—especially one's political imagination.

Sergio Raúl Arroyo is the Director of the Centro Cultural Universitario Tlatelolco (CCUT, Cultural University Center Tlatelolco) where the "Memorial of '68" is located.

PERU: THE BEGINNING OF A NEW WORLD

Oscar Ugarteche

Economic reforms split the country

The market, which was overtaken by transnational businesses in the 1960s, forced Latin American governments to give industry a prominent place in their domestic economies. In Peru, heavy industry, crude oil, and the production of fish meal were regarded as the most important areas of industry. In order to achieve the necessary performance, the government brought foreign capital into the country under unfavorable conditions.

This aggravated the social differences that had divided the population for years; since broad parts of society looked upon the native Indios as a hindrance to development, the latter barely participated in the social life of Peru. Foreign capital ruled the country. The entire situation was summed up by the famous remark of a Peruvian banker: "This business with fish meal always used to stink, but when Mr. Micon [referring to an international mining company] takes an interest in it, it smells like roses."

In the mid-1960s, the economic situation changed and a recession set in, soon followed by inflation. The subsequent military coup did not surprise anybody, and there were no protests whatever on the day it occurred. Early on the morning of October 3, 1968, the army arrested and exiled the president, and occupied parliament and the headquarters of the most important parties and trade unions. Six days later, it then occupied and expropriated the facilities of the International Petroleum Company, the fulcrum of the worst political and economic scandals.

For several years thereafter, October 9 was celebrated as the "Day of National Dignity." Public protests and street fighting began only later, when other large firms were nationalized, big landowners were expropriated, and newspapers were shut down, restricting freedom of speech.

At this point, the government began to carry out necessary reforms, but as it lacked the support of the population, the reforms failed to achieve the desired results. Historians and sociologists still argue over the advantages and disadvantages of the reforms, but everyone agrees that Peru became a new country in 1968. That year marks a watershed in contemporary Peruvian history.

The 1960s were especially prosperous in Peru. These were years of enormous economic growth, of new industrial development driven by automobile manufacturing, and of the emergence of a modern industrial infrastructure that stretched from the middle of the country to its northern border (from the province of Ate Vitarte near Lima to the Panamericana Norte).

In the provinces of Arequipa, Chiclayo, Chimbote, and Moquegua, new industrial sectors arose, generating a modern proletariat that began to get organized into unions. Simultaneously, the boom in mining prompted workers to form powerful and combative unions.

The Cuban Revolution as a model

The drought of 1957 and the unequal distribution of land spurred a large wave of migration in Peru from the mountains to the coast, and especially to Lima. In addition, the middle classes demanded an active role in the urban economy and protested against the oligarchic structure of Peruvian society, in which about one hundred families owned the nation's assets and, thus, determined the country's fortunes.

This tension between the oligarchic structure and the demands of the working and middle classes provided room for the rise of guerrilla movements that sought to mobilize the rural population beginning in the 1960s. Perhaps the most well-known figure from these movements is the young poet guerrilla Javier Heraud, who was killed in 1963. Heraud became very famous when, at age nineteen, he won the national poetry awards, constituting a sort of *enfant terrible à la Rimbaud* of his time. The guerilla movements of the "Sierra Central" and Cuzco in 1965 and the imprisonment of leaders Héctor Béjar and Hugo Blanco marked another episode in a decade in which the Cuban model of insurrection gained momentum and the utopian ideal of assaulting those in power gained validity.

Demanding reforms

In the 1960s, Peru's agriculture and hacienda (or plantation) economy were showing signs of wear and clearly needed to be modernized. The exploitation of the farm workers did not improve the land productivity of the Andes highlands. Moreover, the latifundia of about 100,000 hectares—large land holdings that stretched from the Sierra Mountains, and sometimes from the coast, to the rainforest—were unable to produce enough to pay the wages and allow these workers to free themselves from serfdom. As a result, serfdom persisted, exacerbating the social tensions it gave rise to as modernization increasingly demanded wages for work.

These social conditions carried over to the city, where vertical inequality between whites and non-whites manifested itself in a sort of informal apartheid analogous to that of South Africa. Demands for inclusion in Peruvian democracy came up against racial and ethnic exclusion that was based on the image of Peru as one great hacienda belonging to one hundred families. This resulted in the founding of political parties to the left of the communist party, such as the Vanguardia Revolucionaria [the Revolutionary Avant-Garde], which was probably the most well known, as well as revolutionary student groups, such as the Frente Revolucionario Estudiantil Socialista (FRES [Revolutionary Socialist Student Front]).

Fear of the power of the people

In this context, university students began to take action. One of the most memorable protests was the one that took place in front of the Club Nacional—whose members included the families of the oligarchy—during a debutante ball. Although only a few demonstrators appeared and beat on large drums as the young ladies stepped out of cars and ascended the stairs arm-in-arm with their fathers, this event stirred the oligarchic families' symbolic fear of the power of the masses.

A protest during the annual cardinal's dinner, an elegant event that raised funds for charitable purposes, had a similar effect. Student members of the Juventud de Estudiantes Católicos (JEC [Catholic Student Youth]) stormed the office of the Colegio Maristas in San Isidro and pulled the tablecloth from beneath the set places, causing a great ruckus among the finely dressed ladies and gentlemen. Such direct attacks on the elite generated more fear than the more distant grass-roots movements in the countryside because they plainly demonstrated that the existing social structures had long since lost their legitimacy and that no solution could be found within the system. Rather, drastic change was needed.

Protests against corruption

The economy had slowed down in 1967 after a very long period of high sustained growth, and a devaluation of the currency in

September of that year had sharply reduced the purchasing power of the population. In the meantime, from the early 1960s onwards and increasingly, serfs occupied the hacienda lands they worked. The country's landed gentry refused to consider the possibility of turning them into farm workers in spite of the growing social conflict in the countryside. On top of this, as a result of an international economic slowdown, mineral prices fell, generating additional social tensions while miners in Cerro de Pasco went on strike. Tensions rose even more when, in August 1968, the Peruvian state made a contract with Standard Oil Company of New Jersey (then ESSO, today Exxon). This contract granted the corporation the right to exploit the fields in Brea and Pariñas in the Piura area. However, due to the machinations of Fernando Belaúnde's administration, the congress had not received the complete document when it agreed to the terms.

Students and professors protesting university budget cuts in Lima, Peru, 1967.

Protests erupted in Lima then in light of the blatant corruption of the government in addition to everything else. All through September 1968, there were continual protests by unions and students. At the same time, the media voiced sharp criticism of the government and ceased supporting Belaúnde's democratic administration. Instead, given the political crisis of government, as well as the country's socioeconomic problems, they called for a coup d'état. This actually took place on October 3, 1968, whereupon the military junta led by Juan Velasco assumed political power.

A change in the military's attitude

A decisive shift in the attitude of the armed forces became apparent in the 1960s: they went from seeing themselves as the guards of the oligarchy to caretakers of the people's well-being within the framework of a national security and development strategy. The Centro de Altos Estudios Militares (CAEM [Center for Higher Military Study]), where officers of all divisions attended postgraduate courses in development and security, played a special role in this. In 1965, the Peruvian military had used napalm against the indigenous Asháninka population when they had gotten involved in guerrilla warfare with the Movimiento de Izquierda Revolucionaria (MIR) under the command of Luis de la Puente Uceda. Many in the military had found this method of suppressing the guerrillas inhumane and noted that it failed to resolve the social problems that gave rise to them. This was the backdrop to the memorable phrase junta leader Juan Velasco uttered in a televised speech on "The Day of the Peasant," June 24, 1969, when he announced land reform: "Peasant, your master will no longer feed on your poverty."

The coup of October 3, 1968, marked the irrevocable end of serfdom and of one social order and the start of a new one—to the relief of the many and the regret of the few. Of course, some of the demands from that time have not yet been met. Today in Peru, some people, from intellectuals to domestic workers, still work without wages, and racism, though watered down, persists, in spite of the country's Indian president. Yet the great historical problem of Peru, which has yet to be overcome, is *rentismo*, or rent-seeking. This exploitative practice is keeping Peru from becoming a modern and more just state.

Oscar Ugarteche, a Peruvian national, is a Senior Research Fellow at the Instituto de Investigaciones Económicas, UNAM, Mexico, a member of the Mexican Research System, and a member of LATINDADD, as well as the President of the Agencia Latinoamericana de Información (ALAI).

USA: UNENDING 1968

Todd Gitlin

The nature of Lt. John Kerry's performance on a naval vessel in Vietnamese waters in 1968-69 became a central issue in America's 2004 election. The question of whether the one-time Air National Guard pilot George W. Bush had discharged his military duty after graduating from Yale University in 1968 played a far smaller part.

In October 2008, needling Senator Hillary Rodham Clinton, who had supported a tiny federal appropriation for a museum to commemorate the Woodstock concert of 1969, Senator John McCain brought a Republican audience to its feet when he declared that he had not attended that concert because he had been "tied up at the time"—an obvious allusion to his long imprisonment in North Vietnam after his navy plane was shot down. Barack Obama has periodically told adoring crowds that the culture wars of the 1960s ought to be ended.

Politicians disagree over the consequences of 1968

As in 1992, when Bill Clinton's wartime draft evasion and his claim not to have inhaled marijuana became campaign issues, and as in 1980, when Ronald Reagan gave a speech defending "states' rights" in the county where three civil rights workers had been murdered in 1964, American politicians are still fighting over the 1960s, over what happened, and over its meaning. Were the changes, on balance, good or bad?

This question draws the fundamental divide in American politics today. This history, or wound, is still open because the conflicts that gushed forth during 1968 and the surrounding years went to the heart of American identity. Two visions of America collided—sometimes in the same breast. Opposing ideas about male-female relations, about race and sexuality, about authority altogether, about America's relation to the rest of the world clashed violently. The forces unleashed four decades ago have not ceased to collide.

Protests helped Nixon to power

Again and again in the 1960s, anti-authority charged at authority, and the authorities met the defining test of their rule in a fight against rebels with or without causes. In the imagery of the time, history was either ending or beginning, or both at once. Hope was planted; hope was uprooted. Heroes stepped forward; so did assassins. Recall that in the immediate sense, 1968 was won by the Right—in a year of the savage murders of Martin Luther King Jr. and Robert Kennedy; after black riots in more than 100 cities; after the August police riots in Chicago that were more widely blamed on the demonstrators at the Democratic Convention than on the police and the political authorities who were actually responsible. With one convulsion after another, all amplified by the mass media, it was Richard Nixon who was elected president on the strength of a political backlash, launching a political counterrevolution that lasted almost uninterrupted, and with savage results, for four subsequent decades, and has still not evaporated.

Sit-in at Columbia University on April 26, 1968, protesting the Vietnam War and racial discrimination.

History as a collective nightmare

One of the sublime and strange features of the insurgent '68 was the way it coated differences of intention with an apparently unifying mist—drugs, sexual liberation, "the revolution." But common to the various manifestations of the insurgent '68 was an insistence that, despite all appearances of fixed tradition and immovable authority, life was open and democracy was an uncompleted project.

History was a prologue to freedom, if not an illusion that the moment of freedom had already arrived. Perhaps—thought the utopians—history was a collective nightmare from which we were already beginning to awake! But looming in the background was a political majority that joined the newly Republican South with disaffected white working-class males—Nixon's "silent majority"—insisting that history was very far from open and striving to slam the door.

The "68ers" believed they were the future, but they were not even the present. America's best-selling poet of 1968 was neither Bob Dylan nor the anti-war radical Robert Lowell but a sentimental kitschmeister named Rod McKuen. The most popular television shows were traditional westerns and rural comedies. The musical *Funny Girl* sold more movie tickets in the United States than the countercultural favorite *2001: A Space Odyssey*. As '68's own bards and guerrillas manqués often failed—or refused—to know, not everyone under thirty was swinging together into the age of psychedelic mystery tours, surrealistically stuttering consciousness, and fervent gauchisme.

Discontent about the excesses of the Bush era

Among those who were galvanized by '68 were the likes of George W. Bush, Newt Gingrich, and John McCain, who resolved never to let such foolishness happen again and organized to prevent it. These were the rollbackers: the corporate and fundamentalist artists of Nixon's Southern Strategy, soon joined by the neo-conservatives, all of them triumphant (after an embarrassing pause for impeachment) in the Reagan restoration and then riding high in George W. Bush's administration.

Still, popular currents revolted by the reactionary excesses of the Bush years and eager to resume the progressive project mobilized against them, not without success. It is, as they say, no accident that the two principal rivals for the Democratic nomination in the election campaign of 2008 were an African American and a woman, neither of whose candidacies would have been imaginable without the movements of the 1960s. The efforts, first by Hillary Clinton's supporters, then by the Republicans, to tar Barack Obama with excesses rooted in the '60's—the black nationalism of the Rev. Jeremiah Wright, the terrorism of Bill Ayers, the militant community organizing of Saul Alinsky—failed to defeat him.

Obama has placed himself in the line of progressives; at the same time, he has frequently spoken of the need to transcend the polarizations of decades past. As his first few months in the White House have shown, it is easier to speak of such transcendence than to accomplish it as long as the Republican Party has been captured by its right (and now virtually only) wing. The rhetoric of bipartisanship may be politic, but it cannot be realized. Thus, regardless of his initial intentions, Obama proves to be a child of the '60s. With his win, the Democrats can, at long last, reap some long-deferred harvests from the decade's movements. It is not clear who will get the last word in history, but what is clear is that the fight is still on to inherit that improbable and unrepeatable decade.

Todd Gitlin is a Professor of Journalism and Sociology at Columbia University, and author of *The Sixties: Years of Hope, Days of Rage* (1987) and, most recently, *The Bulldozer and the Big Tent: Blind Republicans, Lame Democrats, and the Recovery of American Ideals* (2007).

VENEZUELA: A SOCIOLOGICAL LABORATORY

Félix Allueva

In 1968, student protests helped bring about changes in participatory procedures in the university community, in the decision-making process, in student co-administration, and in the relationship between university and society. Despite moderate successes for this movement known as the Movement for Renewal of the University, however, Venezuela at that time was held back by its own less developed structures. There were also other hindrances, such as the educational plans drawn up for the country by the United States, a program attuned to the North American model of development. Furthermore, there were continuing battles for power within the universities between the Left and the Right.

New leadership groups regarded the Movement for Renewal of the University as favorable to their own growth and infiltrated it. People in Venezuela also took note of the protests and actions of the youth movements in other countries of the world. From the United States came rock music and the hippie movement, from France and Germany radical philosophies and the vehemence of the student revolts, and from London psychedelic drugs. Prague gave us a spring that held out the prospect of socialism with a human face and generated discussions about leftist dogmatism.

The struggle begins

In June 1968, the university community began its struggle to achieve financing for the university infrastructure and improvement of the teaching staff. At first, naiveté gained the upper hand and a few anarchistic elements briefly carried the day. But as events unfolded, the university increasingly became the principal agent spurring social changes.

The students' activities produced unusual forms of protest as teachers, workers, and assigned officials of the Universidad Central de Venezuela joined in. Communal actions within and outside the university changed parts of everyday life. In June 1968, the Movement for Renewal of the University had become a reality. As the conflict intensified, President Rafael Caldera's administration ordered the military to occupy the Universidad Central de Venezuela.

This act of government interference dampened many of the hopes for the planned changes for renewal.

Rioters attack the limousine of Vice President Richard Nixon and his party during their visit to Caracas, Venezuela, on May 13, 1958.

The more recent Venezuelan protests against the media policies of the Chavez administration in May 2007, however, were more successful, and bear similarities to the legendary Paris May of 1968. Venezuelan students, too, used new political forms. Students took to the streets after decades of apathy and immobility to demonstrate against a government measure designed to shut down a television channel.

In Venezuela, a country divided between the followers of the charismatic president Hugo Chávez and those who oppose him, a new generation of leaders under the age of 25 is emerging. These young students don't identify with any of the existing political parties but don't deny their validity either. They are interested in the democratic system. On the other hand, there is an incipient student front that calls itself "revolutionary." For want of power and significant numbers, its supporters keep reciting the very detailed rules set down by the great helmsman of the Bolivian government.

The Venezuelan May

In May 2007, a national protest movement emerged that unified students on a variety of levels. Universities public and private united; students from different political camps—conservative, progressive, democratic, and even from the so-called ultra-left—different educational levels, middle and higher, and different social classes and regions of the country worked together.

Just as in the French May of 1968, the students took the initiative. They declared themselves autonomous and independent of any party norms; they had no regard for the interests of the government or the opposition. Also parallel to the French May, these student leaders were very naive and lacking in political history and experience. They were accused of being mere puppets of the empire, servants to the ruling classes, and, in the best of cases, "daddies' boys."

A broad-based social movement

But the same Marxist analysis that applied to the decade surrounding the French May pertains in Venezuela as well: Without comprising a social class, the students were an integral part of the people, and so they expressed the interests and struggles of the people. Therefore, the protesting students went beyond making lists of demands and strove to achieve something greater—political debates.

In this way, the student protests, which, after all, began in response to an inefficient and short-sighted government policy, transcended the academic realm and became a broad-based social movement. The strength and novelty of this 2007 movement lay, like that of 1968, in its capacity to communicate situations, needs, and aims without forcing them into previously fixed party schemata.

First, these new social actors took over the streets of the country's main cities protesting the government's sanctions against the media. Weeks later, they became the cement binding the social mortar, which, in turn, generated broader waves of protest. These protests were not only about defending the freedom of speech but also about defending human rights and universities' threatened autonomy. They were also about fighting against repression, and especially against the authoritarian Bolivian leadership's intention of setting the nation on a totalitarian socialist course.

"The other side of the coin"—the student front defending the government—now began mobilizing to stop the "counterrevolutionaries." The arguments were so banal, clichéd, and backward-looking that the students merely managed to isolate themselves. Losing most student elections at schools and universities, the "Chavist" students clearly lacked initiative and impact.

"Boredom is counterrevolutionary"

In 1968, the squares and avenues of Paris, Berlin, Prague, and San Francisco filled with young people who had turned slogans and methods of protest inside out—their creativity knew no bounds.

In 2007, the slogans "Forbid the forbidden" and "Imagination to power" regained their meaning in Caracas and other Venezuelan cities. Whether utilizing surprise tactics, mobilizing commando-style at lightning speed, occupying unusual spaces, or "dressing up" in the official pro-government red, the indie youth movement has always been ahead of President Chávez.

The government's repressive tactics—arrested and wounded students, selective persecution, media attacks and denunciations—are spurring the student movement on, making it larger and stronger. The Internet, communication via SMS, virtual networks, a dose of anarchy, and the nearly 40-year-old democratic tradition have made it possible for the students to withstand the authoritarian ways of their government.

Protests spur change of course

For ten years, the Bolivarian Revolution advanced, but now it has suffered its first defeat. The people of Venezuela rejected the government's constitutional reform proposal on December 2, 2007. Venezuelan students played a major role in bringing about this change of course. In their new leading role and civic engagement, the students have had three direct and positive consequences: first, they prompted voters to reject the constitutional reform; second, they have started up protest activity again for defending civil rights; third, they have stimulated reflection and, above all, self-criticism among those in the government-supporting part of the movement.

These pro-government students realized for the first time that it is necessary to leave behind the "floodlike and emotional" mobilization "created by the leadership of President Chávez." Moreover, they accepted "the mismanagement at all the levels . . . the inefficiency of the bureaucracy, and the disastrous administration of the regional and local governments," as well as the narrow view of the Chavist student leadership. This is not the end of the story, as the protests of 2009 attest. New chapters await us in this Venezuela that has become a veritable sociological laboratory.

Félix Allueva is a researcher and cultural promoter in Venezuela, as well as radio presenter and president of the foundation Festival Nuevas Bandas [New Bands Festival].

ASIA & AUSTRALIA

AUSTRALIA: A NATION OF LOTUS-EATERS

Hugh Mackay

If 1968 was the year that shook "the world," its vibrations took some time to reach Australia. That year began, for us, in a state of shock over the accidental drowning of our prime minister, Harold Holt. His assessment of our mood, delivered shortly before his death, was that we were a nation of lotus-eaters—hedonistic, materialistic, and lazy. That was an echo of the 1964 verdict passed on us by one of our leading public intellectuals, Donald Horne, in his seminal book, *The Lucky Country*, in which he suggested that Australia was a "country run mainly by second-rate people who share its luck. It lives on other people's ideas and, although its ordinary people are adaptable, most of its leaders (in all fields) so lack curiosity about the events that surround them that they are often taken by surprise." Though he changed his mind about us as we began to reinvent ourselves through the 1980s and '90s, Horne had concluded in 1964 that Australia had "not deserved its good fortune."

Back then, Europe seemed far more remote from us than it does today, though most of us claimed European ancestry and recognized the Northern Hemisphere as the reference point for many of our ideas, beliefs, cultural imperatives, fashions, fads, and philosophies. In 1968, our hallmarks were complacency rather than angst; contentment rather than restlessness; optimism rather than dread. Other people's problems were not ours; other societies' upheavals were no harbinger of our own. Our revolutionary spirit was dormant and would remain so, for most of us, until well into the 1970s.

Alarmed but not engaged

Accustomed to the idea that the rest of the world was a long way away, we heard about the student riots in Paris, the strikes sweeping France, the brave resistance of young Czechs to the Soviet tanks rolling into Prague, the assassinations of Martin Luther King Jr. and Robert F. Kennedy in the US, the Tet Offensive in Vietnam, and the upsurge in the Women's Liberation movement. We were intrigued, saddened, even alarmed—but not really engaged.

The country was experiencing a phase of political stability, with conservative governments in power at the national level and in five of our six states. The economy was healthy; unemployment was low. The birthrate had begun to fall after the postwar baby boom, the divorce rate was miniscule, and the prospect of a prosperous, egalitarian society seemed to be coming true in the burgeoning middle-class suburbs sprawling out from our major cities. Our self-confidence was boosted by the sporting triumphs of Australians on the world stage.

Signs of a mounting resistance

While there were signs of mounting resistance to Australia's involvement in the Vietnam War—partly because so many of the troops were conscripts, that is, youths serving their compulsory military service—the majority of Australians, in 1968, still supported Australia's participation in what they had been led to believe was a straightforward struggle against communism. The newly amended National Service Act provided for imprisonment of those who resisted conscription, and a prominent Sydney journalist and pacifist, Simon Townsend, attracted widespread publicity when he was compulsorily enlisted and put on a diet of bread and water for disobeying his first military order.

But an equally prominent young Australian, the rock star Normie Rowe, was widely praised for embracing his call-up. While many Australians in 1968 believed the US strategy in Vietnam was flawed, it would be two more years before a serious mass movement—the Vietnam Moratorium marches—would begin to erode popular and political support for the war.

Protest in London before the Australia House against Australian troops in Vietnam, Jan. 1966.

It was not until 1972 that serious political and social change began to transform Australia. The Whitlam Labor government, elected in that year, brought Australia's involvement in Vietnam to an end, opened a new dialogue with China, introduced free university education, and, in 1975, reformed the divorce laws, removing the concept of "fault" and establishing "irretrievable breakdown of marriage" as the sole grounds for divorce.

During three turbulent years that ended in the dismissal of the Whitlam government by the vice-regal governor-general, Australians became more politically engaged and more open to the idea of reform. As a society, we seemed eager to embrace social and cultural change, having finally begun to pick up the signals from the rest of the world, suggesting that political and cultural change was not just "in the air" but on the ground. Even so, few of us had any idea how radical those changes might turn out to be, or how fundamentally Australian society would be recast as we, too, caught the revolutionary mood.

The mid-1970s found us on the cusp of a series of four revolutions that would, over the ensuing twenty years, effectively reinvent us as a society. The *gender* revolution would fundamentally alter the place of women in our society and redefine the character of relations between the sexes everywhere from marriage to the workplace. The *economic* revolution would change our perspective on the world, bringing Southeast Asia into focus as never before and forcing us to recognize that our traditional ties to Britain and Europe were loosening. It would also challenge our fondly held belief in job security as our birthright and begin a process of wealth redistribution that would see a huge growth in the number of rich Australians, a shrinking of the economic middle class, and a widening gap between wealth and poverty.

The early 1970s also began a revolution in our sense of *cultural identity*, with the concept of multiculturalism being tentatively promoted, along with the idea that it was our ethnic and cultural diversity—rather than our Anglo-Celtic heritage—that would soon define us. The *information technology* revolution was, similarly, destined to change the way we live and work, but it would be another twenty years before we fully appreciated the impact of the emerging electronic technologies on the character of our society.

Women's Liberation Movement

Of all the changes that would reshape us, the gender revolution was by far the most radical. By 1970, the shock waves from the Women's

Liberation Movement were finally beginning to be felt here on a large enough scale for us (especially men) to realize that this was indeed a mass movement with revolution in its sights. Many Australian women had read Simone de Beauvoir's *The Second Sex*, but it was Betty Friedan's *The Feminine Mystique* that gave a voice to a generation of women who became the local pioneers of Women's Lib. Friedan's 1963 classic had inspired many women to ponder their long history of second-class status in Australia, but there were few hints, until well into the 1970s, that Australia was about to embark on the long and painful journey towards sexual equality and, in the process, redefine the institutions of marriage and the family, revolutionize the workplace and redraw the political landscape.

In 1970, the Australian publication of Germaine Greer's *The Female Eunuch* and Kate Millett's *Sexual Politics* added the fuel of anger and outrage to the revolutionary fire. By the late 1970s, the gender revolution was in full swing, aided by the Whitlam government's reform of the divorce laws in 1975 that sent the divorce rate to unprecedented levels. In the ensuing 30 years, Australia joined the high-divorce societies of the world, with between 35 and 40 percent of contemporary marriages now expected to end in divorce.

Falling marriage and birthrates

Along the way, our birth rate plummeted to a record low—partly driven by the rising education levels of women, partly by widespread acceptance of the contraceptive pill, and partly by the attitudes of a new generation of young Australians. These children of the revolution, now adults, appear to be determined to keep their options open and to postpone (or avoid) both marriage and parenthood in unprecedented numbers.

The falling marriage and birth rates and the sustained high rate of divorce rapidly reduced the size of the Australian household. Today, just over 50 percent of all Australian households are either single or two-person households, and the Australian Bureau of Statistics projects that by 2026, 34 percent of all Australian households will be single households. In the past twenty years, the number of Australians living in traditional family households (with a mother, father, and children) has fallen from 60 percent to 50 percent of the population, and is projected to fall to 40 percent in the next 20 years.

Changes in cultural life

The mood that favored change might have been slow to reach Australia, but our cultural life has been transformed in the period since the early 1970s. We've absorbed immigrants from about 180 countries around the world—still predominantly European, though with a growing proportion from East Asia, especially China—and we've also come to see ourselves as part of the Asia Pacific rather than a mere outpost of the UK. Our religious life has been marked by a steady decline in church attendance, the emergence of Roman Catholics as the dominant religious group, and the recent rise of fundamentalism and Pentecostalism. The sectarian bitterness of the past has all but disappeared.

Our revolutionary period might have been gentler and less traumatic than in many other parts of the world, but we, too, have our epidemics of depression and anxiety to show for it. Above all, we no longer feel as remote from the rest of the world as we once did. Our long era of complacency is over.

Hugh Mackay is an Australian social researcher and author. His latest book is *Advance Australia...Where?* (2007).

CHINA: THE PROCESS OF DECOLONIZATION IN THE CASE OF HONG KONG

Oscar Ho Hing-kay

1968 marked a significant change in the governance of Hong Kong under British colonial rule. It was also the beginning of social activism among students and intellectuals who called for decolonization. This new chapter in the history of Hong Kong was ushered in by devastating riots in 1967. The brutal practices of a factory owner in the industrial district precipitated a workers' strike on May 6, 1967. The owner had oppressed his workers by cutting their wages, extending their work hours, and discharging their union leaders. This strike, in turn, triggered a series of riots and bomb attacks that crippled the city for months. While many interpreted the riots as anti-British acts orchestrated by Communist China, which was in the midst of the zealous Cultural Revolution, others regarded them as an anti-colonial movement challenging social injustice and the exploitation of workers.

Up until these events, Hong Kong had operated under the typical colonial marriage of authoritative government and a small but powerful community of businessmen and industrialists. Little attention had been paid to social welfare or the rights of laborers.

Rioting against social injustice

After the 1967 riots in Hong Kong had been suppressed, the British colonial government immediately opened an in-depth internal investigation, which indicated that the unrest had not been motivated by anti-British, Communist sensibilities. Rather, it was prompted primarily by social injustice, having provided an outlet for the accumulated frustration of the youth of Hong Kong.

This new generation, which came of age in the mid-1960s having been born in the baby booms of the 1950s, was better educated and less tolerant of social injustice than the previous one, becoming a significant force for social change. Unlike their parents, who accepted their humble status as refugees seeking shelter under the British, the locally born youth made demands on their colonial government. Ironically, many of them found themselves in a frustrating limbo. On the one hand, they had little historical or emotional connection to China, and, on the other, they had trouble identifying with their birthplace, where corruption, injustice, and harsh governance prevailed. Whether or not they supported the riots of 1967, they shared the desire for decolonization and social change. This generation imbibed the anti-colonial campaign with continuing momentum in 1968.

Realizing the changing composition of the population, and the increased social, political, and cultural discontent with traditional colonial rule, the British rulers recognized that the time had come to abandon the existing mode of governance and introduce softer, more citizen-oriented measures. In the spring of 1968, for the first time in the history of the colony, the Governor's House was briefly opened to the public. The event, which lasted for only a couple of days, was intended as a symbolic gesture representing the end of the century-old segregation of the colonizers and the colonized. Even today, now that the colony has been returned to China, such open house days continue to take place at the Governor's House and remain emblematic of the government's approachability, even though it is not democratically elected.

Chinese demonstrators in Hong Kong wave Mao Tse-Tung's "Little Red Book" outside the residence of Colonial Governor David Trench on May 28, 1967.

Change in cultural policy

The well-being of Hong Kong's non-European citizens had never been of great concern to the British occupiers. Correspondingly, the government had never done much to promote the arts and culture among its citizens. When the City Hall was completed in the central district in 1962, Hong Kong finally had a cultural center. Boasting a theater, concert hall, and museum, this venue, by its mere construction, indicated that the British rulers were contemplating a more modern mode of citizen-oriented governance. The official introduction of cultural activities accompanied the center's opening. However, as in most colonies, the arts fostered at this newly built cultural center remained the exclusive pleasure of a minority of elites and were directed mainly at Europeans and well-educated Chinese. Local culture and the idea of a distinctive Hong Kong cultural identity were not encouraged.

After the rioting of 1967, however, a significant change in cultural policy, which stressed the contemporary and regional culture, was implemented. By the end of 1967, a special office was set up to organize large-scale cultural and recreational programs for the public. In full operation in 1968, this office, for the first time, arranged cultural programs—such as rock and roll concerts, outdoor dancing parties, and the Miss Hong Kong competition—directed not at the elites but at the mass public, and especially young people.

One of the main tasks of the office was to plan the first "Hong Kong Festival" to celebrate the city's new self-image. The festival was launched in 1969 with dance and theater performances, art exhibitions, parades, and all manner of other attractions the government could offer. After decades of indifference, not only did the colonial government begin to care about its citizens and foster the arts, culture, and recreation for its citizens, but it also actively tried to bolster a sense of Hong Kong identity. The government's motivations, however, went beyond smoothing out social relations; they also had a political dimension.

Modern Hong Kong versus backward China

After the suppression of the rioting, the British continued to be wary of the revolutionary zeal still raging in China at the time of the Cultural Revolution. It was, consequently, important, for the sake of effective governance, to nurture a sense of Hong Kong identity to counter the Chinese threat. Using various measures, such as cultural and recreational activities, the government started a long-term campaign to promote Hong Kong as a modern, orderly, international city, in contrast to China, which it portrayed as chaotic, poor, and backward.

At the same time, the influx of Western consumer culture ushered Hong Kong into a colorful era of modern, popular entertainment. The introduction of television shortly after the riots certainly played a role in this as the new medium quickly became an integral part of everyday life.

On the sociopolitical level, this period also saw the first community protest against the colonial government, which demanded that discriminatory colonial structures be eliminated. On January 20, 1968, at the Chinese University, over 100 students, teachers from various universities, professionals from different fields, and social activists attended a forum to discuss implementing Chinese as an official language of Hong Kong, with the same status as English. The forum prompted a widespread campaign to make Chinese an official language, a policy the colonial government finally enacted in 1976.

Discontent with the colonial government

By the end of the 1960s, the new generation of Hong Kong students and intellectuals, discontented with the repressive colonial government and influenced by student movements in the West, started to demand social and political changes at home. The campaign to make Chinese an official language was significant because it not only gave expression to the discontent with the colonial government but also set the stage for a new cultural awareness and the pronounced sociopolitical involvement that would mark the 1970s.

As both the Chinese and the British were aware that something needed to change, the 1970s brought rapid social and cultural transformations. 1968 marked the beginning of this decisive chapter of reforms.

Oscar Ho Hing-kay was formerly the Exhibition Director of the Hong Kong Arts Center and founding Director of Museum of Contemporary Art Shanghai. He has been involved with the planning of a new museum at the West Kowloon Cultural District and is currently the Director for the MA program in Cultural Management at the Chinese University of Hong Kong.

INDIA: OUTSIDERS IN TWO WORLDS

Kiran Nagarkar

Members of my generation were not "Midnight's Children," the memorable phrase Salman Rushdie coined for all those who came into the world at the moment India won independence, 12 AM on the 15th of August 1947, thanks to the nonviolent resistance led by Mahatma Gandhi, Jawaharlal Nehru, Vallabhbhai Patel, and all the other leaders of the freedom movement, not to mention the hundreds of thousands of the common people who participated in it. Rather, we were born at the very tail end of British rule in India. In a sense, we were born between two worlds.

Maybe we just fell between the chinks separating our colonial past from a free mindset. Maybe that is why we would always be half-and-half, mongrel, hybrid, neither here nor there, and neither this nor that. We would always be outsiders in both these worlds.

Need for an Indian identity

English was frequently our medium of instruction, especially in the major cities and towns. Since we had had over two hundred years of British rule, it was quite often the lingua franca that allowed us to communicate among the twenty-odd regional tongues spoken within India. However, by the time they were twenty-five or thereabouts in 1968, many writers of my generation were beginning to feel the need for an Indian identity. One of the ways they chose to search for their roots was to learn their mother tongues and become proficient enough to write in them.

To this day, I have not been able to tell whether I was a mere callow, insensitive youth or just the odd man out. The past was the done, the given. If mine was, willy-nilly, a kind of pidgin culture, I would embrace it with both arms. If I was a half-breed belonging neither to one culture or the other, so be it; I would be an outsider. It is all the more ironic then that I chose to write my very first novel in my mother tongue Marathi, even though it had taken on the color of a foreign language for me—only the first four years of my primary school education had been in this language, and English had almost become the only language I spoke, wrote, and was comfortable with. I wish I could claim an idealistic motive here but it was pure happenstance. A friend mentioned that he had been asked to be the guest editor of a magazine called *Abhiruchi* for one issue. He did not ask me to contribute, so it must have taken a fair amount of unwarranted hubris to sit down that very night to start writing what turned out to be a novel in Marathi.

Encounter with Maoist ideology

By 1968, the Communist Party of India had already splintered into two—one wing loyal to the orthodox Soviet paradigm and the other to the radical Chinese model and Mao's "Little Red Book." My first brush with Maoist ideology was a meeting with an Indian woman married to a Briton who headed a multinational company in Bombay. She lived in comparatively affluent circumstances but worked among the poorest of the poor and oppressed in the villages of India.

I suspect she thought of herself as my mentor since I was an aspiring writer then, and when she was in town, she had me over for tea and sandwiches and read to me from Mao's "Little Red Book" or from his various writings on art and literature. Like many other leftists, she had a kind, pedagogical streak and conveyed to me her ideas, or rather, Chairman Mao's ideas, of what an artist should write about and how, what the tone and tenor should be, what causes to support, and how to undermine the work of the reactionaries and the bourgeoisie. I stopped seeing her after the fourth or fifth meeting because I didn't like to see people as types and didn't want anyone to dictate what I should write about.

On June 12, 1975, the High Court in Allahabad declared the election of Mrs. Indira Gandhi, the prime minister of India and the daughter of Jawaharlal Nehru, null and void. Claiming that she had violated election norms, the court barred her from contesting elections for the next six years. Mrs. Gandhi retaliated in a rather unexpected way, traumatizing the country. On June 25, 1975, she declared a state of emergency and suspended the constitution that had come into force in 1950. The majority of the opposition leaders were put behind bars. One of the thousands of other victims of the "Emergency" was the Maoist woman I had known. She was imprisoned and brutally tortured. Marxism and its Maoist incarnation may have fallen on hard days now, but it would be foolish not to respect the courage of this woman and the tremendous price she paid for her convictions.

1968: Tailor-made for conspiracy theories

There's something comforting about looking back. Hindsight allows thinkers, critics, and historians to detect grand designs and trace trends, patterns, movements, and to discover conspiracies, real or imaginary. For example, there was a haphazard and bumbling but honorable attempt to unseat a dictator called Batista in Cuba. When a band of men led by Fidel Castro and Che Guevara fortuitously succeeded in unseating him after many previous attempts, it surprised—or, rather, shocked—everybody. Over the years, this story became a master narrative maintaining that Batista's overthrow was not a happy accident but an ideological uprising with an elaborately planned guerrilla strategy that could not fail.

The year 1968 saw ideological protests in the United States, and in many parts of Europe, especially France and Germany. In retrospect, 1968 was indeed tailor-made for conspiracy theories or all-encompassing master narratives that could claim that these seemingly disparate movements were linked— inspired and planned by a diabolical, communist, evil genius. But regardless of the utility of elaborating these links, it is true that the various protest phenomena had a common core: they were symbolic of an intense dissatifaction with the existing order, a deep concern for the deprived, and an overwhelming desire for change. In the US, it was the Black Panthers, Woodstock, and the agitation against the Vietnam War; in France, it was the student rebellion, Régis Debray, and Daniel Cohn-Bendit; in Germany, it was groups like Baader-Meinhof.

Indian Prime Minister Indira Gandhi greets children and hands out garlands during a public appearance, Aug. 20, 1973.

A Maoist revolution in India: Suppression by the zamindars

Oddly enough, the protest movements were not confined to the Western world. There had been considerable ferment and dissension in the leftist segment of the political spectrum on the Indian subcontinent, as well. One of the breakaway parties propounded a radical agenda based on the teachings of Chairman Mao and opted for violent revolutionary methods. As with the parallel movements in the West, the motives of this party's members were lofty. They wanted a more equitable society where justice and fairness would prevail, especially for the most underprivileged and deprived. Some of the brightest intellectuals from

Calcutta, Bombay, Delhi, and other parts of the country gave up their promising careers and joined this extremist crusade.

For hundreds of years, the zamindars, as the landlords in India are called, had treated farmhands, bonded laborers, tribal people, and small farmers, the lower castes and the outcasts who are now called Dalits, as little more than slaves. They lent money at unthinkably exorbitant interest rates whenever these laborers had a birth, marriage, illness, or death in the family. The workers were in no position to pay the rapidly spiraling interest on interest, let alone to repay the principle. In short, they were trapped in perpetuity. Their women were abused and raped, their houses burned, and every sort of atrocity was committed against them. One of the earliest revolts occurred in a village called Naxalbari. Hence, these revolutionaries from the extreme left came to be known as Naxalites. They were also called Maoists since they drew their inspiration from the Chinese leader and this nomenclature differentiated them from the Marxist-Leninist line followed by the mainstream leftists who had close ideological links with the Soviet Union.

The immediate reaction to the first signs of the serfs' revolt among the ruling classes was shock and disbelief. The serfs had never had any say, and their only job was to do as they were told. It was inconceivable that they could think for themselves or, worse still, turn upon their masters. Shortly thereafter, the landlords' incredulousness turned to rage, and their response was swift and unambiguous. They crushed not only the rebels but entire villages as a warning to others. But while this tactic was effective in the short run, it merely added fuel to the fire in the long run. The Naxalite movement has continued to spread steadily.

Radicalization by the Naxalites

The pace of the revolution, however, proved too slow for some of the members, and the unity of vision was lost. Gradually, the group divided into smaller and smaller units, each convinced that they alone were the keepers of the true faith. Some, believing that only a far more extreme form of retaliation could yield any substantial results, raised the bar on brutality and atrocities. A tooth for a tooth, an eye for an eye, a life for a life—that was their philosophy. In truth, they wanted to up the ante even further because their objective was to strike terror in the hearts and minds of the landlords and the upper classes and speed the revolutionary process.

The Maoists indoctrinated and radicalized villagers, manufactured crude arms and bombs, and inflicted heavy losses on the landlords and the police. In time, their ideology was exported to Nepal and took hold among the oppressed there. For the first time, they were able to withstand the sustained campaign launched against them by the king and the military, and in the end, they were able to bring the monarch to heel. Today, the Maoists comprise one of the legitimate parties represented in elections in Nepal. However, whether the party can maintain its unity and continue to participate in the democratic process remains to be seen.

The return of the Maoists

After its initial successes and the hysterical media coverage, the Naxalite movement in India seemed to lose some of its momentum. Many of its top leaders were sent to jail, grew frustrated with the lack of substantial progress, or were disillusioned by the in-fighting and returned home. Moreover, the landlords had proved to be a formidable enemy: they were not only tremendously wealthy but were just as prone to violence as the Naxalites. On top of that, they had unlimited resources and private militias that would stop at nothing. But around 2004 and 2005, the splinter groups realized the folly of operating separately and joined forces once again. They had learned their lesson. They were now far better organized, better trained, and better armed. Their communication systems were technologically more advanced and their hit-and-run tactics more effective. They turned professional and were just as comfortable using lathis or wooden staffs as AK47s.

In 2008, film director Sudhir Mishra introduced *Red Sun*, Sudeep Chakrabarty's book on the resurgence of the Naxalite movement, in words that had the flavor of a film trailer: "Coming soon to a locality near you." It was, however, not a facetious comment. The Maoists had indeed infiltrated every state in the country, and the government, despite all its bravura, had been mostly ineffective in inhibiting or preventing their steady encroachment. Even more important, the authorities had failed to address the fundamental issues that had allowed the Naxalites to expand their operations so rapidly and recruit more and more members of those living below the poverty line in the country.

The terrible truth about violence is that it brutalizes the victim as much as the victimizer. In the land of the Buddha and Gandhi, the Naxalites were declared terrorists, long before we knew of al-Qaida and the Taliban. The extremists started out in the late 1960s with noble intentions, but that idealism has long since turned into something as repugnant as the viciousness and malevolence of the very people they wanted to fight.

Kiran Nagarkar, born in 1942 in Bombay, has published numerous novels, plays and film scripts. His first novel *Saat Sakkam Trechalis* [Seven Sixes are Forty-Three] is considered a milestone of Indian literature after independence.

JAPAN: "1968"–HISTORY OF A DECADE

Claudia Derichs

The history of the "1968" movement in Japan is really the history of more than a decade because the first radical political event of the postwar period occurred in 1960. The US and Japan intended to extend a bilateral security agreement that year that Prime Minister Yoshida Shigeru had negotiated simultaneously with the peace treaty of San Francisco in 1951. Part of the prime minister's "Yoshida Doctrine," a political program that initiated Japan's ties with the West, the security agreement firmly linked Japan to the US, giving the US special conditions. For example, it did not even need to consult the Japanese government if it chose to engage in military actions from Japanese territory. Opposing the proposed ten-year extension, the Japanese populace erupted in protests, which undoubtedly presented a test for the young democracy.

In the political Left that had developed in Japan since 1945, a tightly organized Communist Party as well as an effective union movement arose. Later, the Socialist Party of Japan also formed a part of this camp. In retrospect, this Left made up the "Old Left," because in 1957, the "New Left" was formed, directing itself primarily against the stultifying hierarchy of the party organizations and their "Stalinism." The early New Left derived most of its members from student circles; its groupings were understood as *tôha*—party factions. Over the course of a decade of splits and new foundings, four dominant, ideological strands emerged by 1967 in the whole New Left movement: the Trotskyist, structural reformist, Maoist, and socialist strands spawned in association with the Socialist Party. Common to all these New Left groups was a confrontational stance toward the Japanese Communist Party (JCP), which they believed could no longer claim to be avant-garde. Nevertheless, the "old" (JCP) and New Left worked together to fight the extension of the security treaty in 1960. Yet despite storming the parliament and forcing President Eisenhower to cancel a visit due to lack of security on June 14 that year, the New Left was not able to prevent the extension from being ratified.

The mass demonstrations of the 1960 movement suggest that 1968 was not the year that launched the Japanese student movement and the militant and terrorist groups that followed it. The late 1960s, to be sure, contributed to these developments, and especially, thereafter, to the Japanese Red Army, but a dynamic shaped by events other than Japan's efforts to come to terms with its ultra-nationalist past had already emerged before that time.

Loose and spontaneous: Beheiren and Zenkyôtô

The protest and organizational structures of 1960 had been dominated by established parties and unions. The well-rehearsed zig-zag march—the *snake dance*—of the student umbrella organization Zengakuren, not only made it famous but virtually symbolized the group's rigid organization, for example. In the mid-1960s, however, spurred by the Vietnam War and later by the global wave of *student power*, protest structures were transformed. In civil society, a movement against the Vietnam War developed that had a markedly loose organizational structure. Led by Oda Makoto (one of the most prominent social critics and peace activists in the country), this movement, known as Beheiren (Betonamu ni heiwa o! shimin undô [Citizen's League for Peace in Vietnam], was nonpartisan, emphasizing voluntary, non-binding participation in demonstrations. Zengakuren [All-Japan Federation of Student Self-Government Associations] and Zenkyôtô (Zengaku kyôtô kaigi [All-Campus Joint Struggle]) constituted the opposite poles of the student movement of the late '60s. Zenkyôtô members, unlike their Zengakuren counterparts, consciously avoided grouping themselves into party factions, calling themselves *non-sects*, or *non-poli*, to strengthen their apolitical stance. In fact, primarily concerned with particular demands of university students, they were principally geared toward the "Campus Struggle," which, nonetheless, was just as militant as the street fighting.

However, New Left groups tried to infiltrate the Zenkyôtô associations to recruit them for the political struggle. Consequently, in

Masked and armed with wooden sticks, Zengakuren members participate on Oct. 21, 1968, in a demonstration on International Anti-War Day in Tokyo.

1969, an all-Japan Zenkyôtô was founded in which eight New Left factions forged an alliance, although it didn't last long—despite dramatic and militant street and campus battles, the movement petered out by the end of the year. With the decline of the student movement in sight, controversial, ideological strategy debates erupted, resulting in a few, strong cadres, and later in the terrorist branch, the Red Army of Japan. The various cadres of the New Left thereafter competed with one another in recruiting new members and for the hegemonic leadership of the movement. Two prominent ones were the Chûkaku and Kakumaru factions, which continued to use violence to wage their ideological battles even after 1969.

Such violence was typical of the phase of *uchi-geba* [internal violence] that lasted from the late '60s and early '70s. In retrospect, *uchi-geba* can be regarded as one of the specific characteristics of Japan's New Left. In 1971, most cadres had begun to form armed "guerilla units," whose activists went underground. They perceived themselves as being in a state of war against enemy cadres within their own movement, as well as against the Japanese state. The spiral of violence escalated after 1970, becoming a much-discussed topic among Japanese intellectuals. Professionalized mechanisms of retaliation were deployed, accompanied by ritualized self-criticism and the ideological justification of attacking and killing people.

Japan's "1968" took place within this mix of factors and factions. Students protested conditions at the mass universities but, for the most part, did not address the war generation's failure to deal with its past. For the Left, the emperor remained the symbol of the fatal, imperial war, yet even the large leftist parties did not succeed in dethroning him while he lived. Clearly, behavioral continuities with the prewar period contributed to this: even if the emperor had become merely human after the country's defeat in 1945, he still deserved respect and loyalty. The debate about his war guilt never evolved into a wide, public discussion during his lifetime (he died in January 1989); no historians' dispute (like the one in 1986 in Germany) was carried out in the national newspapers and journals to come to terms, vehemently, with past events.

The Japanese Red Army: Japanese perceptions

As the student movement lost momentum in 1969 and "internal violence" reigned, protesters asked themselves, "What next?" Some chose the cadres mentioned above; others opted to take up the armed struggle beyond Japan's borders; and, on activist Shiomi Takaya's initiative, the Red Army Faction (RAF) of Japan was founded. Yet when Shiomi was arrested, the group found itself without a leader. As political leadership in Japan is exceptionally personality-oriented—even in official politics—this circumstance had a profound effect on the remaining activists and sympathizers, whose views on how they should carry on diverged. Those loyal to Shiomi, who continued to call themselves the Red Army Faction, espoused concerted action in Japan. To this end, they allied themselves with a group within the so-called United Red Army that specialized in stealing weapons.

In the West, the conception of the Japanese Red Army primarily derives from a group, Nihon Sekigun [The Japanese Red Army], led by Shigenobu Fusako, which went to the Middle East. In Japan, however, the image is shaped much more by the United Red Army because of the dramatic and widely broadcast events triggered by this group there. Fleeing police persecution, about two dozen activists of the United Red Army had absconded to the Japanese Alps north of Tokyo in the winter of 1971 amidst ice and snow. They had to stay "underground" because warrants for their arrest had long since been issued for armed attacks, theft of weapons and money, and serious bodily injury to others. In this situation, the question of control and hierarchy within the group became more important than the revolution they strove for. To hold the group together ideologically, a system of ideas had to be created to give the group a *raison d'être* and lend legitimacy and necessity to its actions. At issue was the survival of the collective, which was to be preserved by a process of "communist transformation." Although the details of the process were not given, all the members had to subject themselves to it, critically examining their own bourgeois attitudes and behaviors and eradicating them to become better revolutionaries. The collective investigated personal flaws and weaknesses, whereupon individuals tried to overcome them, yet no one managed to do this to the satisfaction of the leaders, who then punished them with increasing severity: fourteen members died from the tortures inflicted upon them, and all the others surmised that they would be next.

This internal murder ended in February 1972 when the police battled these Red Army members in a resort town in the Japanese Alps. As the conflict was broadcast live on Japanese television, the images, above all, took root in popular memory. Five members of the United Red Army had taken a hostage, preventing the police squad from storming their hideout right away. On the tenth day, the police squad leader decided to proceed with water cannon and tear gas, freeing the hostage.

This episode left indelible traces in Japan's collective memory. The wave of horror over the murders and the armed conflict with the police washed all the way to the Middle East, where the Japanese Red Army was active. Its "reaction" to events at home consisted in planning and executing a suicide attack at Israel's Ben Gurion Airport in May 1972. Whereas the attack is commonly regarded as an expression of the Japanese terrorists' solidarity with the Palestinian liberation war, Shigenobu's personal descriptions emphasized its connection to the events in the Japanese Alps.

"Aftereffects" of the "68ers"

The lynchings and the United Red Army's battle in the mountains paralyzed the entire New Left movement. This paralysis must have been at least partly to blame for the failure of sections of the New Left to become integrated into the "new social movements" of the 1970s. No political party arising from transregional, social movements—like the Green Party in Germany—was founded in Japan.

In short, the political influence of "1968" in Japan does not seem to have been very great. When asked about it today, most students consider the influence of the movement on later political occurrences "marginal" in comparison to the developments in Europe (such as the Green Party). Rather, it was the events and episodes themselves that continue to have aftereffects in Japan's collective memory: among others, the spontaneous protest against the Vietnam War (before 1968), the founding of Zenkyôtô to counter Zengakuren, internal violence, and especially the history of the United Red Army.

As some of the cadres from that time are still active—they have been "converted" to peaceful environmental NGOs and critics of globalization that now get along, by and large—it seems that no concluding evaluation of their early activities and influence can be made at this point in time. Late reconciliations and cooperative endeavors among them have nearly obscured their violence-prone phase from memory. Nonetheless, the '68 movement in Japan—1960,

Vietnam, and the 1970s, for example—certainly gave Japanese society a "shove." However, ever since that time, the movement has been unable to prepare proactively for action but has only been able to react to events in society.

To be sure, Japan has movements—women's, environmental, and anti-nuclear power ones, for example—that would see their roots in "1968," yet with very limited causality. Consequently, the discourses on anti-authoritarian child-rearing, women's emancipation, and other such themes have made their way into other contexts for which the direct descent from the events of the late '60s can hardly be discerned. The members of the New Left were "conformist" in their organizational structures, and also in their lifestyles and value systems. These facts contributed to the comparatively low level of influence they exerted. At the same time, the events of that time may have had triggered impulses that will only be visible in the future.

Claudia Derichs is a Professor of Political Science at the University of Hildesheim, Germany, with a PhD in Japanology and numerous publications on a broad range of Japanese and Asian political themes.

PAKISTAN: THE YEAR OF CHANGE

Ghazi Salahuddin

1968 was a year of great change for Pakistan. The country seemed uniquely plugged into the spirit of that time as it manifested itself in the West. As a young reporter in Karachi, I was a participant-observer of a social and political upheaval that became the seed of momentous events in Pakistan's history.

Bangladeshi independence

In 1968, what is now Pakistan was West Pakistan. Separated by one thousand miles of India was East Pakistan, which is now Bangladesh. The beginning of the creation of this nation is one event that can be traced back to this decisive year. In the first week of January 1968, the central government accused Bengali leader Sheikh Mujibur Rahman of conspiring with India to make East Pakistan a separate country. Sheikh Mujib was arrested, and East Pakistan was pushed into a protracted phase of political uncertainty marked by violent agitation. Following Bangladesh's independence in 1971, however, Rahman, who was never convicted, was released and became the leader of the new nation.

Protest against propaganda

The issue of social and economic disparity in Pakistan society also came to the fore in this pivotal year. Ayub Khan, the military leader who had seized power in a coup in 1958, and his government inaugurated a propaganda campaign celebrating "the decade of development." But this propaganda merely underlined the disparity between the classes as it grew ever more evident that the fruits of economic progress had not filtered down to the lower classes. One memorable slogan of the year was "22 families." The Chief Economist of the Planning Commission, Dr. Mahbubul Haq, had revealed in a document that a mere 22 families owned or controlled 66 percent of the nation's industrial wealth and 87 percent of banking and insurance wealth. Khan's propaganda campaign thus greatly annoyed the majority of the people, prompting a strong backlash.

The national language, Urdu, was deployed in the popular movement, especially by the poets. One rebel poet, Habib Jalib, a Marxist-Leninist who tended toward communism and was not afraid to express his views openly, won great acclaim for his readings at political meetings. Jalib, of course, had a provocative take on "22 families." The poetry of socialist Faiz Ahmed Faiz, perhaps the greatest modern Urdu poet, illustrated the major political events in a classical diction. This protest poetry, in a way, was a Pakistani echo of the pop music that enthralled the defiant youth of the West in 1968.

Year of the television

1968 was also the year of television in Pakistan, ushering in a cultural explosion. Three television stations were set up in Karachi, Lahore, and Rawalpindi in late 1967 and a fourth was inaugurated in Dhaka, East Pakistan, in early 1968. Though television, like radio, was state-controlled and the news was highly censored, the medium conveyed its own message. Suddenly, a largely illiterate population was exposed to living images from the far corners of the world. It was assumed that Ayub Khan wanted to use television to promote his own agenda, but like "the decade of development," its actual effect ran counter to its intent. Social critics noted how television, irrespective of its content, stimulated popular discontent. Shows made in Hollywood projected a world of unbelievable opulence and convenience that exacerbated the sense of deprivation among the populace. The rage that played out on the streets may have had its roots in the forbidden glitter of lives lived in the West.

Pakistani President Zulfikar Ali Bhutto on Februrary 20, 1976, in Bonn, Germany.

Bhutto founds the Pakistan People's Party

Most significantly, 1968 was the year in which charismatic leader Zulfikar Ali Bhutto (1928–1979) developed a large following. He mobilized the youth to challenge the status quo and awakened deep yearnings for social emancipation among the masses. Bhutto's name still functions as a red flag in Pakistan politics, with many describing him as the prince of the country's political disorders.

In 1958, Bhutto became the youngest minister in Ayub Khan's cabinet. However, Bhutto resigned in late 1966, gradually emerging as the main figure opposing

Khan's government. On November 30, 1967, he formed the Pakistan People's Party (PPP) with a revolutionary, socialist manifesto. The PPP constituted an alliance of the progressive intelligentsia and the oppressed masses. With the slogan "All power belongs to the masses," Bhutto provided the people with a sense of agency.

Through his vocal opposition, Bhutto emerged as a cult leader for the youth and decisively changed Pakistan. It was only natural that he would be a polarizing figure. Just as his followers revered him deeply, the ruling establishment saw him as the incarnation of evil. And like most charismatic leaders who emerge in times of crisis, he radicalized public opinion in an aggressive manner. He was intellectually brilliant and often subtly calculating in his politics. The first leader to cover the entire length and breadth of (West) Pakistan, Bhutto had phenomenal energy, holding a dozen or more speeches a day. Throughout this year, Bhutto found himself in and out of jail.

In rural areas, with ordinary people responding to his call, the entire political landscape was transformed. I remember running into the streets of Karachi watching the police disperse rallies staged by students, lawyers, or trade unions, with baton charges and tear gas. There was a lot of stone-throwing, as well.

This agitation culminated in the catalytic event of November 7, 1968, when police opened fire on students gathered to greet Bhutto in Rawalpindi. One student was killed. Demonstrations erupted in all the cities of the country, and there were many violent confrontations. In Rawalpindi, the army had to be called in and a curfew imposed. At this point, factory workers joined in the students' protest. Bhutto and other leaders were arrested.

But people's dissatisfaction could not be ignored. Not long after the year ended, in March 1969, there was another military intervention; Ayub Khan handed power over to his military chief, General Agha Mohammed Yahya Khan; martial law was imposed with the promise that democracy would be restored.

When East Pakistan won independence with the help of the Indian army in late 1971, Bhutto became prime minister of Pakistan, and, although the history of these recent decades is quite complex and Bhutto was eventually executed by military ruler Zia-ul-Haq in 1979, the Bhutto phenomenon and the Pakistan People's Party has survived to this day. In 1973, Bhutto's title changed to president under a new constitution. Then, in 1977, he was ousted from power by a military coup following allegations that the election was rigged in favor of Bhutto's PPP. His 1979 execution was a traumatic event in the country's history. But in spite of repeated attempts by the "establishment" to crush the PPP, Bhutto's daughter Benazir inherited his charisma and became the head of government twice—in 1988 until she was removed in 1990, and in 1993 until she was removed in 1996. After eight years of exile in London, she returned to Pakistan in 2007 and warned of mass protests as the leading candidate of the opposition. Though she was assassinated during an election rally in Rawalpindi on December 27, 2007, the PPP went on to win numerous seats in the general elections the following February, so that the Pakistani president, Nawaz Sharif, signed an agreement to form a coalition government between his Pakistan Muslim League party and the PPP. In this way, Zulfikar Ali Bhutto's spirit lives on.

In sum, 1968 was a watershed year for Pakistan. The country's youth became angry and restless. And in the midst of all that tumult, they were excited and hopeful about the future. They could see the rainbow in the sky. I know because I was one of them.

Ghazi Salahuddin is the Editorial Director of the daily paper *The News International*, a large, English-language newspaper in Pakistan, and editor of "Geo TV."

THAILAND: THE "OCTOBER MOVEMENT" AND THE TRANSFORMATION TO DEMOCRACY

Kittisak Prokati

In the 1960s, following years of military dictatorship in Thailand, the country's connection with the United States, which it viewed as a protector from the communist revolutions sweeping neighboring states, prompted broad swathes of society to discuss Western values with their reformist impetus. With the beginning of the Vietnam War in 1964, massive amounts of military and economic assistance flowed into the country, supplemented by the presence of American military units.

By 1968, there were 50,000 American soldiers in Thailand. Conversely, numerous young Thai officials, scientists, and scholars received scholarships to study the United States. The rising surge of modernization and continuing economic growth enlarged the middle class, as well as the number of young people studying at universities. The close relationship to the US brought not only classical liberal values to Thailand but also the alternative lifestyles of American youth, such as the hippie movement.

The longing for democracy, freedom, and the rule of law grew. At the same time, despite being drawn to the liberal values of American culture, students vehemently criticized American racism—embodied for them in the murder of Martin Luther King Jr. (1968). They also criticized developments in America's involvement in Vietnam, particularly the "My Lai Massacre" of March 1968, in which hundreds of unarmed South Vietnamese citizens, including children and the elderly, were mercilessly slaughtered. Countering official anti-communist propaganda, students now started to call the American government the "White Peril." Gradually, sympathy for socialist values spread, inspired, in particular, by the Chinese Cultural Revolution.

Although military dictator Thanom Kittikachorn ruled Thailand from 1963 to 1973, Thailand briefly became a constitutional state in 1968. Still, Kittikachorn appointed himself prime minister after elections in 1969, and then, in 1971, revoked the constitution with a staged inside putsch in 1971, supposedly to purge communist infiltration. Protests now swept campuses, particularly at

Thammasat University in Bangkok, where student organizations demonstratively set a black wreath at the monument to democracy. This event laid the symbolic foundation stone of the student protest movement.

October Movement and social change in Thailand

A clear transformation of values began in Thailand at this time, such that voices of protest became louder and more numerous, demanding democratic structures and an end to corruption. This transformation sparked a shift in social and political consciousness that has endured to the present.

Between 1971 and 1973, violent clashes erupted at many universities. When the military government issued a decree to place the independent judiciary under its control, students organized an ongoing protest until the decree was revoked. When nine students at Ramkamhaeng University were expelled in 1973 for criticizing members of the government for their illegal conduct at a hunt in a nature reserve, students at several universities took to the streets. This spurred the nullification of the expulsions and the resignation of the pro-military government director of the university.

In October 1973, however, the spirit of protest peaked with a violent three-day uprising that ended Kittikachorn's military rule. Students and intellectuals publicly demanded a new constitution. When the demonstrators were arrested, students at Thammasat University called for a mass protest against the military government. The student protest soon widened into a national revolt: on October 13, more than 500,000 people peacefully demonstrated in Bangkok, demanding the immediate release of the arrested protesters and the completion of

A Thai soldier in a gas mask orders protesting students away from tanks as a massive demonstration turns to riot in Bangkok on Oct. 15, 1973.

a constitution within six months. The next day, October 14, the police and the military broke up the demonstration in a bloody clash. Resistance nevertheless continued until Prime Minister Kittikachorn and the commander-in-chief of the armed forces resigned all their offices and went into exile.

A euphoric wave of democratization and liberalization then swept across Thailand. The general population called for political safeguards of social justice. On the left margin of society, socialist and communist ideals enjoyed considerable popularity among students and intellectuals.

Established institutions react

To be sure, not all were happy with this "spirit of change." The old elite and some segments of the general population alike felt threatened by this revolt against traditional values. To counteract these changes and maintain their established positions of power after 1973, some of the old elite mobilized, ready to use their connections to groups that would even use violence against the student movement.

Then, the circumstances changed, turning a much greater portion of the population, including the lower and middle classes, against the student protest movement: the oil crisis triggered inflation, American troops retreated from Southeast Asia, and communists took over in Laos, Cambodia, and Vietnam, exacerbating fears. Feeling insecure, broad swathes of the population blamed the student protest movement for all the problems.

At the beginning of October 1976, the situation reached a head. Kittikachorn had returned to Thailand as a novice monk, and outraged student protestors had mobilized. Eventually, on October 5, when a newspaper ran a photo of a mock hanging by protesters that had been doctored to look like the crown prince, the student protesters were accused of *lèse majesté*. A massacre at Thammasat University, wherein hundreds of protesters were killed, and a military putsch ensued on October 6, returning the country to military rule and eradicating the student movement. Most students returned to everyday life or left the country to study in Europe or America. Several hundred members of the active core of the movement fled to the communists in the jungle. However, only a few years later, they would return to be respected politicians or professors at Thammasat University when they were granted amnesty and returned to mainstream society.

In sum, it may be said that the events of October 6, 1976, slowed down the "spirit of change" but did not put a halt to it. Although the student movement was eradicated, the "spirit of change" survived. It could no longer be banned from public and intellectual discussion. Nearly twenty years later, in 1992, when representatives of the generation of 1973 had become part of the academic avant-garde and had assumed influential positions in public media, administration, and the economy, the movement for democracy began again, renewing resistance against a military government. Since then, the political situation in Thailand has shifted many times, but one thing has remained constant: the spirit of liberal-democratic development entered directly into the Thai constitution of 1997 and continues to be an integral component of the contemporary discussion of law, politics, and society.

Kittisak Prokati is a law historian at Thammasat University in Bangkok.

AFRICA & THE MIDDLE EAST

EGYPT: FROM ROMANTICISM TO REALISM

Ibrahim Farghali

"My fathers and mothers go back to the pyramids and to histories of parrots, and even as far back as Mayan culture. So I don't feel that I belong to a specific generation ... However, as far as the 60s generation is concerned, I believe I only wished to have experienced May 1968—just as I would have liked to have been involved in the 1972 student demonstrations in Egypt."

These words by poet and translator Huda Hussein, taken from an interview published in *al-Sharq al-Awsat*, not only summarize the influence exerted by the "'68 movement" in Egypt but also show that such influence has now, for the most part, vanished. The present generation, born around 1968, is not moved by Egyptians who directly experienced 1968; there is only a sense of a "nostalgic" connection with student demonstrations at Egyptian universities in the early 1970s. The real influence that the 1990s generation feels (those now entering college) derives directly from the '68 movement as originally manifested in Europe.

Mixing politics and ideology with culture

Allow me to turn for a moment to a leading personality who exemplifies the enthusiastic objector: the late Ibrahim Mansur, an intellectual who was one of the founders of the celebrated *Gallery 68*, a journal that played a significant role in providing roots for the writers of the '60s generation. In addition, in the 1970s Mansur was one of the best-known opponents of the policies of Anwar al-Sadat, then Egyptian president. He is now established in Egyptian intellectuals' collective memory as the "national conscience," whose keen sword of criticism descended on anyone who opposed the nationalist feelings held by most of the population.

Mansur embodies the paradigm of the Egyptian intellectual who mixes politics and ideology with culture. This mixture is typical of the '60s generation, making it a general characteristic of Egyptian culture. But this is precisely what the '90s generation openly rejects in pursuing individualism and favoring aesthetics at the expense of ideology.

More liberty for student associations

While it is true that the Mansur generation played an important role in the '60s and '70s—as a result of some circumstances, such as the Arab defeat in the Six-Day War of 1967—it is, nonetheless, not improbable that the '68 movement in France was the main influence on the November demonstrations in Egypt. These demonstrations gained such momentum that Egyptian President Abdel Nasser yielded to students' demands and conceded greater independence, effectiveness, and freedom of movement to their groups. Student associations were also allowed to be politically active.

Che Guevara meets Egyptian Premier Nasser in Cairo on June 19, 1958.

Nevertheless, this generation, successful in exerting pressure on its president, did not play any great part later in influencing the modernization of Egyptian society. Despite all its political and ideological activities, it was not in a position to effectively counter corruption and the population's marginalization in political life—a state of affairs Egyptian society had to struggle against during the '80s and '90s. Literature was affected, too. Perhaps this was the reason the '90s generation rejected its predecessors in the spheres of ideology, creativity, and politics.

Movement of the urban population

When the '60s generation was growing up, it profited from the 1952 revolution, which had led to free education and welfare benefits. On the other hand, this generation was also shaped by the revolutionary atmosphere that became characteristic of Egyptian society as a whole, in which people trusted by those in power were given precedence over those better qualified. Another consequence of the revolution was the fact that young people from rural areas now enjoyed the advantages of education. In addition, work opportunities arose in Cairo, so that people brought their customs, traditions, behaviors, and values to the city, adhering to these instead of exchanging them for modern urban ways. In other words, the capital imported values from the regions instead of the city spreading urban standards to rural areas.

So what happened in Cairo at the end of the 1960s cannot be compared with the '68 movement in Europe since the latter involved an urban population with all that this implied in terms of culture and patterns of behavior. The Egyptian student movement was fundamentally different. There is an essential difference between intellectuals and citizens in the two cultures, and, in fact, between European and Third World cultures more generally. The Egyptian is essentially a countryman [*muwaatin*], a son of the homeland, whereas the European is a citizen, a son of the city.

Perhaps this unclear understanding of culture and its relationship to the land (i.e., to the homeland) rather than to the given realities was one of the reasons the Egyptian generation of '68 no longer influenced succeeding generations and thus failed to play its part in revolutionizing and modernizing society. This generation was equally incapable of liberating itself from the roots of traditional culture, founded on a dualistic value system of the permitted [*halaal*] and the forbidden [*haraam*]. Its thinking was bound by this dualism.

Romantic representation of the revolt

The second reason this generation failed to significantly influence subsequent generations was its lack of will to record ideas in writing so that they could be discussed more widely and further developed. In my opinion, Ibrahim Mansur, an emblem of oral culture, exemplifies this disparagement of the written word. As a result, his influence was limited to a small circle of people in direct contact with him who repeated his words without writing them down. Reflecting on Ibrahim Mansur thus involves a kind of romanticism—which seems to be a general characteristic of both the '70s generation and its predecessor, as Sharif Younis emphasized in his study of the Egyptian student movement: "The different circumstances of the '70s led to the rise of a student movement characterized by romantic and abstract representation. The romantic hero is someone who does nothing but fight; he does not eat, drink, or work." (*Al Hewar Al Motamadden*, December 16, 2002).

However, there were many exceptions, particularly within the student movement itself, including the late intellectual Ahmad Abdallah, who played a salient part in the student leadership during this revolt.

Abdallah, who studied economics and politics, headed the students' national committee that directed the January 1972 upheaval—seen by many, especially on the Left, as preparation for the 1973 war against Israel. He also led students' most important campus protest, which the security forces could only bring to an end by using their truncheons. Abdallah was arrested three times in 1972 and 1973. Yet even though Abdallah surmounted many of his generation's afflictions, he had little influence on later student generations because they associate him with populist culture, which they—particularly the intellectuals among them—do not appreciate.

Influence of the European '68 movement

Nevertheless, we cannot view the influence of the European '68 movement and modernization attempts in Egypt as separate phenomena. It does not matter whether such attempts involved the clothes worn then, open relationships, and the start of a new era with a different understanding of relations between the sexes, or perhaps concerning an alternative way of life, borrowing from the hippies by, for example, growing long hair. However, the spread of Islamic fundamentalism at the end of the '70s counteracted this wave of modernization. Then President Anwar al-Sadat used this trend to suppress leftist and communist tendencies—with the outcome that conservatism and religious leanings gained acceptance in Egyptian society.

The '90s generation, likewise, was divided by opposing tendencies. Some of its members seem to have been influenced by '68, but there are also many intellectuals from rural areas whose writings and behavior are rife with contradictions. Some of these intellectuals are traditional conservatives who view themselves as enlightened and avant-garde, but they are far from it. However, this identity crisis affects not only this conservative group of intellectuals and artists but also another stratum of rebels who wanted to undertake a different experiment. Perhaps the most prominent of these experiments was one carried out by the "Grasshopper Group," headed by Ahmad Taha, a '70s generation poet. He attempted to foster a number of '90s poets who had broken taboos in literature with the magazine *Al Garad* [The Grasshoppers], but this group did not survive artistically.

Criticizing the government

Although the European movement of 1968 appears to have had little effect on Egypt, it does have affinities with the modern Egyptian protest movement. For example, both reject prevailing values concerning power or society's traditionally conservative code of behavior. However, the Egyptian protest movement of today can only be observed using modern technological means like the Internet—and within the past few years, blogs. Here, many open-minded young people reveal a different awareness in how they think and live, consciously and courageously criticizing the government.

Currently in Egypt, another new phenomenon is emerging: the formation of political, social, cultural, and artistic groups in cyberspace, particularly via the increasing popularity of Facebook. Among the virtual groups established recently is "Support Sawiris." It aims to assist Egyptian businessman Naguib Sawiris, whose "Sawiris Institution for Social Development" supports a variety of cultural projects. Most strikingly, he established an Egyptian television channel that shows uncensored cinema films, arousing the rancor of some religious groups.

To me, the Egypt of today seems influenced by the '68 movement in its call for change, the surmounting of traditional values, and liberation from oppression, whether political, social, ethical, or religious. The current generation of young people seems to be launching new movements dedicated to liberation and modernization without any great commotion, inflammatory words, or revolutionary slogans. Rather, things are happening quietly with real dialogue and the development of new ideas that must spread to create a climate suitable for liberalism.

Ibrahim Farghali is a journalist and author from Cairo.

ISRAEL: 1968 AND THE "'67 GENERATION"*

Gilad Margalit

To a large extent, Israel was left out of the protest wave in 1968. No students or young people's demonstrations demanding reform and change were registered. It was definitely the 1967 "Six-Day War" rather than any other event that was the formative generational experience of Israelis born in the years 1938-1948 (the age group typically called the '68 Generation elsewhere). In Israel, this generation is mainly associated with that war, and thus, tends to be called the '67 Generation.

Before the 1967 conflict, many Israelis had feared that a new violent conflict with the Arab armies would have disastrous consequences. The unexpected military victory evoked a nationalist euphoria, accompanied by an economic boom that ended a severe economic recession. Too many Israelis, young as old, felt an exaggerated sense of national self-confidence, adored their generals, and held the defeated Arabs in contempt.

Although 1968 does not mark any dramatic shift in public opinion, it does delineate the beginning of multiple waves of deep changes in Israeli society, culture, and politics, in which the local "'67 Generation" was very instrumental. These changes modernized Israeli society, turning it into an integral part of the West during the 1970s and 1980s.

The new Zionist society

Since its foundation in 1948, Israel has been a multicultural migrant society with a majority of Jews and a large Arab minority of about 20 percent. In the first decades, this heterogeneous Jewish society consolidated its identity. During the pre-state Yishuv [settlement] period (1880-1948), and up to the 1960s, the vast majority of Israeli elites consisted of Zionist immigrants from Eastern Europe. Many integrated their nationalist convictions into a socialist vision. The socialist parties, which dominated Zionist politics for decades up to 1977, constituted the backbone of the Israeli coalition governments and ran a centralized and highly regulated economy. The country had no TV, and essentially only one, government-owned radio station. Only in 1960 did it inaugurate a second station that broadcast light, foreign music. Trips abroad were rather an exception. This relative cultural isolation contributed to the comparatively late naturalization of Israeli pop and rock in local popular music, as well as of other Western ideas and fashions. Until the late 1960s, the popular music scene was deeply influenced by Eastern European music, the French chanson, and Bedouin shepherd songs. The military entertainment units enjoyed enormous popularity in the Israeli musical scene and in the local hit parades.

Internationally, in the early 1950s, Israel became part of the Western bloc in the Cold War conflict. However, in the late 1950s and early 1960s, Israel tried to affiliate itself with the newly liberated African countries while developing close military ties to France, which was simultaneously fighting to retain Algeria.

The Jewish community had a strong sense of mission: its goals were to "build and protect the new Zionist society," absorb significant waves of immigration of Holocaust survivors and Jews from Arab-speaking countries, and establish a thriving economy against serious odds. The prolonged conflict with the Arab world and the economic problems produced existential fears. Consequently, the society was characterized by a high level of public consensus and identification with Zionist collectivism. It felt the necessity to socialize its youth accordingly.

Similar to other European nationalist and socialist movements, Zionism aspired to create a new type of Jewish human being in the land of Israel that was to be the antithesis and negation of the mythical "Diaspora Jew." "New Jews," the so-called Zabars named after a local cactus *Opuntia ficus-indica* to indicate their native-born status and outward toughness, would be free Hebrew speakers, healthy in body and soul, and untouched by the devastating influence of European anti-Semitism.

Expectations about the young generation

Israeli elites had high expectations of this young, Israeli-born generation, deeming it essential for the very survival of the Jewish society and state. Hence, the young generation had a very clear vocation in the Zionist revolution. To assure success, the Jewish society had implemented strong institutional controls on young people consisting of a formal, nationalist education system and a complementary informal system of youth movements ideologically connected to the various Zionist political parties. The common maxim for all these institutions was that young people should be deeply committed to the state and nation, even at the cost of their individual development and personal well-being.

In the same vein, the Israeli government made every effort to shield the youth from exposure to "harmful" foreign influences that might divert them from their national vocation by imposing censorship and controls on media and culture. Israel's founding father, David Ben-Gurion, opposed the introduction of TV broadcasting in Israel because he thought it might harm young people, spoiling their good reading habits and undermining the development of their national identity. In 1965, a government commission responsible for allocating foreign currency for inviting foreign artists prevented the Beatles (who had already enjoyed popularity in the Israeli hit parades of foreign music) from visiting Israel when it ascertained that the group did not comply with the country's cultural and artistic standards!

The so-called 1948 Generation [*Dor Tashach*], a first generation of Zabars, consisting of those who fought in the 1948 "War of Independence," seems to have conformed better to the Zionist aspirations than its successor. The members of the second generation, who had been socialized in the young state during its first decade, seemed to Zionist observers to be less committed to fulfilling their national mission. In 1960, the famous author Izhar Smilanski (1916–2006), who was also a member of the Knesset (parliament) on behalf of the dominant Mapai Party, lamented the individualistic, mediocre, petit-bourgeois aspirations of the urban youth of this generation. Citing the Jewish author Arthur Koestler, he named them the "Espresso Generation," noting that they seemed to be wasting their time in cafés instead of engaging in national missions, as his own 1948 Generation had done. Ironically, this was the first attempt to define the Israeli generation contemporary with the so-called '68 Generation. After the victory of the Six-Day War of 1967, this generation had been "vindicated" and came to be known as the "'67 Generation," just as the "'48 Generation" had been named for its heroic victory in the 1948 Arab-Israeli War.

Israeli soldiers advance in armored personnel carriers toward El Arish in Sinai during the Arab-Israeli Six-Day War, June 7, 1967.

Political change and reform

A gradual process of change and reform was started under the leadership of prime minister Levi Eshkol, who replaced the old patriarch David Ben-Gurion in 1963. Most notably, in 1966 the Eshkol government abolished the military regime, which had controlled the lives of much of the Israeli-Palestinian population since 1948. In 1968, the government introduced a government-owned TV channel (broadcasting in black and white).

Throughout the formative years of Israeli society, non-conformist Jewish voices from the left criticized the dominant political body. Since 1948, the Jewish members of the Israeli Communist Party [Maki] represented such a voice, especially regarding to the Palestinian question.

Another prominent oppositional voice belonged to Uri Avneri, a member of the '48 Generation. Avneri led a tough, non-Marxist anti-establishment line with his controversial weekly *Ha'olam Haze* [This World]. In 1965, he founded a political movement, establishing a political party that bore the name Ha'olam Ha'ze—Koach-Chadash [This World—New Power] and getting elected to the Knesset. This party became an address for young radicals of the '67 Generation.

The Israeli Socialist Organization, better known as the Matzpen [Compass] group in reference to its newspaper, was a tiny splinter group that split from the Israeli Communist Party in 1962 after it had objected to the lack of free and open discussions within the party and protested against its ideological collectivism. This Marxist organization was always very marginal, but it started to resonate with a wider public after 1967. Its members were—and probably still are—regarded by the majority of Israelis as outcasts. Nevertheless, they introduced a unique and unprecedented contribution to the Israeli political discourse. The late Professor Ehud Sprinzak claimed that the Matzpen people were the first to break the Israeli—and probably Jewish—taboo on exposing Israel's "dirty laundry" (the economic, civil, and national discrimination against the Israeli Palestinians) in front of the Western public, including in Germany. On June 8, 1967, in the middle of the Six-Day War, Matzpen jointly published a political manifesto in the London *Times* with members of the Democratic Front for the Liberation of Palestine, regarded by most Israelis then as a terrorist group aiming to destroy Israel (many still see it this way today). This strongly anti-Zionist manifesto called for the establishment of a binational state that would replace Zionist Israel. However, it emphasized Jews' right to live in this state, and similarly opposed Arab and Jewish nationalism.

Similar to developments in other Western countries, certain splinter groups in the Israeli protest movement of the late '60s condoned the use of violence and terror by the Palestinian liberation movements as a legitimate means to achieve their goals. A small number of Jewish radicals of the '67 Generation belonging to one of Matzpen's splinters, the Chazit Aduma [Red Front], expressed their wish to participate in the armed Palestinian struggle for a socialist binational state in Palestine, and two of them even went illegally to Syria and participated in armed training there. The vast majority of Jewish society perceived this unprecedented phenomenon as severe and alarming high treason.

Between protest and consensus

The earliest, calloused voice of protest by a member of the Israeli '67 Generation was that of Hanoch Levin (1943-1999), who would later become one of Israel's most creative playwrights and poets. At the age of twenty-four—in August 1968, in the midst of the post '67 war euphoria—he staged an anti-militaristic cabaret in Tel-Aviv: *You, I and the Next War*. Following Brecht, this cabaret sharply and wittily criticized Jewish-Israeli society for its sanctification of death and its militarism, mocking Israel's most sacred values of sacrifice and heroism for the nation's cause, and ridiculing its pompous generals. Like many creative minds of his generation, Levin seemed eager to slaughter holy cows and did not shy away from using slang and rude words in his works, thereby shocking Israelis. This cabaret and two additional political plays he wrote between 1968 and 1970 evoked fierce public debates in Israel, which usually focused not on the militaristic character of the society but on the legitimacy of expressing criticism against it.

A bit later, in 1971, a group belonging to the '67 Generation of *Mizrachiim* [Jews from Arab and Muslim countries] founded a protest organization named the Black Panthers under the influence of radical American Jewish students in Jerusalem (some of these American Jewish students were also members of Matzpen). This was the first radical *Mizrachi* protest against the Ashkenazi (Jews of European background) establishment and the discrimination of the Oriental Jewish migrants in Israel. Contrary to Matzpen, the Panthers managed to attract thousands of supporters at their demonstrations. They heightened public awareness of the social discrimination against the *Mizrachi* communities in Israel and augmented the resources directed to ministering to their needs.

Notwithstanding the protest movements, Zionism was still consensual in 1968 among young people, who did not challenge the old leadership either in politics or other fields, even though most Israeli politicians of the time were senior citizens. They never called the commitment to the young state into question. For example, until the Lebanon War of 1982, pacifist refusal to serve in the army (which is compulsory for three years for men, and about two years for women) was a very rare and marginal phenomenon.

While Israeli society was governed by socialist parties, and the collectivist Kibbutz Movement enjoyed extremely high standing, most Israelis perceived the communist bloc during most of the Cold War as a direct enemy of the young Jewish State. The Soviet support of the Arab world and the Soviet anti-Semitism gave rise, as well, to animosity towards the New Left in Europe, which had adopted what most Israelis viewed as pro-Soviet and anti-Israeli positions. Many young Israelis identified with the US, which had equipped the Israel Defense Forces since the French embargo on arms and ammunition to Israel of 1967. They completely misunderstood the struggle of their peers on American campuses against the war in Vietnam, a war they considered an integral part of the fight to free the world from the communist threat.

Young Israelis exhibited the same reservations about the social messages of the '68 protest. The Israeli '67 Generation was quite familiar—directly acquainted, even—with socialist and communal ideology and models (e.g., the Kibbutz Movement). While many Western '68 protesters attracted to the way of life in the kibbutz came to Israel as volunteers, young, educated, urban Israelis were much less enthusiastic about the communal way of life. They wished to escape collectivism, possessing a strong urge to pursue individualistic self-fulfillment and to freely express their personal feelings.

It is also notable that feminism did not play any central role in Israel in 1968. The radical groups described here consisted mostly of young men; extremely few women had participated in their protest activities. This may have been due to the Zionist movement's support of gender equality (manifested, for example, in the requirement that women, like men, serve in the army).

The legacy of the "'67 Generation"

The generational conflict in the Israel of 1968 did not attain the dimensions it had acquired in the West. Young people did not challenge their parents, many of whom were immigrants, among them Holocaust survivors. They perceived them as weak rather than powerful and oppressive figures who, therefore, deserved their protection instead of their belligerence.

Despite these remarkable differences between the developments in Israel and in other parts of the world, the '67 Generation avant-garde brought pacifist, civilian, and, above all, individualistic voices into Israeli discourse, counterbalancing its former hegemonic militarist, nationalist, and collectivist characteristics. Their efforts helped liberalize Israeli society, making it more polyphonic, pluralistic, and basically Western.

* I am very grateful to my friend and colleague, Professor Benjamin Bental, himself a member of the "'67 Generation," for his thoughtful comments on drafts of this paper.

Gilad Margalit, born in 1959, is an Israeli historian, and Deputy Director of the Haifa Center for German and European Studies (HCGES) at the University of Haifa. His research focuses on German history since 1945.

LEBANON: OF THINGS THAT REMAIN UNSAID*

Rachid al-Daif

Without a doubt, a great deal was said in Lebanon about the student revolts in France in the year 1968. However, there are undoubtedly some things that remain unsaid—in particular, because these events took place following the defeat of the Arabs by Israel in 1967 and the rise of the Palestinian Fatah movement under the leadership of Yasser Arafat, a time when a revolutionary atmosphere hostile to the West and to America prevailed.

Not only we, the Lebanese left-wingers, but also the Arab left-wing in general, perceived in this student revolt tremendous support for the path of modernity and secularism that we believed Arab societies would confidently, assuredly follow, even if progress was so leisurely that we lost patience and, on occasion, our equanimity, too. This revolt, which we imitated and allowed to inspire us, fascinated us.

Effects of the revolt on everyday life

Many things, then, have already been said about these events; and many things still remain to be said. Yet I cannot remember reading or hearing anything about the way this revolt changed our everyday lives, our individual development, particularly in terms of our bodies and our clothes, as well as our relationship—especially the sexual one—between men and women of our generation. This is, in my opinion, highly significant, and because no one has yet paid adequate attention to the topic, I intend to concentrate on this alone.

I clearly recall this everyday impact. I went to bookshops to look at the photographs of events in the French newspapers and magazines. I imagined myself with the students in the Latin Quarter, felling trees and setting fire to tires to erect barricades in the streets; I saw myself digging up cobblestones to throw at the police, the instrument of bourgeois repression. The hair and sideburns in these pictures were long, as were the beards, which the students allowed to grow wild, completely ungroomed.

Long hair as a sign of rebellion

In the early days of our youth, we used to wear suits and matching ties, each according to his parents' material circumstances. We never wore clothes that were not ironed, and every couple of weeks we would get our hair cut by a professional barber. We shaved our beards almost every day, and I and my friends from the same modest background bought razor blades, which we sharpened repeatedly when they became blunt.

Then, in the course of the events of 1968, we grew muttonchops and grew our hair long. We no longer paid great attention to our clothes, as we had done in the past; sometimes we didn't even pay much attention to how clean they were, and we were very proud of all this, because it was revolutionary. We implied that comrades who did not behave as we did were still prisoners of bourgeois thinking and bourgeois traditions, which were the remnants of a bourgeois view of the world. Sooner or later, one had to free oneself from this.

Our devoutness decreased

Our piety also waned further. This development had begun long before with the advent of the Arab modern age and continued through the age of the great reformers and on into our time. Throughout my entire time at university, which I entered in 1966, I never saw anybody pray or fast, neither Muslim nor Christian. If it became known that someone was fasting, that person would make reference to his parents or grandparents and claim only to be fasting out of obedience to them or something of the kind.

What was remarkable about all this was that we expressed our rejection of bourgeois norms although we never suffered from them, because, quite simply, we had never experienced them. Most of our families were poor or lived in modest circumstances: off the land or from casual work, or else on donations from family and relations abroad. Even to the well-off amongst us, such societal rules were not familiar.

Rejection of traditional customs

We let our hair and our sideburns grow until our families compared us to girls and made fun of us. It made them angry, but the reason for this anger was not that our behavior constituted a rejection of their customs and behavior, which indeed was not the case. My mother, for example, looked long and hard at my long hair and muttonchops and laughed uproariously. She exclaimed, "If only you'd been born a girl!" From time to time she would get slightly annoyed because my long hair made the whole towel wet when I took a bath on Friday night or Saturday morning—once a week, as was usual in our house. If my brothers and sisters took a bath after me, they could no longer use the towel. This was a problem for my mother, because towels in our house were in extremely short supply. She therefore took to cutting up our old cotton shirts and sewing hand towels out of them; I had to use these as a punishment for my long hair and to avoid creating problems for those who bathed after me.

Lack of cleanliness among pupils was something that infuriated the teachers at our school. I remember that one teacher threatened to hit us hard on the tips of our fingers if he spotted dirt under our nails. Many of the pupils always had dirty fingernails because they helped their families in the fields. This teacher said to one pupil, who was a neighbor of mine, "Scrub your hands morning, noon, and night for a good long time with soap and pumice!" I will never forget this because my friend's skin was very raw from working with his father every day before and after school and on school holidays. He mowed the field so that their three cows had something to eat. He helped his father milk them, mucked out their stall, and did other jobs that go with keeping livestock and farming. This pupil sometimes scrubbed his hands so long that they bled.

Before our rebellion, I had to wait patiently until my father, after much careful deliberation, bought me a suit, which I treated as if it had to last forever. And it did have to last almost forever, because I only got a suit every two or more years. I did not even wear it every Sunday but only on certain Sundays and on special occasions so that it still looked like new. Nonetheless, when we rebelled, we refused to wear suits and ties; our wardrobe now consisted solely of jeans. Jeans were avant-garde and revolutionary.

We heard a lot about sexual freedom, free love, and a free attitude to the body. That stimulated our imagination: we were young people starting out in life with all our vitality and vigor, and so we embarked on this adventure. One student who was studying at one of the French universities at the time told us that he had witnessed a provocative demonstration on one of the squares by advocates of sexual liberation performing sexual acts in a public square. The sex acts involved naked young men and women, young women on their own without men, and one young woman and her pet.

In our country, people had begun to call for the liberation of women in the mid-nineteenth century. Over time women had won many rights, while conservative moral traditions gradually retreated: the veil was discarded, and women gained the freedom to choose a husband and equal educational opportunities, for example. We, however—the generation of Palestinian resistance, Vietnam and Guevara—were fascinated by the 1968 student revolt in France because it involved a rejection of sexual prohibition.

So we pounced on women in an unprecedented manner, and in doing so realized our dream of liberation as well as our dream of being a progressive people. Yet for us (or, to be more precise, for some of us), women became a sort of prey that had to be hunted en route to attaining freedom. When I now think back on our behavior towards the young women, I feel a certain shame. Most of us were from the countryside, or from small towns that were even more countrified than the country, and our (progressive) view of women was prisoner to several-thousand-year-old traditions of manliness, patriarchy, chastity, shame, the forbidden, motherliness, emotionality, tenderness, and the clear division of gender roles. Thus, women were not equal partners in sexual liberation but conquests of the forbidden under a patriarchal order.

Demonstration for the Palestinian Liberation Organization (PLO) on Sept. 23, 1970, in Beirut.

Sexual liberation at the women's expense

Looking back on our behavior towards women, which was influenced by the news from France in 1968, I believe that we were cruel, sometimes even brutal, towards them. We men were experimenting, we men had the pleasure; they were the instruments of our experiments and of our pleasure, and we often treated them with a double standard. For example, one comrade in a left-wing Marxist movement believed that the body of the woman whose belly would contain his child had to be "pure." For this reason, he had a "serious" relationship with the girl he had decided to marry but had flings with other girls he did not want to marry. Noteworthy was that he preserved the virginity of the one who was to become his wife and the mother of his children until after the marriage ceremony. This was at the start of the 1970s.

This was no isolated case; many comrades behaved in exactly the same way. Hunting women was a deed of glory. I remember that one of the comrades had impregnated a woman "by mistake" or "out of laziness." When she told him, he left her to her own devices, so that she was forced to ask close friends for help. While they stood by her in seeking and getting an abortion, his role was limited to boasting to his close friends, his breast swelling with pride, about this "achievement." Other comrades thought differently about this. They behaved as if the woman really did have the freedom to choose what she did with her body and did not lose her "purity" or "chastity" if she exercised this freedom. They regarded the others as reactionaries, but of course they numbered only a few.

Nonetheless, at the time following the revolt of 1968, women's liberation in general and sexuality in particular received a powerful boost. Discussions on these topics were heated compared to those in the past, and they were held in much broader circles like the Lebanese Communist organizations and parties, as well as in the Palestinian ones in Lebanon; they were also held in the nationalist parties influenced by left-wing Marxist thinking, some of which were very large and influential.

A consequence of such widespread sexual liberation, of course, was that the number of abortions rose dramatically, as did the number of doctors semi-officially performing them, often under unacceptable medical conditions. In the mid-1980s there were rumors in Beirut that a doctor who had specialized in offering almost official abortions had been murdered in mysterious circumstances. It was said that his murderers were fundamentalists who rejected this procedure. In fact, this event marked the beginning of a sea change toward piety in the city.

Signs of increasing devoutness

By the 1990s, religiousness was apparent everywhere. Sometimes the number of women in lecture halls wearing the veil was higher than the number without. The number of those fasting increased until they constituted an absolute majority. In many universities, prayer rooms were established under pressure from the students (prayer rooms for women, and separate ones for men), and in the month of fasting, almost every sign of eating, drinking, or smoking in public disappeared from view.

Nonetheless, I do not believe that these signs can be taken as decisive proof that all traces of the events of 1968 have disappeared. I am almost certain that these traces are there, because the new attitudes and behaviors stimulated by the revolution, which represented a reawakening of a development that had begun long before, had become deeply ingrained, putting down roots in the ethics and culture of the Lebanese people. It seems unlikely that all traces of these events could have been completely eradicated, despite the turn to piety of the last forty years.

* An earlier version of this article was published in the Goethe-Institut cultural magazine *Fikrun wa Fann*.

Rachid al-Daif, born in northern Lebanon in 1945, is one of Lebanon's greatest contemporary authors.

PALESTINIAN TERRITORIES: DISCOVERING FREEDOM IN A REFUGEE CAMP*

Hassan Khadr

At the start of the 1970s, we all read *Mourir d'aimer* [Dying for Love], a novel written by a Frenchman whose name still sticks in my memory: Pierre Duchesne. Using "we" to speak about this reading describes the reality better than "I," since reading was a communal activity forced on us by the fact that books were very expensive—at least for senior pupils living in a Gaza refugee camp, and also because we took turns reading books. Talking about books was one of the most precious of pleasures and—done crowded against the walls of houses in semi-dark streets during long evenings—one of the most exciting.

This novel impressed us so much that some of us still remember it. There are various reasons for this: First, it was a novel about love—and when you are sixteen, raging hormones electrify that word, cutting you to the quick as soon as you feel this emotion or talk about it. Secondly, this novel was concerned with an "unnatural" relationship between a female teacher and one of her pupils who, as luck would have it, was the same age as we were. Of course, we identified with this fortunate beloved, despite his sad fate (he and his teacher kill themselves in the end). Perhaps that fate drove us to dream of a similar, and even greater, experience of seduction. The third reason was that the novel was set against the background of the 1968 student uprising in France.

A right to our own values

We had heard and read about the demonstrations that erupted in the French capital and then spread to other European cities, but *Mourir d'aimer* was the best and simplest opportunity for both grasping the significance of the student rebellion and discovering a connection (whatever that might have been) between us and the uprising. The love between a teacher and her pupil challenged the social rules that determine individual behavior and lay down the conditions for belonging to society.

When the two lovers decide to kill themselves in response to a society striving to protect a degenerate morality from disgrace, their action really does arise out of the individual's freedom to reject dominant values. They assume the individual's right to adopt one's own values and moral standards out of free will and act out the desire to discover and try out something new rather than adhere to imitation and instruction.

Decline of paternal authority

Our enthusiasm for speaking about freedom and values certainly cannot be interpreted abstractly, and if we attributed excessive importance to this, it surely did not come from any cultural sensitivity. The truth is that when the Israelis defeated the Arabs in the Six-Day War of June 1967, a year before the student revolt, we came to admire any criticism of traditional values and discussion of moving beyond them.

One of many attempts to explain the defeat included the idea of a decline in paternal authority, which most immediately affected us. Paternal authority did not refer to paternity in a narrow and direct sense of the word but rather to society as an extended father endowed with all possible powers. It was this society—with its ideas about morality, its social structure, its hypocrisy, and its carelessness—that had caused and suffered the defeat.

Finding words for the rebellion

At that time, *Self-Criticism after the Defeat*, a book by Syrian-born Sadiq Jalal al-Azm published soon after the end of the 1967 war, enriched our thinking with valuable ideas. Al-Azm wrote about "slick operators," people who are superficial, deceitful, and lacking in morality and culture—qualities necessary for success in diverse societies. They could be politicians, intellectuals, soldiers, administrators, or presidents, and it was they, he wrote, who had led the Arab world to defeat.

These reflections imparted credibility to our ideas and enabled us to adhere to views perhaps inappropriate to our age, but we had an empathy with them and understood them in an instinctive and profound way. These texts gave us the words to justify our rebellion and to familiarize ourselves with our true opponents.

Connection to the international community

In this spirit, our enthusiasm for anything that called prevalent values into question, even if it occurred in a distant country and was embodied in a relationship ending in death, was not just a cultural response. It was also our way of taking part in an international movement that, though lacking clear-cut characteristics, spanned large parts of the world.

Among the books we passed around at the end of the '60s were remnants from a library plundered during the war. One of them was entitled *A Dictionary of Communism*, published by a Beirut company, which, I learned later, comprised part of a US project designed to combat the dissemination of leftist ideas in the Arab world. The compilers of this dictionary, who even wanted to discourage people from using terms like "the Left," concentrated on the dangers morality and society faced when destructive ideas spread. Despite these warnings, or maybe because of them, we became leftists even before we had read the final pages of the dictionary. After all, the Left, as described in the book, promised to change morality and society.

Ban on long hair

As many of us found expression by means other than words, long hair, tight clothing, and particularly bell-bottom pants became a kind of territory under dispute between ourselves and society, represented by school, people's gaze in the streets, and sometimes also the family. In high school, we were punished if we allowed our hair to grow long, or wore colorful shirts and bell-bottoms. Some kids were skillful and wore two shirts and two pairs of pants simultaneously, but no solution could be found for long hair. At least until our schooldays came to an end, this remained one of those forbidden things that could not be concealed.

Returning to the past is akin to visiting an old house we once lived in, and which we believed we knew everything about. But when we visit this place, we always discover a

Palestinian refugee camp near Amman, Jordan, in March 1969.

corner we never saw before. For example, it is remarkable to recall high school pupils forty years ago spending long evenings in the semi-dark streets of a refugee camp discussing freedom and invoking such names as Sartre, Marcuse, and Simone de Beauvoir. We were busy with the struggle against colonialism and imperialism wherever that occurred—as if that were a personal or almost a family affair that had to be dealt with immediately.

Great change in small worlds

Some years ago, I met an Israeli who was a member of Matzpen (the Israeli Socialist Organization), who told me about growing up at the end of the '60s. Surprisingly, he and his cohorts, about the same age as I was, were interested in the same books and individuals, and had the same dreams—just in another language, of course. It is not difficult to imagine innumerable students in different places across the world who did likewise and believed that an uprising against real or imagined fathers should not be delayed.

The widespread nature of revolutionary thinking at that time prods us to make comparisons between generations, or talk about the world of high school students today. Yet I have no particular inclination to do so. One can only say that those who can be called the '60s generation in our country brought great change to their little worlds. Perhaps they even achieved at least symbolic success in overthrowing real and imagined fathers. However, today it is indisputable that this success was short-lived.

* An earlier version of this text was published in the Goethe-Institut cultural magazine *Fikrun wa Fann*.

Hassan Khadr is a Palestinian journalist who lives in Germany.

SENEGAL: MAY 1968, AFRICA'S REVOLT

Andy Stafford

On May 27, 1968, the Association of Senegalese Students and the Dakar Association of Students in the nation's capital called for a strike of indefinite length and for a boycott of examinations. Police quashed riots on campus, and foreign students were expelled from the country by armed force. In the street fighting that followed, one student was killed and over 900 were arrested. Student demonstrations developed into an opposition against the ideology of the ruling-class Senegalese Progressive Union's (UPS) monopoly of power, and the regime's submission to the former French colonial power when the trade unions went on strike to support the students. Senegalese President Léopold S. Senghor, who was also an award-winning poet, closed the university in Dakar and declared a state of emergency across the nation.

How can we conceive of these events in Senegal in May and June 1968? Were they related to the nearly simultaneous events in the former colonial power, France, or were they more independent? It would seem that the activists, the agents of history in Senegal, and the subsequent explanations given for their revolt have been conditioned in reaction to France, and so we must attempt to understand the complex relations between former colonial master and newly independent African countries across the events of May 1968. How then does the experience of revolt in Senegal affect the French and Francophone memory of '68?

Writing the history of 1968 in Senegal

Senegal is not generally included in histories of events concerning 1968. This exclusion seemed to occur from the very start. Famous posters appeared in Paris in 1968 that linked the revolt with the former colonies ("Brisons les urnes colonialistes" [Smash colonialist vote-rigging]; "Travailleurs français immigrés unis" [French immigrant workers united], etc.), yet the events in Senegal were largely ignored. In the maelstrom in France in May and June 1968, this is not surprising. In Senegal, too, in recent years, there has been no mention whatsoever of the events of May 1968 nor of the subsequent backlash of Senghor's government.

There are a number of reasons for this. First, the revolts in May 1968 in Senegal's capital, Dakar, tend to be characterized as "internal." Even a radical critic with internationalist leanings such as Jean-Pierre Ndiaye insisted that Senegal's May '68 did not arise in imitation of France's revolts, which had begun a few weeks earlier. Ndiaye conceded in 1971 that Senegal was the most incorporated of all of France's former African colonies, heavily dependent on the fortunes of the former colonial master's economy, but since such a revolt did not take place in other Francophone countries, something else must have been going on in Senegal. Here, ironically, then appear the deeper parallels with France, rather than the simple notion of cause and effect. Like France, argues Ndiaye, Senegal had a working class that, though stymied by intermediaries, had not lost its class hatred. This was the smoldering situation that both French and Senegalese students encountered, becoming the spark in 1968. As in Paris, the uprising surprised Senegalese authorities, who were caught short for forty-eight hours, in part because political power relied heavily on Paris. As May '68 unfurled in France, President Senghor apparently saw de Gaulle losing his grip in France, and so he reacted more resolutely, barricading himself in as soon as he saw Senegal begin its own revolt.

Crucially for Senghor's tactic of isolating the Dakar uprising, it was American and Chinese nationals who were swiftly extradited from Senegal as the revolt began to grow. Senghor was adroitly cynical in blaming outside influences for the events in Dakar in May-June 1968. However, when the movement picked up again in May-June 1969 and France showed no signs of a major rerun, Senghor could no longer use these arguments. Ndiaye offers a neocolonial explanation of the absence in France but persistence in Senegal of the movement in 1969, but it merely increases the autarkic nature of his analysis: France could offer workers reforms and carefully marginalize the *gauchistes* and then increase neocolonial exploitation as a payback; but Senghor clearly did not have this last option. So, in order to shore up his one-party rule, he cannily launched a "new society" in 1969, incorporating young intellectuals into the democratic system. In a bid to head off mass political challenge from below, Senghor hoisted many of the intellectuals who had led the movement into government, as he looked to—or made it seem like there was—a fresh start for the newly independent Senegal. In particular, this "new society" made loud noises about the "Senegalization" of the economy, all the while maintaining strong European connections, which, for some, such as radical filmmaker Sembene Ousmane, was merely a shift to a neocolonial policy (see the opening sequence of Sembene's 1974 film *Xala*, a film about economic and sexual impotence).

There were a number of further factors that increased the autarky of the events in Dakar. Running a few weeks later than Paris (Dakar's uprising began May 27, 1968) and ending much more abruptly on June 11, Senegal's May '68, like a slicker version of Paris's but able to straddle two calendar months, ended with the same sorry tale: one demonstrator dead, huge but fragile pay increases, and a perceived "sellout" by pliant and pliable mid-level organizations (just like the French Communist Party) grouped around conservative Islamic leaders.

The longue durée

Naturally, one could always find the origins of May '68 in Dakar in earlier periods than the final explosion of May 27, 1968: the failed coup of 1962 by Prime Minister Mamadou Dia; the shooting of up to fifty student demonstrators during the 1963 elections; Senghor's concentration of presidential power after 1964, which now looks very similar to General de Gaulle's in the 1958 referendum and launch of the Fifth French Republic; the perceived "abuse" of "Negritude" with which to wed all the social classes under the one, national "Senegal" banner. Luckily for Senghor, as a poet and intellectual, he was beholden to none of the (Maoist) cultural-revolutionary suspicion of intellectuals that Sekou Touré might have displayed in neighboring Guinea-Conakry. But Senghor did not see social class as a problem internal to nations, a view that underpinned his version of "African socialism" in which Marx was deemed "anti-nationalist." This suited Senghor's autocratic rule but also made him blind to social conflict. Indeed, in a manner not dissimilar to André Gorz in France—who, in 1967, ruled out any hint of a social or political rebellion in France—Senghor misjudged the simmering anger in 1960s Senegal. But this is not to say that Senghor was unaware of challenge.

Senghor had outlawed the most radical parties in Senegal, the African Regroupment Party of Senegal (PRA)—its leaders were arrested during the 1963 elections but then courted and incorporated into his government after 1965—as well as the Party of African Independence (PAI), which articulated a mix of Marxist-Leninism, pan-Africanism and "nationalism." Abdoulaye Bathily, the only person to have chronicled the events of May '68 in Senegal in a book-length study, *Mai 68 à Dakar, ou la révolte universitaire et la démocratie* (1992), had been a key leader of the PAI and a student activist during Senegal's May '68. But like his counterpart in Europe, Daniel Cohn-Bendit, Bathily has since reassessed his view of Senegal's May '68.

Though not condemning the events, Bathily has seen them as an escapade designed to win more student rights and to reform the Senghor government into a democracy. Similar to Ndiaye, Bathily has considered the revolt an internal one, and not an extension of that in France. Yet despite this similarity in their analyses, we must not conflate Bathily's later view with Ndiaye's account. For Ndiaye, writing in 1971, Dakar in late May 1968 represented the first direct confrontation between *le pouvoir* and students. It was, after all, workers in solidarity with students in Dakar who triggered the events.

On May 27, 800 workers were arrested after demonstrations following the occupation of the university campus by Senegalese paratroops. Then General Bigeard's nearby French troops were drafted in, which led to more demonstrations, Molotov cocktails, and to 2,500 student arrests. At the same time, Jean Colin, France's interior minister, who had been dispatched to Senegal by France's African "fixer," Jacques Foccart, called the French air force in from its base in Senegal to help out the Senegalese army. At the height of the events, President Senghor gave a radio speech on May 30, 1968, and, using a tactic typical of beleaguered politicians, blamed outside influences for undermining Senegal's independence and accused Dakar's students of merely copying the French students. The tactic seemed to work. Senghor cynically (and selectively) used the practical nonalignment that was Senegal's foreign policy to deflect the movement. With the student movement and trade unions at least partly accepting Senghor's "neocolonial" maneuver, the president succeeded in heading off a more serious challenge to his state power.

The ambivalent relationship to France

Despite the internal causes of Senegal's revolt, we can now see that the links with France and its own uprising were undeniable. One example is the continuously popular figure of Senegalese legend Omar Diop (aka Diop Blondin). Diop Blondin started his militant career as a key Paris activist, having also had a major part in Jean-Luc Godard's radical 1967 film *La Chinoise*. Returning to Senegal after the 1968–1969 events (apparently deported at Foccart's behest), Diop was arrested in 1972 for using Molotov cocktails when French president Pompidou visited the Centre Culturel Français in Dakar. Though his comrades supported him in the Maoist "Gauche Prolétarienne" and in the "Révolution Afrique" group in Paris, Diop died in mysterious circumstances in a Gorée jail in 1973. Diop's transcultural experiences and specific targets mirror the interconnectedness of the French and Senegalese culture of protest.

Georges Pompidou (1911-1974), president of the French Republic, and Léopold Sédar Senghor, Senegalese statesman, in Dakar, February 1971.

At the same time, Senegal's revolt expressed a critique of neocolonialism with respect to France and the wider international community. Much of the political content of the demands from the movement was phrased in anti-French, anti-foreign language. Ironically, Senghor, too, blamed the events on foreigners trying to undermine the national sovereignty that Senegal's independence from France was enjoying. Senghor and the student movement fell over themselves to be the bigger critics of external influence. Senghor used it to suit his divide-and-rule policy; the students isolated their own struggle by lining up (behind Senghor, ultimately) to decry France and its "neocolonial" project.

Yet the autarky of the movement in Senegal was not endemic. In 1966, when Kwame Nkrumah's anti-colonial regime fell in Ghana, Dakar students had besieged the British and American embassies for being behind the coup and called Senghor's "a reactionary, feudal and neocolonial regime." For the Left in Senegal (and elsewhere), the "Festival d'Arts nègres," held in a Dakar in 1966, merely confirmed this: supported by the US, France, and the UK, but boycotted by China, Cuba, and the Non-Aligned Movement, the festival marked the beginning of the end of the Négritude movement, to which Senghor's power in Senegal and his own intellectual and artistic achievements owed so much. If we add this to a long series of student demands for union recognition, for a reform of higher education across 1967, then we can see that the events of May 1968 were well prepared in Senegal. By May 1, 1968, workers and students were demanding lower rice prices, more jobs, an end to the links between Senegalese bosses and Senghor's party, the UPS. This challenge to Senghor and to Négritude was just like the challenge to de Gaulle in France in May 1968: younger, more militant sections no longer accepted that Négritude (or Gaullism in France) was really about liberation (the former from colonialism and racism, the latter from the Nazi Occupation). The revolts in both countries were also concerned with the leader's own person, his beliefs, and use of history.

The radical economist Pierre Jalée pointed out that de Gaulle had to be supported economically, grudgingly bailed out, by the US in June 1968. With the French franc in free fall across the 1968 period, it was finally subjected to devaluation in August 1969. Given that many economies in Africa had their banks and currencies pegged to the French franc, the integration of Francophone Africa into European and North American economies had already begun long before May '68. Thus, May '68 in France had an enormous effect—political, social, economic, and ideological—in parts of Africa. It was a conscious strategy by Senghor to isolate the movement, precisely by blaming outside influence. In other words, Senghor played his last card: using a rhetoric of "the Third World against Europe," of the new Senegal fighting against French neocolonialism, his tactic worked. Autarky of the Dakar movement from France was used by Senegal's rulers in May '68 in order to "recuperate" (or "negate") the challenge being made by the masses of students and workers alike. The movement, in turn, followed Senghor's critique of neocolonialism—not that surprising given that only eight years before the Senegalese had fought hard for their independence from the colonial master. The difference between ruler and ruled, however, was that the former, Senghor, was markedly more "dialectical" than his revolting opponents in the students' and workers' movement. That is to say, African rulers like Senghor could at once denounce outside influences, all the while relying on foreign powers (France, the US) to supply the crucial policing and military role. Their opponents—the thousands, millions, radicalized by world and domestic events and local conditions—needed to have been more dialectical in *their* attitude towards imperialism and class society. For, though it was imperative to denounce France's continued neocolonialist policy in Africa, this critique by the Senegalese Left needed to be linked much more tightly with the revolt in France's May 1968; and more importantly, Senghor's "anti-imperialist" rhetoric needed to be exposed for its opportunist ability to deflect criticism away from the Senegalese ruling class.

Describing the Paris Commune of 1871 as a *trésor perdu*, Bernard Noël could easily have applied the same metaphor to May '68 in Senegal: its "failure," in real and representational terms, merely increases its potential for success in the future. And although France has been slow to adopt postcolonial approaches to history, politics, and literature, it seems that the lost treasure of May '68 is now being reconsidered in this light. The publication of volumes such as Blanchard's *La Fracture coloniale* in 2005 has begun to draw links between "home" and "out there." But more important events in France and its cities since 1995 have encouraged an adjustment of the historiographical picture. Just as in Senegal in the late 1960s, workers, students, and now immigrants (from Africa and from elsewhere) and their children growing up in France risk coming together in a new uprising, for and in which autarky, in France or elsewhere, will not be an option.

Andy Stafford is a senior lecturer in French and Francophone studies at the University of Leeds. A member of the editorial board of *Francophone Postcolonial Studies*, he has taught and published on several Francophone African countries.

SOUTH AFRICA: WHERE WERE WE LOOKING IN 1968?

John Daniel and Peter Vale

A joke and an anecdote drawn from apartheid's rich but tragic archive both sets the mood of this essay and explains how it was that what was then arguably the world's most political country, South Africa, largely escaped 1968, potentially the twentieth century's most political year. Here is the joke: from the cockpit, passengers in the cabin of a full jetliner that has just landed at Johannesburg international airport sometime in the apartheid era hear this announcement: "Ladies and Gentlemen, we have just landed in South Africa. Please turn your watches back five years."

The anecdote relates to an intelligent University of Natal student, the late Monica Fairall, who was Miss South Africa 1968 and thus South Africa's entrant in the Miss Universe competition, which happened to be held in her home country that year. After the opening ceremony, Ms. Fairall was asked by the event's South African organizers not to wear her evening gown again because it was considered "too extreme" as it showed too much "back."

Backdrop to 1968

The years between 1964 and 1972 were ones in which the relationship between apartheid and modernity deepened. The country's economic growth rate averaged between 6 and 8 percent per annum. This fed a frenzy of construction and pointed the country's constitutional politics towards the Cold War authoritarianism that would follow in the 1980s.

It was a boom that followed a four-year period of unprecedented repression. A campaign of defiance led by the Pan-Africanist Congress (PAC) against the highly restrictive pass laws ended in March 1960 with the shootings at Sharpeville that left 69 dead and 150 wounded. This left no doubt that South Africa's minority government would use violence to quell resistance. Thereafter, the two largest political groupings—the African National Congress (ANC) and the PAC—representing the African majority, were banned, and draconian security laws that gave the police unfettered powers were enacted. It was clear that, in the eyes of the regime, non-racial protest had become "communist agitation."

It was at this time in 1960 that the ANC's Nelson Mandela, who would eventually become South Africa's first democratically elected president, went underground. He traveled abroad and visited, among other places, Algeria, where he met Ahmed Ben Bella, the country's newly elected president. This was not an incidental meeting: the successful Algerian war of liberation had sent a strong message to similar movements throughout the world, which is why its impact on the events in Paris in 1968 was indisputable. On his return, Mandela was arrested, convicted, and sentenced to five years in prison on relatively minor charges. But he was soon brought to trial again following a police raid of a house in Rivonia (near Johannesburg). The trial, which ended in June 1964, saw him and eight others of the High Command of the recently formed revolutionary army, Umkhonto we Sizwe, sentenced to life imprisonment. He was to spend the next twenty-seven years in prison.

In 1966, South Africa's National Party government obtained a clear majority of seats in parliament—astonishingly, this was close to two decades after it was first elected to government. That year, the intellectual behind apartheid's quest for modernity, social psychologist Hendrik Verwoerd, who had been elected prime minister in 1958, was stabbed to death on the floor of the same parliament. His replacement was the no-nonsense John Vorster, who had previously been the Minister of Justice and whose early-1960s crackdown on opposition had turned South Africa into a police state. A biographer has described Vorster as a "cold, formal, even rude" man who was "unsmiling, inflexible, fearsome and intolerant" towards opponents and critics.

In many ways, these same adjectives could be used to describe South Africa in 1968. It was a stark and grim place. Political repression had all but defeated opposition to apartheid; high levels of control and censorship prevented the spread of any literature that hinted at the emancipatory goals that would mark the events in Paris in May 1968. So, to use an apposite example, the reading of Mao, whose book *Quotations From Chairman Mao Tse-Tung*, which was known as the "Little Red Book," was so important in Europe in 1968, was almost unknown in South Africa.

Not much recognized at the time, however, events in the southern African region were signaling the possibility of change in South Africa. In 1965, the minority-controlled government of neighboring

Rhodesia had unilaterally declared independence from the United Kingdom and had been made subject by the United Nations (UN) to a regime of strict international sanctions. In October 1966, the UN General Assembly resolved that South Africa had forfeited its right to administer South-West Africa and terminated the mandate originally granted by the former League of Nations. In its place, it set up an eleven-member UN council to take over the administration of the territory. In June 1967, the General Assembly resolved to change the name of the territory to Namibia, a name that soon gained international currency everywhere except in Pretoria, a city located in the northern part of South Africa. By late 1966, guerrilla fighters were engaged in armed conflict against what they considered to be illegal regimes in both Rhodesia and Namibia. The slowly deteriorating situation on South Africa's borders was marked in 1967 by South Africa's commitment of police forces to combat infiltration into Rhodesia. A year later, counterinsurgency training was introduced into both police and military training with police units also being deployed to Namibia to battle the insurgency there.

International influences and new protest tactics

Let us now consider the direct impact the events of 1968 had on the South African public and on its politics. Overall, only a small but informed public, both black and white, followed these events as they unfolded, but they remained largely peripheral in terms of the political process itself. Still, they had some effect.

Student activists at the time—John Daniel was then serving as president of the National Union of South African Students (NUSAS), an anti-apartheid grouping of white English-speaking and some black campuses—followed the events in France in May and June 1968 with awe and fascination. In those pre-television days in South Africa, hourly news bulletins of the BBC World Service were the only dependable source of information. The idea of a student-worker alliance toppling a major Western government seemed impossible to South African students confronted with an intractable government at home. But "Danny the Red" (Daniel Cohn-Bendit), Rudi Dutschke, and Columbia University's Mark Rudd provided new heroes and a new set of protest tactics that students at the University of Cape Town would soon put to use.

Probably more influential than the events in France in the minds of the larger South African public, however, were the back-to-back assassinations in the United States of Martin Luther King Jr. and Robert Kennedy. The liberal promise of the US during those years meant that South Africans closely followed political developments on the other side of the Atlantic. The Cold War notwithstanding, the US was regarded then as a potential ally in the struggle to end apartheid; black South Africa, especially, identified intensely with the American civil rights campaign. When Martin Luther King Jr. railed against the denial of rights in the United States, he was seen as speaking for black South Africans and their inequalities, too. Though banned by the local censorship authorities, copies—in the form of a long-playing record—of Dr. King's 1963 "I Have a Dream" Washington Monument speech had been smuggled into South Africa and circulated like Soviet samizdat texts (individually produced and uncensored dissident texts distributed in the Soviet Bloc).

The 1966 NUSAS congress listened with great admiration to one of these smuggled recordings. King's assassination in April 1968 sparked a wave of deep sorrow and emotion in South Africa's black townships. Hundreds wept openly at memorial services. Few who heard it will ever forget how the state-controlled, South African Broadcasting Corporation announced his death in its 7:00 a.m. news bulletin. Without even a perfunctory gesture towards the message of King's lifework, but with menace, it proclaimed in a racist tone with barely concealed relish that "Widespread rioting has broken out in the United States following the assassination of the Negro civil rights agitator, Martin Luther King."

Sen. Robert F. Kennedy and his wife Ethel arrive at the Roman Catholic Cathedral of the Sacred Heart in Pretoria during their visit to South Africa, June 5, 1966.

Two months later, the murder of Robert Kennedy unleashed a second wave of sorrow among South African activists. Kennedy's whirlwind campaign-style visit to South Africa two years earlier had, in the words of a press commentator, Stanley Uys, "blown clean air into a dank and closed room." Wherever he went on that visit, he attracted huge and enthusiastic crowds, even in the government-supporting student heartland of Stellenbosch. His tour of Soweto sent out a clear message to black South Africans that in his eyes, they mattered, and that what they stood for was right. His helicopter visit to the then isolated Natal village of Groutville—to which ANC president and Nobel Peace Prize laureate Chief Albert Luthuli was restricted—was seen as an endorsement of all the ANC stood for. His description of the chief as "the most impressive man I have ever met" outraged the regime and thrilled those who had no voice in the government. Prime Minister Verwoerd's sulky refusal to meet with Kennedy diminished the premier and made him seem small-minded and petty.

For the National Party, Kennedy's visit in June 1966 was a propaganda disaster, but for the anti-apartheid opposition it was both a timely reminder that the world was on its side and a much-needed morale booster after the jail sentences that had recently been imposed on Nelson Mandela and other ANC leaders. While difficult to quantify, one should never underestimate the power of hope even in bleak times—Kennedy's visit was certainly one such pillar of hope.

Explosive events at the University of Cape Town

While these tragic killings in the United States had a significant impact on the political consciousness of some South Africans, it was developments at the University of Cape Town (UCT) in August 1968 that promised, albeit briefly, to bring home the explosive events in Europe. On August 14 approximately 1,000 overwhelmingly white students met and condemned the decision of the highest decision-making body, the University Council, to withdraw an offer of a senior lectureship in anthropology to a black South African, Archie Mafeje, then completing his doctorate at Cambridge University. After the meeting, more than 300 students marched on the administration building, but instead of the customary pause in the courtyard to petition the principal, they pushed through the front doors and took possession of the building. It was South Africa's first sit-in, which lasted ten days. Supportive UCT academics, as well as a recently-returned graduate from the Sorbonne and witness to the events of Paris in May, Richard ("Ric") Turner, conducted non-stop seminars introducing a whole new generation of student activists to the works of Marx and prominent leftist scholars of the time. Nine years later, in January 1977, Turner, then a lecturer in political science at the University of Natal in Durban, was gunned down by an apartheid assassin.

Led by student body leader Duncan Innes and Radical Society chair Rafi Kaplinsky (immediately dubbed "Red Rafi" in the media), the sit-in outraged the government but captured the media's interest more effectively than any previous student protest. It acutely embarrassed the university administration and exposed the cowardly political nature of the leadership of this self-proclaimed anti-apartheid institution. Having originally appointed the best applicant for the post, the university administration capitulated, in the face of a threat from the government, to legislate a prohibition on the employment of black lecturers in white universities. Instead of standing firm, the council did the government's dirty work for it and reneged on its original principled stance. The council's decision split the campus: the dean of the Humanities Faculty, Professor Maurice Pope, resigned from the university in protest. He, as well as a minority of demurring voices in the council like Leo Marquard, and the student occupiers of the administration facility, deserve to be remembered with credit for their actions.

But why were South Africa's universities so intimidated whereas universities in much of the rest of the world were the cauldrons of new ideas, if not battlefields? To reflect on this, we need to consider the prevailing culture of South Africa's universities of the time.

Challenging the university system from within

In South Africa's English-language universities, the hold of the "network of imperial knowledge," as the South African historian Saul Dubow has put it, was strong. Their cultural roots drew them towards the intellectual conservatism of Oxbridge. In the words of Laurence Wright, an English professor at Rhodes University in the Eastern Cape, they were instruments for "transmitting metropolitan knowledge and excitement in a colonial situation."

Arguably, this imperial mold was only broken in Britain by the intellectual ferment (and the progressive politics) that followed upon the establishment of the University of Sussex in 1961. Not coincidentally, a number of South Africans who were to make a deep impression on both South African scholarship and the anti-apartheid struggle in the 1970s and 1980s did postgraduate work at Sussex; it was from this institution that the country's president from 1999 to 2008, Thabo Mbeki, graduated with an MA in economics, as did two brothers who were to become his closest political confidants—Aziz and Essop Pahad—and the scholar/activist, Robert Davies, currently Minister of Trade and Industry in President Jacob Zuma's administration.

Some aspects of the role Mbeki played in the events of 1968 from his base in Sussex have recently come to light. His biographer Mark Gevisser claims that Mbeki used the mood of the times to insert the anti-apartheid message into other political developments. "It was classic entryism, and it worked: Mbeki would be meeting with the likes of Daniel Cohn-Bendit and Rudi Dutschke, the leaders of that year's student uprisings in Paris and Berlin, and the ANC would be represented on the steering committee of the coalition that organised that year's massive anti-Vietnam war marches in London."

In South Africa itself, inspiring teachers often challenged the status quo by instilling, in the words of the late American philosopher Richard Rorty, "doubts in the students ... about the society to which they belong." These departures were openly political, and, interestingly, they drew on European thinking. In 1968, a course called "Freedom and Authority," which was almost entirely devoted to the work of Hannah Arendt, was offered at the University of the Witwatersrand. But those in power did not appreciate such dissenting approaches. Academics and students who pursued them were often censured both within and without the university walls.

South Africa's black universities

What was the position with students at other South African universities? The oldest of South Africa's black universities, Fort Hare, was founded by Scottish missionaries in 1916; in 1946, it gained semi-autonomous status with its degrees issued under the supervision of Rhodes University. But the University of Fort Hare played a much larger part in ending apartheid than this mundane and linear narrative suggests. It was here that Nelson Mandela and numerous leaders studied: Mandela, who had organized a boycott, was expelled by the college's principal during his final year of study. The institution's social and political capital, however, was obliterated by the 1959 Universities Act that, despite according it full university status, effectively curtailed its academic and intellectual authority at the very moment that four other universities for "non-whites" (those of Zululand, the Western Cape, Durban-Westville, and the North) were established.

These "tribal colleges," as they were derisively dubbed, were staffed by Afrikaner academics deployed to them almost as a form of "national service." Administratively, these institutions were tightly controlled: leadership positions were primarily filled with ideologues, and budgets were drawn, not from the national education budget, but from that of the state department designated to deal with black affairs. For almost a decade and a half, these institutions operated outside the academic mainstream. As a result, they seemed to have no real stake in the national conversation that was at the very heart of the country's future until probably the most seminal event in South Africa in 1968 liberated them from this netherworld.

This was the action of a young medical student, Steve Biko, who led South Africa's black campuses out of the white-dominated student federation NUSAS to strike out on their own in the form of the South African Students Organisation (SASO). SASO reflected a new assertiveness on the part of young black South Africans. It reflected, too, the view held by postcolonial theorist and revolutionary Frantz Fanon that for a people to be free, they have to believe they deserve to be free. SASO challenged the mental self-enslavement of black South Africans. It called upon blacks to stand up to "whitey" and to reject internal oppression. It was an idea whose time had come as reflected in the youth rebellion that spread across the country in 1976, sparked by events in Soweto. Again with the benefit of hindsight, it is now possible to see the Soweto uprising as a watershed in the struggle to rid South Africa of colonial and minority domination.

Afrikaner perspectives

The position in Afrikaner circles was different. The project of uniting Afrikaners as a collective into a coherent white "nation"— "imagining a community," to twist Benedict Anderson's phrase— was strong. They were encouraged to follow the ideal of a *volksuniversiteit*, which Afrikaner intellectual Van der Merwe Scholtz defined as "a university which belongs to the *volk* and must therefore be of the *volk*, out of the *volk* and for the *volk*, anchored in its traditions and fired by the desire to serve the *volk* in accordance with its own view of life." In this intellectual project, scarcely a discipline failed to encourage the idea that a university education provided students with the anchor of, in Stellenbosch University Professor Johan Degenaar's words, "being bound to the people."

Breaking with this line of thought was difficult, if not impossible, as poet and literature professor N. P. van Wyk Louw described in a convoluted fashion: Effective criticism, he argued, "emerges when the critic places himself in the midst of the group he criticises, when he knows that he is bound unbreakably ... to the *volk* he dares rebuke." Although this *"loyale verset"*—or loyal dissent—was the early form of breakout, Afrikaner intellectuals eventually became more daring. In 1964, the farmer and novelist Etienne Leroux published a novel called *Sewe Dae by die Silbersteins*, which many came to regard as the founding of a new writing movement, *Die Sestigers* [The Sixties Generation]. Although many saw Leroux's book as a breakthrough for an Afrikaner New Left, revisionist interpretations now see it as "giving literary expression to the Afrikaner nightmare." Another poet, the intellectual and activist Breyten Breytenbach, who was jailed for high treason in the early 1970s and who lived in Paris in 1968, was the most famous example of a rebelling writer. Another Afrikaner writer, novelist André Brink, also lived in Paris at that time. The eventual revolt of Afrikaner youth, however, would come in the 1980s with a fusion of protest rock and political activism known now under the generic term *Voëlvry* [Free as a Bird].

Boycotting South African cricket

The other event that got caught in the political breeze in 1968 was Prime Minister Vorster's decision to veto the selection of black South African émigré Basil D'Oliviera as a member of the English cricket team, which was due to tour in the summer of 1968-69. A brilliant cricketer denied the opportunity to represent the country of his birth on account of race, D'Oliviera had moved to England and qualified for British citizenship. Vorster's veto outraged British public opinion and forced a reluctant and historically collaborationist English cricket administration, kicking and screaming all the while, to cancel the tour. It was a decisive moment in the campaign to isolate South African sports. More than twenty years were to pass before a legitimate national team would again play cricket against a South African national team. The international sports boycott of South Africa is acknowledged to have been a crucial pressure point in the increasingly effective campaign of comprehensive sanctions directed against the apartheid system.

Overall, however, 1968 was a low time in the struggle for democracy in South Africa. Many historians have referred to the period between the sabotage trials of the mid-1960s and the labor unrest of the early 1970s as one when nothing significant happened in opposition circles. For example, Julie Frederikse has described this period as "the lull." However, hindsight is a wonderful thing, and it is now possible to see how seemingly unrelated occurrences in South Africa in 1968—the student protest at UCT, the emergence of black consciousness under the leadership of Steve Biko, the D'Oliviera affair, the rise of cultural resistance inside South Africa, and the growing armed insurgencies in the region—set developments in motion that contributed significantly to ending the apartheid system. Not recognized as such at the time, each of these events or developments was a critical harbinger of change.

John Daniel is a retired Professor of Political Science who taught at the University of Durban-Westville. In the mid-1960s, he was the President of the National Union of South African Students, and in June 1966, he hosted the visit of Senator Robert F. Kennedy to South Africa.

Peter Vale is the Nelson Mandela Professor of Politics at Rhodes University in South Africa.

SYRIA: THE CHILDREN OF THE SIX-DAY WAR

Mouaffaq Nyrabia

With a population of about 18 million, and one of the highest growth rates worldwide (2.4 percent—with previous estimates of even 3.3 percent), 52.2 percent of Syrians are between 15 and 54 years of age, and 44.8 percent are under the age of 15. The unemployment rate of the youth between the ages of 20 and 24 is officially 34.4 percent, but unofficial sources claim that unreported cases, if added, would greatly increase this percentage. Teaching outside of the state curricula has become ever more unthinkable. The number of attractive learning opportunities is severely decreasing for an ever growing group of young people. Syrian's contemporary educational institutions are falling behind in respect to modern curricula and teaching methods around the world.

By contrast, the number of expensive, private universities is growing steadily, although there are no established standards for their curricula. Membership in the Revolutionary Youth Organization and in the National Union of Syrian Students is compulsory and monitored by officials. Students in schools and universities are rarely able to refuse to become members of the Baath Party. For university students, political activities beyond the Baath-organized National Front of Progress have been forbidden since 1972, even for the parties of the Baath-controlled Progressive National Front. One result of this situation is that Syrian youth overwhelmingly dream of emigrating.

June 5, 1967: It was the second day of my final examination in school. Suddenly, the teachers entered the classroom and told us to pack up our things and to leave school immediately. The Arab-Israeli War had broken out. We ran out to the streets, shouting and ready to take up arms.

We were totally convinced that winning the war would be easy for us, due to the propaganda our governments and political leaders had made. Our Palestinian brothers would be able to return to their homeland, from which they had been expelled in 1948. We Arabs constituted a large community, connected on the basis of a common history and culture, in sharp contrast to the people coming from all over the world to build a state only nineteen years old.

But what happened was something different—something terrible in its effect on the enthusiasm and conviction of the youth: we were beaten with incredible ease, and Israel was able to occupy new territories that enlarged its original area by a factor of five. The Arab armies retreated extremely quickly. Arab identity thus suffered its greatest shock in modernity. Being desperate, some of us sought sanctuary in religion, trying to find explanations and solutions. Others joined the leftists and focused on upbraiding those who led us to defeat. Still others fled into their own seemingly absurd worlds, completely rejecting everything around them.

The Palestinian Resistance

The Vietnam War began to cast ever longer shadows. A popular song from that era went: "In Vietnam, half America has vanished—we will take care of the rest!" That is, fighting was seen as the answer. At the end of 1964, the Palestinian Resistance entered the scene, calling for support and participation. Blaming the sovereign classes and the so-called Generation Nakba (*Al-Nakba* is the official name for the loss of Palestine and the founding of Israel in 1948), it united leftist ideology and the will to fight for the nation. The Popular Front for the Liberation of Palestine (PFLP) was founded, which aimed to participate in direct action in neighboring Arab states.

Then a splinter group called the Democratic Front for the Liberation of Palestine (DFLP) formed, which, ironically, was socially more radical and nationally more moderate. Syrians were also among its founders, including Sadiq Jalal al-Azm, a famous researcher and philosopher, as well as Saadallah Wannous, who later became the most important dramatist in the Arab world.

Armed resistance and students

Even more important, however, is the fact that young people quit their education to join the armed resistance. They, like others, drifted more and more towards the Left, fascinated by concepts like "alienation," "privation," "loss," "refusal," and "generation conflict"—hot topics that were often discussed at universities. So, the preconditions for "1968" here were different from those in Europe, partly contradicting the course and message of the European revolts. For example, the question of nation was very urgent for us, as was the issue of the armed resistance, but we also perceived Zionism as the cause of all our problems and defined the Soviet Union as our most vital support in the world.

Although the ideas and demands of the European students often ran counter to ideas that were important to us—for example, the role of Israel or the criticism of sticking together with the forceful "socialist brother" and his satellites—these students, especially in their tremendous enthusiasm and expressiveness, were crucial points of reference for many of us. Others had scarcely any reservations, identifying strongly with European students in their attitude of rejection, as well as their leftist tendencies, and fully embraced these new characteristics from Europe, though adapting them to their own purposes.

Transitions in cultural life

Influenced by the defeat in the Six-Day War and the student revolutions of 1968, an essential shift in cultural, intellectual, and political values occurred in Syria. People suddenly claimed that the songs of Um Kalthoum, who had been the queen of Arab singers of the twentieth century, had been responsible not only for our defeat but also for our backwardness. Political songs, which had been marginal up to then, suddenly gained great popularity, especially among the youth. These songs heaped scorn on the governments and expressed the unrest of the Arab nation. The images of Che Guevara or other symbolic figures hung nearly everywhere.

After taking the Syrian city Quneitra on June 11, 1967, Israeli soldiers round up and search the local Arab population.

This time also revitalized poems of resistance and politics and led to the further development of their form. Many young poets became well known, and some of them are still counted among Syria's leading poets today. Many were motivated by the feverish excitement nearly everyone felt, among them Mamduh Adwan, Ali Kanaan, and Nazih Abu Afash. New trends toward nihilistic and stingingly sarcastic plays arose in theater. After returning from France, Saadallah Wannous published his *Declarations of a New*

Theater and performed his play *Evening Entertainment for the Fifth of July* in a new form. It was the advent of modernized theater, presenting itself in a new, revolutionary light to its audience.

The committed art

Syrian cinema also sparked new art forms. The Public Establishment for Cinema was founded to bolster new film trends. Young students went to Europe to study the art of film-making, and, upon their return, formed a group including the now most widely known Syrian directors, such as Omar Amiralay, Samir Zikra, Haitham Haqqi, Muhammad Mallass, and Osama Muhammad. The wave of new art forms was also manifested in the visual arts. Old forms were vehemently called into question, and innovative styles were introduced that gave free reign to experimentation. The number of exhibitions increased and new art societies were launched, which also had influence on a political level.

In general, one can say that Syrian young people experienced the social and political events of the European revolts from another point of view. Those who studied in Europe experienced them first hand. Abu Ali Yassin, for example, was a member of a commune in Frankfurt, Germany. After coming back to Syria, he published his work, *The Taboo Triad: Religion, Sexuality and Class Struggle*, in which he raised exceedingly bold questions. He also came out with the study *Democracy in Education*, establishing his reputation as one of the most important representatives of the new Syrian generation of researchers.

The film director Omar Amiralay and theater director Saadallah Wannous, at that time both living in France, mutually planned the production of several crucial films, including the film *Daily Life in a Syrian Village* (1976), which is still banned in Syria today. At the same time, Saadallah Wannous, as mentioned above, began to work on his innovative theater pieces and took an active part in the Palestinian Resistance. In those days, many Europeans, like the French dramatist Jean Genet, came to participate in the Palestinian cause or, at least, to experience the resistance movement first hand.

Between the poles

All these developments occurred in conflicting political circumstances. On the one hand, there was a leftist, separatist, and authoritative system that observed the aftermath of the 1968 upheavals with cautious optimism. On the other hand, there was a powerful pan-Arabic faction that called for people to take up arms and fight. This tempted many youth, especially, to express their anger using weapons. Moreover, leftist Arab intellectuals were struggling to find their own modernity but were unable, without uprooting themselves, to produce powerful revolutionaries in leftist groups and Trotskyist, Maoist, and Marxist circles.

There were also many activists in the Palestinian Resistance who were enthusiastic about helping to shape the forms of public life, arts, and culture. Political organizations were established, among them the Arab Communist Organization (ACO), which was responsible for bomb attacks in Damascus where its members took people hostages in a hotel located in the city center. Some members of the ACO were executed while others were kept in prison for twenty-nine years.

Students go on strike

Even in the ruling Baath Party, there were young people who were averse to any right-wing authoritative tendencies. Some of them left the party in 1968; others defended the party leadership, and in 1969, a coup was within reach under the leadership of Hafez al-Assad. In 1970, this was completed with the "Correctionist Movement." The leftist and Baathist students subsequently went on strike and organized demonstrations in a central place in Damascus but were brutally suppressed by the security forces.

Only isolated demonstrations followed these incidents. The engineering students went on strike for a week, insisting that their demands be met. Likewise, art students provoked the authorities with critical posters and caricature drawings circulated under anonymous names. Some of these artists are now considered great representatives of the Syrian art scene.

Turning point in political thinking

The events of the years 1967 and 1968 marked a turning point in the political thinking of Syrian intellectuals. A comprehensive revision in political thinking in the form of modernization started, spurred by intellectuals such as Yassin al-Hafes, Elias Mirqos, and pragmatic politicians like Odei and Jamal al-Atassi and Riad al-Turk. This development transformed into a deep and reality-oriented process of modernization. By the mid-1970s, this process manifested itself in the demand for democracy. Up to today, this remains one of the core demands of different oppositional groups.

The events also released a tremendous energy within the young generation. The system clearly recognized the message of this, as shown by its legal prohibition of any political activities by students, even those who were members of the coalition parties. In reaction, it established its own student and youth organizations, more or less forcing children and young people to join. This gave it a monopoly in youth organization activities, which helped generate a climate of suppression and manipulation that, at the same time, offered preformed political solutions and the illusion of stability.

In the present, the ban on political action by young people makes it very difficult to integrate the younger generation into the activities of the democratic opposition. Considering the educational system devoid of meaning, the high rate of unemployment, everyday worries, and the constant search for a change in the situation, the youth today seem like an explosive gas tank—ready to disperse their energy at the slightest provocation.

The opposition today

On December 1, 2007, 167 members of the democratic opposition assembled for the first time in recent Syrian history. They formed the National Council of the Damascus Declaration, calling for the state to change into a constitutional democracy according to the political standards of modern times and to leave the totalitarian one-party system behind. The meeting was held under exceptional circumstances involving tight control on the part of the security forces, which created an atmosphere of intimidation and oppression. The signatories averaged 54 years of age, which indicates that, in 1968, they were 15, an age when people in our country begin to get interested in politics. In a way, then, one can say that the children of the Six-Day War and the youth revolts of 1968 comprise the opposition in Syria today.

Mouaffaq Nyrabia is a Syrian political analyst and civil rights activist.

EASTERN EUROPE

CZECHOSLOVAKIA: LINES OF TANKS IN PRAGUE*

Petruška Šustrová

On many occasions, I have been told by people from other post-communist countries how much the events that unfolded in Czechoslovakia in 1968—the Prague Spring and the ensuing Soviet occupation—meant to them.

The first couple of times it happened, I was astonished. Surely, all countries in the former communist bloc had their own landmark years and dates that Czechs were often not even aware of. Why did people relate so much to Czechoslovakia and to the year 1968? Having heard several times from various former opponents of communist regimes in Romania, Poland, Georgia, and Ukraine, and even from those in faraway Soviet republics in Central Asia, that the Soviet tanks in Prague had crushed their last hope for a humane Soviet-type socialism, I began to understand. Czechs, however, have traveled down some strange and winding roads when reflecting on 1968 in the years of freedom after 1989.

Relaxation within the system

The grip on political and social life in Czechoslovakia started gradually loosening in the mid-1960s, which culminated in a "reform process" in the spring and summer of 1968. It happened for various reasons: subsiding international tension, significant changes in the membership of the Czechoslovak Communist Party, and appointments of pro-change people into positions of power and influence. Of course, most of these people wanted to keep the Communist Party in power and operated within the system. Still, the society at large responded enthusiastically to the relaxation of control.

Censorship was abolished, and a powerful torrent of hitherto suppressed information, criticism, and points of view gushed out through the media, even though the same people were in control of them. The Kremlin and its allies in other communist bloc countries first responded with warnings, then with threats, and ultimately with a large-scale, armed invasion.

Hopes crushed by tanks

It is now difficult to judge whether Czechoslovak communists would have eventually curbed the shifting popular mindset and calls for more changes, adapted to it, or ended up using violence themselves to crush the desire of Czechs and Slovaks for freedom. But this is not relevant in this context. The important thing is that the atmosphere of freedom—or at least much greater freedom—raised great hopes that were then crushed by the invading tanks.

Protesters surround a Soviet tank in front of the construction site for the parliament building in Prague on Aug. 22, 1968.

Czech society at large was powerfully galvanized in August 1968 and immediately thereafter. People felt the importance of being a community. Instead of viewing themselves as mere objects of history, they suddenly felt that they could make decisions and act freely, even if the impact of their actions was limited and the future held no promises that the situation would change.

Caricatured memories of 1968

We often hear that the Prague Spring was simply a battle of two communist cliques—the conservatives and those who called themselves progressives—and that it can be dismissed as an effort to make changes within the system. Many others, myself included, disagree, arguing that the opportunity to take a deep breath and experience a whiff of freedom, as well as the newspapers, magazines and books that were allowed to be published in 1968 and for a while thereafter, gave people back the self-confidence they had lost in the tough and cruel 1950s. It reminded them that all was not lost.

There is no denying that the two decades of "normalization" that followed the invasion ate away at and stifled that self-confidence, having suppressed pro-change elements and brought to power, for the most part, people of inferior intellect and integrity. Still, memories of 1968 persisted, though often merely as caricatures; people remembered Alexander Dubček and other Prague Spring figures as their heroes. In the late 1980s—in fact, even in November 1989—you could still hear crowds cheer "Dubček!" at demonstrations, although Dubček had personally signed legislation in August 1969 authorizing the use of police, militias, and weapons to crack down on public resistance.

Documents from 1968 guarded like a treasure

We tend to judge the situation at that time by what we know today. It is difficult enough for those who lived through it to empathize with this history, let alone for the younger generation that cannot remember it. This kind of historical anachronism is very common. This said, we must not ignore that the fact that 1968 has boosted our social memory and given us new sources—old copies of newspapers and magazines that people guarded like treasure, books discarded from public and private libraries that passed from hand to hand, as well as samizdat literature and exile magazines; publishing companies, too, have worked tirelessly to fill in the gaps. Nor must we overlook the fact that the atmosphere of the Prague Spring made it possible to establish numerous contacts among like-minded people. Although the ensuing normalization broke off some of those contacts, it could not dissolve all of them.

In the intentionally atomized and corrupt society, however, there were groups that did not seek to make communism more human but to move beyond it toward democracy. The assumption that memories of 1968 must be linked to those who wanted to reform but not overthrow communism is false. In the week after the occupation of August 1968, people's actions were conscious, organized, and courageous. The community showed itself at its best. Memories of that did not disappear either; they gave many people hope and energy when the next opportunity to resist presented itself at the end of the 1980s.

Climate of free exchange of opinions

Of course, twenty years later, it was politically and economically impossible to continue where we had left off in 1968; the times had changed, and so had the people. Surely you could find among those communists who lost power and influence after 1969 some that still dreamed of going back to building a socialism with a human face, but the fall of 1989 was not the spring of 1968. However, life is made up not only of economic, political and power arrangements, but also of the atmosphere in which people live and meet.

It is the atmosphere of freedom, trust, and exchange of views that defines the Prague Spring, despite its limitations, even decades later. After all, in the fall of 1989, you could literally feel the touch of historical memory and reminiscences of the months lived in greater freedom in 1968. Surely those who recall the warm welcome lavished on the iconic figures of 1968 in 1989, such as Karel Kryl or Marta Kubišová, even though they had been absent from the public eye for twenty years, will agree.

* The author writes from the present Czech Republic. The title of the contribution, however, reflects the political alignment of the country in 1968.

Petruška Šustrová is a publicist, signatory, and spokeswoman of Charter 77. After 1990, she briefly served as the vice minister of the Ministry of the Interior of the Czech Republic.

EAST GERMANY: "SOLIDARITY WITH RED PRAGUE"

Philipp Gassert and Elisabeth Piller

In the German Democratic Republic, 1968 seemed like a non-event. In his book about 1968 in East Germany, *Der Traum von der Revolte* [The Dream of Rebellion], Stefan Wolle, then an 18-year-old student, remembers the eerie quietness of East Berlin's streets during that summer. As Soviet tanks were rolling into Prague, nothing seemed to be happening in the realm of East German state leader Walter Ulbricht. Yet it was precisely this stark and depressing contrast between the calm surface and inner revulsion that would linger in people's memories for years.

1968 in East Germany does not evoke dramatic images of protesting students, angry crowds, and countercultural discourses about Vietnam or sexual revolution. Still, 1968 was a significant turning point in East Germany's history. While the small-scale protests against the Warsaw Pact invasion of Czechoslovakia never reached the larger public, the Prague crackdown destroyed whatever illusions people still harbored about "real existing" socialism. Furthermore, in 1969 the cautious reform politics of the 1960s effectively came to an end. In retrospect, communism's inability to accommodate dissent became unmistakable in the events of 1968.

The East German 1960s: Reforms and the youth

The East German 1960s were an era of concerted reform efforts: Life was supposed to become more attractive, socialism more efficient. Greater freedom in the work place was meant to spur productivity. These economic reform efforts were flanked by a new approach to youth. More liberal policies were intended to direct the aspirations of young East Germans toward the socialist state.

Beginning in 1963, Western-style music, clothes, and leisure activities became more acceptable. In 1964, a three-day festival in East Berlin attracted 560,000 young East Germans and 25,000 West German visitors. The West German weekly *Der Spiegel* described the event's atmosphere as one of "sun, sex, and socialism." In early 1965, the East German label "Amiga" published a Beatles record. Under the slogan "real love belongs to the youth" [*Echte Liebe gehört zur Jugend*], sexual norms were liberalized.

These new freedoms raised hopes for a more democratic future. Yet, the ruling Socialist Unity Party soon became nervous about the more independent styles. At the Eleventh Party Congress in 1965, writers and intellectuals were accused of corrupting the youth. Books, records, bands, and films were banned. The party unleashed a campaign against Westernization. As the East German writer Brigitte Reimann remembers, "There were demonstrations; the police used water cannon, arrested people; there were prison and work camps. The laughter in us disappeared."

1968: "Russians out of the ČSSR"

This aborted liberalization prepared the ground for the East German 1968. Events in Prague extended their influence into the GDR. Czech writer Ludvik Vaculik's manifesto "2000 Words," which famously advocated stepping up reform efforts in the ČSSR, sparked discussions about the democratic socialism in the GDR. Dissidents like Robert Havemann seemed to give credibility to the SED's worst fears when he stated: "Socialism is Democracy—the great word has to be realized. This is, given the exciting development in the ČSSR, our ardent hope." Graffiti that read "Russians out," "Hands off," and "Solidarity with Red Prague" appeared on the walls. A whiff of Central European independence vis-à-vis the Soviet occupier was in the air.

East German demonstrators express their solidarity with the Prague Spring on May Day 1968 in East Berlin.

Opposition to the suppression of the Prague Spring came from all strata of East German society. It was the protests of the children of high functionaries that received most of the attention. Yet the backbone of the rebellion consisted of young workers, who made up more than 70 percent of those persecuted after the crackdown. Often, they had refused to sign official declaratory acts [*Willenserklärungen*] designed to force them to state their agreement with the invasion of Czechoslovakia.

The impact of 1968: Silence and the end of reform

Even though the GDR seemed to be on the way to its own short spring, dissent never got beyond the safeguards that the East German security services had put in place. Different from its response in 1989, the regime in 1968 was willing to suppress dissent before it gained momentum. Suspicious persons were jailed, and the security apparatus was further expanded. Young protesters were barred from universities. The protesters also lacked effective lines of communication. With no space for dissent, East German youth lacked public access and the media, which could have given resonance to their demands.

While the East German security apparatus succeeded in quelling dissent, disenchantment with socialism grew to an all-time high. The ambitious reform projects of the 1960s were aborted. Erich Honecker soon replaced Walter Ulbricht as head of state and party chief. Honecker's long reign became one of continuous economic decline. For many East Germans, the gulf between the country's ideological claims and the lived reality had become painfully clear. East Germany's participation in the Prague crackdown was thus tantamount to a declaration of bankruptcy. As the East German historian Hartmut Zwahr put it, in 1968, the dream of a socialist society "shattered in the heads of the people."

The legacy of 1968, therefore, was one of heightened repression and a growing petrifaction in the East German system. While it did not directly lead to the events that ended socialism in 1989, it became a catalyst for growing disenchantment. In addition, it forced the East German regime to give up any hopes of reform from within. The frustrations of 1968 lay dormant for 20 years. They finally found an outlet in 1989, when East Germans would take to the streets once again. And this time, their revolution would succeed.

Philipp Gassert, a former Deputy Director of the GHI, is currently a Professor of Transatlantic History at the University of Augsburg.

Elisabeth Piller is a graduate student in modern German and American history at the University of Heidelberg.

HUNGARY: THE YEAR OF DISILLUSIONMENT

László Márton

From the People's Revolution to the "Happiest Barracks"

On October 23, 1956, in Budapest, a demonstration by students demanding free elections and protesting against the regime developed into an armed revolution, with broad swathes of the population joining in. That same night, the Politbüro appointed Communist reformist Imre Nagy prime minister, but at the same time called for assistance from Soviet troops. In the short term, Nagy got the situation under control; the Soviets withdrew. However, on November 4, the Soviets invaded Hungary again, this time to overthrow the Nagy government.

Afterward, Moscow installed a regime of collaborators led by Nagy's comrade-in-arms Janos Kádár. The uprising was quashed; Kádár's justice system had hundreds of revolutionaries executed, among them Imre Nagy. Around 200,000 Hungarians left their homeland. Nonetheless, after years of such retribution for the uprising, Kádár started to allow reforms and relaxations within the system. Hungary became the "most liberal" country in Moscow's sphere of influence—it was known as "Goulash Communism," or wryly as the "happiest barracks in the camp." On January 1, 1968, the "New Economic Mechanism" was introduced in Hungary, but, after the suppression of the Prague Spring in August of that year, in which Hungarian troops were also involved, it could hardly be implemented as planned.

In Hungary, where I live, the most significant event of 1968 was the invasion of Prague, which units of the Hungarian People's Army were involved in. I was nine years old at the time. My own personal memories are clearly distinct from what I would later learn about these sociopolitical events.

From mid-August of that year, I was at a Pioneer camp—a camp of the party-based youth organization—in northern Hungary near the border. On the last Sunday before returning home, my school's soccer team played against the local technical training school, suffering a defeat. During this (for us) shameful game, we watched military convoys moving along the highway. They resembled the military parades that streamed by Budapest's City Park, but this was no parade. In a quickly arranged political lesson, we were informed that it was friendly international assistance.

Silence about the invasion

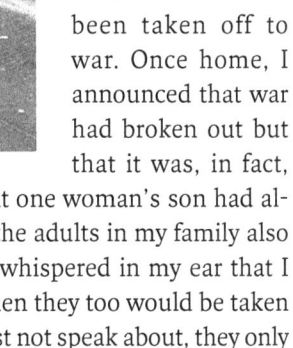

A Soviet tank moves through Budapest quelling the demonstration that began on Oct. 23, 1956. The torso of a vandalized statue of Stalin lies in the background.

As we made our way home, I saw women of the village standing along its main street with alarm on their faces. One was even crying; she said her son had been taken off to war. Once home, I announced that war had broken out but that it was, in fact, friendly international assistance, and that one woman's son had already been pressed into service. At this, the adults in my family also seemed alarmed, or rather, afraid. They whispered in my ear that I dare not speak of such things, because then they too would be taken away. When I asked what it was that I must not speak about, they only replied that merely discussing what one should or should not discuss could get one taken away.

For me, 1968 was, independent of the friendly international assistance and this brief interlude, the year the world turned dark and serious, the year things took a quick and powerful turn for the worse. An incident in my family at that time brought home to me that the protection and emotional security a family offers could vanish in a single moment. I got a taste of being at the mercy of my surroundings; I now had to understand that good was bad, bad was good, and that both were strictly forbidden: in a word, I came face to face with obligation and compulsion. What began for me in 1968 was what bad lawyers use to exonerate criminals in court: a "difficult childhood." Or perhaps it would be better to put it this way: my childhood ended in that year, a little earlier than it should have. All of this remains clearly distinct from what I perceive today, as a writer, citizen, and thinking person, about the aftermath of 1968.

After 1968, years of stagnation and isolation followed in Hungary. The economic reforms initiated shortly before that year were now suspended. Advocates of these reforms were ousted from their posts, overthrown, or intimidated. In the arts, particularly in literature and music, censorship, which had been relatively mild in the preceding years, now became oppressive. The press, on a short leash, now occupied itself with the typical pseudo-debates, at the same time revealing symptoms of deceitfulness and collective intellectual decline. Official control of scholarship, particularly in the social sciences, became extremely strict. Centers of sociological study that had become more active in the 1960s were shut down; scholars in philosophy, psychology, history, and literary studies found themselves under direct state control.

Although there was no wholesale liquidation of the cultural elite as in Czechoslovakia, the apparatus of the Ministry of the Interior and the party managed to expel a great many outstanding scientists and artists from the country in the decade that followed 1968. At least as many more committed suicide under the burden of their maladjustment or hopeless prospects. Many would become alcoholics, and many became marginalized. The greatest number, though, were those who abandoned their moral compass, or simply adapted to the narrow-mindedness and drab mediocrity of the regime.

Society under the guardianship of the state

I reflect on all of this, simultaneously aware of the undeniable fact that after 1968, in the mature years of the Kádár regime, order, tranquility, and even moderate prosperity prevailed. Yet all of these things, which cause many to think back with nostalgia on this period, went hand in hand with a paralysis of society, with its citizens subjected to the guardianship of the state. The decade in the wake of 1968 was not malicious, bloody, and brutal like Stalin's terror, but merely malicious, mendacious, and moronic. This was only heightened by the ingratiating ideology of the "happiest barracks." On the one hand, this ideology conveyed a cynical scorn for the Soviet occupiers and their other colonies in the region (because our misery was made to seem like prosperity and freedom in comparison to their greater misery); on the other hand, it contained an unspoken threat: this could all get worse—much worse, in fact, if the party leadership should so decide.

At the same time, 1968 was the year of disillusionment. Young intellectuals who, in the ferment of the 1960s, had thought that the communist dictatorship could be reformed, could be gradually improved, were now forced to cast off their illusions. Those of sound mind and moral sensibility could no longer believe that what we had was anything but "true socialism," or that what "existed in reality" could be improved and given a "human face." Such delusions lost all credibility at one stroke. The devastating realization dawned on these intellectuals that this was indeed true socialism, and that it was rotten from the core.

Wary of ideologies

Whoever joined "the party" before 1968 ("the party" as it was the only one: the Hungarian Socialist Workers' Party) might even have been an honorable person though perhaps a bit too naïve or optimistic. After 1968, however, such a person was either blind or a devoted careerist. Then the next great cathartic realization came: that scholarly thought, and indeed philosophy itself, could be conceived of without Marxism. Just as the cultural elite of the time dropped Marxism in an instant, the Marxist utopia was flushed from Bolshevik ideology, too. All that remained was the raw exercise of power. Next, a few important questions gradually began to be raised. Like this one: in the absence of freedom in the political and public spheres, could one eke out a small corner of intellectual freedom?

I feel this to be the most significant positive legacy of 1968, one that still survives today: the freedom from illusion, the wariness of ideologies, and the striving for intellectual freedom. Whether the reflexes of solidarity that have imbued this positive legacy of 1968 will survive in some form, or merely become objects for the archeological study of intellectual history in a few decades' time, I am, unfortunately, unable to predict.

László Márton is a Hungarian author.

POLAND: THE MARCH EVENTS OF 1968

Jerzy Eisler

The fortieth anniversary of the so-called March Events that occurred in Poland in 1968 provides an opportune moment for reflecting on their meaning. At the same time, it must be remembered that the "March Events" sum up many different, not necessarily connected, and sometimes contradictory tendencies. In practice, all they had in common were the time (Spring 1968) and place (Poland).

Observers looking back on the March Events concentrate on whatever aspects personally impacted them the most, or on the crowd they kept company with. Thus, it is not surprising that the youth uprisings are the most salient memories for the students of 1968. Protests in one form or another were held in nearly all institutions of higher learning in Poland, with street demonstrations and violent clashes with the state police occurring in several cities.

The student component of the March 1968 events is often compared to the wave of student protest in the West. However, despite a range of apparent similarities (university strikes, vigils, clashes with the law), the Polish events can only be accurately compared to the reform movement that was taking place in Czechoslovakia. Under the banner of freedom, the Polish students struggled for the same values and goals as their Czech and Slovak brethren.

The students in the West, on the other hand, were battling a different state system. They did not first need to fight for the freedoms of speech and assembly as these were fundamental principles of a democratic state. Still, it is worth noting that, despite these differences, French students in May 1968 made a point of emphasizing their solidarity with their Polish counterparts by chanting "Rome, Berlin, Warsaw, Paris!" Moreover, the French translation of the "Open Letter to the Party" by the intellectual leaders of the movement, Jacek Kuroń and Karol Modzelewski, was then one of the most popular readings at the Sorbonne.

Nonetheless, it must be borne in mind that the students in the West could be sure that their protests would be widely covered in the national press—and with a modicum of goodwill—whereas Polish students, who lived in a country where the state had nearly monopolistic control over the mass media, could not count on such coverage. Instead, they were forced to challenge an onslaught of misinformation, lies, and slander in the press, on the radio, and on television.

Whereas student leaders in the West immediately became heroes of the crowds, often becoming even more popular than rock stars or athletes, their Polish counterparts, subject to political baiting and persecution, were thrown in prison. Utilizing leftist rhetoric, the Polish students struggled to democratize and liberalize the communist system, as well as for the right to acknowledge the true nature of their circumstances.

Student demonstrators run towards the Communist Party Building in Warsaw, March 8, 1968.

Their efforts contributed to the development of the concept of the "'68 Generation." Many people from this generation went on to become anti-communist activists in the 1970s and later activists and advisors in the Solidarność trade union movement.

Attack on artists, scientists, and Jews

Many people in the Polish worlds of culture, science, and arts perceive March 1968 and the years following from a different angle, namely, as a pogrom against the intelligentsia. Authors and scientists—often extremely well-respected and highly esteemed individuals—were brutally attacked in the media. Such open attacks, like party functionaries, not only denied the ideological and moral integrity of those they maligned but also called their professional qualifications into question.

Finally, those who left Poland after March 1968 often associate the era with the disgraceful anti-Semitic campaign, which officials ineffectively disguised as a form of "anti-Zionism." Anti-Semitism has long roots in European history and will most likely continue to exist, but it was difficult to openly espouse such beliefs in post-Shoah

Europe. In democratic countries, these elements have often been pushed to the margins of society where they can only anonymously voice their opinions in small niche publications. In communist Poland, with preventive censorship and a police force that guarded the interests of the state, the publication of anti-Semitic materials was officially banned but, as it turned out, not impossible.

In the context of Polish communism, anti-Semitism was able to find its way onto the front pages of the newspapers as well as onto prime-time radio and television in 1968. As a matter of fact, from as early as the beginning of the 1960s, the Ministry of the Interior had begun to exhibit a growing interest in the Jewish community, even though no more than 30,000 Jews or people of Jewish heritage lived in Poland by the middle of the decade. In the spring of 1968, Jews were "cleansed" from practically all areas of public life: the party apparatus, national and regional governmental offices, state administrative bodies, the armed forces, mass media outlets, the educational system, as well as cultural and academic communities. This wide-scale "aryanization" of the security apparatus (as the operation was called internally) had already begun a few years before but now grew more intense. In Warsaw alone, between March and September of 1968, close to 800 people were dismissed from leading posts, whereas between 1965 and 1967, about 600 people had been.

Emigration of intellectuals from Poland

In this political climate, 15,000 people emigrated from Poland between 1968 and 1972. This emigration is significant not so much in terms of the number of people as in their intellectual caliber: of the 9,570 adults who applied for emigration, 1,832 of them had university degrees and another 944 were students. Of those who wished to emigrate to Israel (at the time, it was the only emigration destination one could indicate, even if one did not truly intend to go there at all) 217 were former university employees and 275 had worked at various academic institutions. This wave of emigration was therefore very much an emigration of the intelligentsia.

Those who initiated the anti-Semitic campaign surely failed to consider, 25 years after German Nazis had carried out the Holocaust on Polish ground, how the international public would regard their actions. The West judged the campaign uniformly negatively, and a wave of protests broke out. For this reason, Poland at that time had an undeniably bad reputation in many countries.

March 1968 witnessed one of the deepest political and social shocks in Poland since the end of World War II, and the many aftershocks have affected events up to the present day. The year 1968 ushered in a decline of communist ideology in Poland, and thereafter, ideological zeal lost ground to cynicism, opportunism, and impassive pragmatism. At the same time, Poland evolved into a nationally homogeneous state to the greatest extent ever. Over those years, a new political elite sprouted up and began to challenge the communist regime. As indicated already, many representatives of this new elite played an active role in the system transition toward the end of the 1980s and continue to be major players in the Polish public scene even today. Assessing the balance of events from the present perspective, we can now plainly see the overarching outcome of Poland's 1968.

Jerzy Eisler is a historian and Director of the Institute of National Remembrance [Instytut Pamieci Narodowej, IPN] in Warsaw.

RUSSIA: THE PHILOSOPHY OF THE LONG-HAIRED REBELLION

Victor Yerofeyev

In 1968, I was not in Paris or in Prague, but Paris and Prague were inside of me. Both revolutions were my revolutions, the revolutions in my life. Living in the Soviet Union in the center of Brezhnev's Moscow on the main avenue then known as Gorky Street, I somehow seemed out of place and was alone: no one around shared my ideas.

The students of Moscow State University, where I studied philology at the time, were mostly indifferent to the revolutionary events in Europe. They were not rebels by nature. They were not even Soviet conformists: they merely wanted to be left alone; politics frightened them with its unpredictable consequences. Where did my rebellious passions come from?

No relationship to freedom

I grew up in a family of diplomats. My parents were Soviets but decent people, and my father was connected with France through work. We lived in Paris for a few years before the 1960s, and the whole family fell in love with France. My father was a liberal in family life, and my mother was no stranger to cultural liberalism. These facts might seem insignificant to the development of my future worldview, but it was my parents' decency and their taste for liberal decisions that set the stage for my inclination toward freedom.

My love of literature and my wish to be a writer were no less important. But how many bibliophiles and writers have nothing to do with freedom? Every individual has a rebellious strain. There are limits to everyone's patience and obedience. But a rebellion only makes sense when it is based on a clear understanding of what freedom and justice are.

"The whole system had to be broken up"

Perhaps I was the only person in the Soviet Union to combine the principles of both revolutions within myself. In 1968, I had already met a few writers and philosophers with a capacity for independent judgment who were prone to intellectual dissent. Obviously or latently anti-Soviet, they reacted negatively to the May movement in Paris, thinking that the students were far too well off, that their Maoist slogans were deeply amoral in a political sense. On the other hand, naturally enough, they supported the Prague Spring. Even my mother secretly supported "socialism with a human face" and was privately outraged when Soviet tanks entered Prague. By the way, the famous drawing of Lenin shedding a tear because of the Soviet invasion was as politically naïve as my mother's liberalism. Making cosmetic changes to the Soviet system was not possible. It had to be totally destroyed, not in cooperation with Lenin but against him.

Drawing upon the principles of freedom and justice

Military and political leaders take part in the 54th anniversary celebration of the October Revolution on Nov. 7, 1970, at the Lenin Mausoleum. Brezhnev stands 7th from the left.

Soviet propaganda always thrived on anything that destabilized the West, and so it was naturally interested in the Parisian barricades of 1968. This also explains the Soviet intelligentsia's negative reaction to the barricades. The Prague Spring, on the other hand, was a direct threat to the political system of the Soviet Union, and Brezhnev did everything he could to make it appear vile and grotesque. I was equally passionate about both revolutions, though it seemed impossible to reconcile them inside of me. Their aims were too different, not to mention opposite, but they both drew upon the principles of freedom and justice.

The Parisian barricades were dear to me first and foremost because they constituted a joyful protest. It was not a somber, unenlightened protest, like the one that led Russia to the Bolshevik Revolution, but a happy, mischievous affair. In France, I had become familiar not only with the beauty of Paris and the Côte-d'Azur but also with the pettiness of the petty bourgeoisie, the suspiciousness and the stinginess of small merchants, the arrogance and prudery of the elite. Already in my student years in Russia, all of this seemed ossified and off-putting. There was not enough fresh air. Long-haired students created a new culture of humor and sex, which appealed to me. Now that it has become fashionable in France to condemn 1968, to complain that it destroyed the foundations of family and education, I still think that the Parisian barricades were an indispensable part of the cultural and political development of Europe.

Against dry teaching and stagnation

Instead of machine guns, students used Maoist slogans as weapons of provocation. Looking from the Soviet Union then at the Maoist badges on the chests of long-haired students, I realized how explosive they were, yet I did not take them seriously but more as a joke. Even now, I prefer the young students in this story to their masters, like Sartre, who were looking for the philosophical roots of rebellion. The philosophy of the Paris rebellion could not be reduced to the anarchist ideas of Mikhail Bakunin or the existentialism of Jean-Paul Sartre. Rather, it was the demand of human nature in its adolescence, not always logical, but intolerant of dry teaching and stagnation. The protest on the barricades was not just against old morals but also against nationalism. Without 1968, the united Europe of today would not be possible.

The idea of stagnation was also important for the Prague Spring. Whereas Parisian students were fighting against their own bourgeois imbecility, the stagnation in Prague resulted from the continued export of a false revolution that was only disguised as a revolution, being in fact an instrument of Soviet imperialism. Every day in my university library in Moscow, although I did not speak Czech, I read the chief communist newspaper of Czechoslovakia, *Rudé Právo*, in order to understand what was going on there.

Divested of the last Soviet illusions

For me, Alexander Dubček, the Czechoslovakian reformist politician who presided over the country during the Prague Spring, has always been the polar opposite of Che Guevara, a legendary figure similar to the martyrs of early Christianity. In Prague, the young rebels were long-haired, just as in Paris. I, too, had let my hair grow by then, which I was harassed for at university; sometimes outward marks of distinction become symbols of rebellion. Since then, everyone has short hair and has become terribly reasonable, but at that time only Soviet soldiers had shaved heads—the targets of tomatoes and cries of indignation when Soviet troops invaded the capital in August.

The invasion of Prague started the true dissident movement in Russia. The delusive hope of liberal changes showed itself to be downright nonsense. A few people went into the Red Square to protest the invasion, but this was just the tip of the iceberg. My mother did not cry over the death of "socialism with a human face" in vain. Deprived of the last Soviet illusions, shocked by the cruelty and the madness of the system, the intelligentsia, to which my mother belonged, refused to cooperate with the authorities. An abyss opened up between them and the system, which was a catastrophic harbinger of change. Without Prague, there would have been no perestroika.

Victor Yerofeyev is an author and literary scholar from Russia.

TURKEY: THE LOST GENERATION*

Zafer Şenocak

He was referred to simply as "Hodscha." I saw him for the first time at the Turkish table in the cafeteria at the University of Munich. He was a haggard man, with dark eyes and a three-day beard, surrounded by attentive, patient listeners. He was too old to be a "professional student." He spoke slowly and so quietly that one had to concentrate to hear him in the loud cafeteria. As far as I could follow, he was speaking about the emergence of socialism in Afghanistan. My communist phase was behind me, and I could no longer get excited about that sort of thing, even if it was presented with the fervor of a whirling dervish. It was the first time I saw some of the people in his circle. Had he brought them along? A fellow student whispered to me that he had stood next to Mahir Çayan.

Mahir Çayan? Wasn't he the student leader who had been shot by the army in 1972? Çayan was more that that. He was the head of the Turkish student movement—a well-read, quick-witted young man with a head full of ideals. How to construct a more just system in Turkey, how to break the hold of the oligarchy and establish a people's democracy—these were questions that preoccupied not only him but an entire generation that paid more dearly for these seditious thoughts than those of a similar persuasion in other countries.

1968 was an important year in Turkey, too, and as in the rest of Europe, students took to the streets. But the state's reaction in Turkey was more severe and repressive; many of the old "68ers" migrated to Germany. The resurgence of Islam in Turkey began as a reaction to the leftist students; one of the central figures among the era's right-wing students is Abdullah Gül, the current president of Turkey. The people didn't want a people's democracy. In 1971, there was a military coup. The students were imprisoned, tortured, and broken; three of them were hanged.

A heated atmosphere on the streets

1968: My father is publishing a conservative political periodical in Istanbul. He is staunchly anti-communist. The mood is heated. His office is in the Old City, directly opposite the student union dominated by right-wing youth. The big mosques are not far, and the university is also just a short walk away. The streets are piled with sandbags. The police, wearing armor, look like Martians. There are demonstrations in the streets every day. The leftist students like to march in front of the right-wing student union. Will they be able to occupy the building? Stones are thrown; windowpanes shatter. My father's office is in an old building; it is in a large room with a bay window. I am seven years old, and for hours on end I sit there in suspense at the window, watching the events unfold.

Turkey is a NATO member and opposes the communist students. Tensions run high. Turkey is a poor, underdeveloped country. The differences between the rich and the poor are overwhelming. The "simple" people in the country have been told for generations that poverty and wealth are God-given. One must resign oneself to one's destiny. But Turkey has begun to undergo industrialization. The population is moving to the cities in search of work. For the leftist students, the conditions are decidedly revolutionary. The works of Marx and Lenin are extremely significant. Mao is also popular. Marcuse is meaningless.

Driven by Vulgar Marxism

Turkey's 1968 is guided by Vulgar Marxism. Relations are strained and the climate rough. Communists, members of the Worker's Party, sit in parliament for the first time, having been elected in 1965. They don't refer to themselves as such. Communism is forbidden. Communist thinking is punishable by a minimum of five years in prison. Turkey is, however, a practicing democracy. The 1961 constitution is based on that of West Germany—a strict separation of powers, a constitutional court. But the situation in Turkey is more reminiscent of South American countries than of West Germany.

Communist Turkey is an illusion. In the Cold War, no weight can be shifted without triggering an international crisis. The world is rigidly divided into camps. The Russians are allowed to march on Prague, and Turkey will accordingly remain part of the West. It is a superpower deal that goes above the heads of the people. Turkey is a cornerstone of NATO, a stronghold against communism. Industry is still too precarious. Conservative traditions and values are still dominant in the countryside. Turkish farmers are not waiting for salvation. When "anarchists" (as the leftist student cadre is called) appear, the farmers go straight to the police. The anarchists are godless and engage in free love, or so it is said. They have no morals or decency; they trample all over the holy Koran. The state should make short order of them.

Resistance is quickly overcome

It is not difficult for the regime to suppress the student revolt after the military coup in 1971. The resistance is quickly overcome. A state of emergency is declared across the country. The courts are controlled by the military. The elected government is deposed. The military appoints an emergency government. The violent atmosphere, however, continues into the 1970s and brings the country to the brink of civil war within a few years. Left-wing and right-wing students wage war against one another. Every day, there are new dead and injured to report.

The events of the 1970s remain unresolved to this day. They served as a pretext for the next military coup in 1980. This coup is the most severe Turkey has experienced. It brings the nation to its knees. Turkey is made fit for globalization. Above all, it is important that labor remain cheap. Turkey should be integrated into the global market. Foreign capital needs to flow into the country. The traces of the military's authoritarian rule are still felt today: an undemocratic constitution and an atmosphere in which the very notion of politics has become taboo. All this has prevented Turkey from undergoing a comprehensive, lasting democratization up to the present.

Street fight between students on the Right and Left in Ankara on Apr. 14, 1969.

Coup forces intellectuals into exile

The coup in 1980 drives many Turkish intellectuals and student leaders abroad, into exile. Before this, they had increasingly shaped Turkish culture. Many publishing houses had been founded in the 1970s and 1980s by "68ers." Production had not been limited to political literature; international literature had been translated, and, above all, so-called progressive authors from around the world had been discovered. In South American literature, for example, authors like Carlos Fuentes and Gabriel García Márquez had become popular. But after the military coup, all books are banned. There are book burnings. Nâzim Hikmet's poetry once again disappears from bookstore shelves. Many left-leaning poets are no longer allowed to publish.

A large number go to Germany, where many Turks already reside. They do not all just sit in cafeterias, as Hodscha did, who always willingly answered all of our questions about the conditions in "those days" with a certain tinge of pride in his soft voice. Many of those who were politically active then become involved in cultural circles, publish periodicals, establish small libraries, and hold seminars. A rivalry arises between the mosque circles and the small cultural centers of the Turkish Left in Germany.

The decade of German asylum

I do some of my first readings at these Turkish leftist centers; my poetry is classified as too middle class. I write in German. Most listeners do not understand German. I notice how alien these people have become to me, how alien and distant Turkey is. But my translations of Turkish folk poetry are well received. The Turkish folk poets of the past decades are seen as progressive. They resisted the rule of the sultan and opposed conservative Muslim theologians.

In the 1980s, Germany becomes a center for Turkish communists. In Turkey, prisons are overflowing with them and their sympathizers, and more than a few of them end up on the gallows. In Germany, however, even the Evangelische Studentengemeinde [Protestant Student Association] worries about the persecuted. It is not that people are interested in Turkish communists' way of thinking; it is enough that the Turkish state is persecuting them. It is the decade of German asylum. Germans' naïveté is convenient for Turks who are not prepared to critically evaluate their own past.

Relentless ideological warfare

Was the Turkish revolt of 1968 an emancipation movement at all? Or, to put it differently, was it not controlled by self-appointed "leaders" with macho allure who had long since lost touch with reality? Without question, Turkey was a repressive state. But the opponents of that state, splitting like sects into countless factions, thought and behaved no less oppressively. They could not abide contradictions; even differing interpretations of the Marxist worldview did not lead to open discussions but to spiteful ideological battles.

The worldview of the revolutionaries did not call gender relations into question, not even in regard to violence. This is probably the greatest difference between the German and the Turkish generations of 1968. The latter preferred to assemble brigades over communes. Joie de vivre and humor eluded them. Private life was not revolutionized. It simply did not exist. A revolutionary who wanted to be taken seriously did not fall in love.

Leftist sects enamored of themselves

The Turkish student movement did not give rise to the "Greens," but rather to many leftist sects enamored of themselves, which trumped one another in their lack of meaning. It is not the groups in this movement that deserve respect but the many individuals whose engagement, self-discipline, and courage to think critically distinguished them from the masses. These individuals make sure that the legacy of the Turkish revolt is not entirely forgotten. In Germany, the central question for the Left was how a society could be changed, how living conditions for people could be improved; it was called the "the march through the institutions." In Turkey, there was no such march. Only the military marched.

In the meantime, the battle between the leftists and the mosque circles in Germany has been lost. Many of the people who were culturally active in the 1980s have withdrawn from public life. They are politically disillusioned, perhaps broken. Some of them run restaurants and concern themselves (at least!) primarily with their personal well-being. They are no longer role models for the young. The mosque groups, conversely, have become well organized and attract the youth.

The silence of the 1968 generation

The situation for Turks in Germany perfectly reflects the situation in Turkey. After the military eradicated the leftist movement, undermined labor unions, and prohibited political activity at high schools, a network of religious groups spread across the country. Many of them were illegal but not as loud and rebellious as the leftists. Mystical orders, Muslim self-awareness groups, and self-styled gurus of the Islamic way of life have increasingly become important cultural forces. Independent thinkers are isolated and marginalized. Turkey is recalling its Muslim identity. The only opposing force worth mentioning is the tendency towards the world of consumption, the day-to-day culture of globalization.

The silence of the generation of 1968 about this development is remarkable. Vulgar Marxist paradigms lead us no further. Taking action against this "reactionary" development seems futile. The collapse of totalitarian socialism left a great deal of bitterness but did not lead to critical self-reflection.

The garish colors of the ideologues

But in the 1980s, as we democratically minded Turks fought in Germany and Turkey against the Turkish state, people like Hodscha were still authorities, living (and surviving) exemplars of resistance, of hope for better times. Hodscha spoke French well but not a word of German. He did not want to learn German. He wanted to return to Turkey and once again take up the fight against the oligarchy. He could summon only a tired smile for German comrades who strove to achieve political influence and recognition in parliament. He saw parliamentary democracy only as a playground for the spoiled middle class. This middle class, merely masquerading in Germany as democratic, was showing its true face in Turkey.

Weren't Germany and Turkey allies? Yet how did he explain the fact that Germany offered him asylum? He simply ignored such questions. Revolutionaries gladly push aside such questions because they disrupt their ideological worldview. The revolution cannot tolerate gray areas but demands clarity. But that is roughly comparable to attempting to lighten a photograph of deepest winter by overexposing it. The print is always a failure.

Ideologues have always disturbed me. I have always seen them as enemies of poetry. For poetry is borne of shades of gray, of the voices between the lines, of the nuances of color. Ideologues, on the other hand, always require sharp pictures, garish colors, resolutions of words' secrets and ambiguities. I let Hodscha speak, but I never read him one of my poems.

* An earlier version of this article was published in the Goethe-Institut's cultural magazine, *Fikrun wa Fann*.

Zafer Şenocak was born in Ankara in 1961, grew up in Istanbul and Munich, and currently lives in Berlin. He is one of the most prominent authors of Turkish heritage in Germany and writes in German and Turkish.

YUGOSLAVIA: "DOWN WITH THE RED BOURGEOISIE!"*
Želimir Žilnik

The Yugoslavian "1968" began on the night of June 2-3 in that year with a clash between the students and the police in Studentski Grad, a student district in the capital of Belgrade. Hundreds of young people wanted to go to a concert for which there were not enough tickets. When they began to riot at the door, the police intervened with guns, and the situation escalated into a street battle. The brutality the police had exhibited prompted several thousand students to march to the city center some six kilometers away. During this march, the conflict intensified and the police opened fire. Many people were injured including 130 students and 20 policemen. Dozens of students were arrested. Politicians were brought in to talk to students, but in one intervention, the police even beat up some of these mediators! Meanwhile, the student battalion chanted "Down with red bourgeoisie," "We're sons of working people," "We need jobs," "Students—workers."

The next morning, Belgrade seemed deserted and quiet, as if a state of emergency had been declared. Street demonstrations were banned. Newspapers reported that there had been "incidents caused by a group of hooligans," whereupon students and professors had "occupied" the university and declared an all-out strike. On June 4, the Student Assembly had decided to rename the Belgrade University "the Red University of Karl Marx." Slogan-bearing banners were hung on the façades of the buildings. They read "Down with corruption" and "Our problems are also workers' problems." A list of demands soon followed: freedom of the press and assembly, the dismantling of the bureaucracy, and punishment for those responsible for the police brutality. The events in Belgrade immediately prompted similar actions in Zagreb, Ljubljana, and Sarajevo.

The biggest protest movement since World War II rocked the political system. It took a week of striking for Tito, the head of state and party leader, to publicly praise the young people's commitment in the media and agree to meet the students halfway so that they could be persuaded to allow teaching to resume.

Interpretations of the Yugoslavian 1968

The year 1968 in the former Yugoslavian political universe, and particularly in Serbia today, has been transformed into a myth.

Its interpretations vary widely according to one's political leanings, and the purposes to which one wants to put this historical moment.

Right-wingers today say that the occupation of the University of Belgrade was a Maoist means of applying pressure to restore Stalinism and thus to "rectify" Titoism. Moreover, they perceive the students as tools used by dogmatic elements within the ruling party.

Student rally in Belgrade on June 3, 1968, to demand higher education reform and protest the military's brutal treatment of student demonstrators.

Technocrats of "new capitalism" in Serbia claim that the rebellion halted economic reforms that were supposed to have led to the development of a market economy and political pluralism in Yugoslavia.

The apparatchiks of Milošević's regime and the organizers of the "Anti-bureaucratic Revolution" say that Belgrade students lived in worse conditions than their peers in Zagreb and Ljubljana, and that Belgrade was brought "under control" after the protests.

Nationalists add that the students euphorically welcomed speeches by Serb writers and criticized Yugoslavia as an artificial creation that sought to wipe out national cultures.

Formerly disciplined members of the Communist League and some former party officials have their own viewpoints. Now enriched with new experiences, they say that the student rebellion could have been a basis for dialogue, but that its methods were disturbing and anarchic. They say that the students and professors assessed the situation in society unrealistically and that they unwittingly contributed to the escalation of conflict. Moreover, they provoked reactions from outside and brought the country under international pressure (which is to say from the Soviet Union).

The better part of the activists of the anti-war and anti-nationalist movements in the 1990s knew from experience that the 1968 protests imparted important lessons in the struggle against despotism and for freedom from the risk of political persecution, from arrests and trials. The events of that time made it quite clear that the state constituted a repressive mechanism and its ideology an officially propagated lie. The regime had exposed its weaknesses and its resistance to democratization with its response to the demonstrations, but the revolt had had a very simple motive: the younger generation sought to make more room for itself in a country increasingly under pressure from a geriatric elite. They struggled against the privileges of the party elite and against the poverty of workers and students. In a nutshell, the students were the first to demand public dialogue on the contradictions of the process of "building up socialism."

The claims and interpretations of these various groups hit upon truths in particular ways.

Persecution of people who thought differently

The ruling elite, which had been narcissistically self-confident and untouchable up to June 1968, was overwhelmed by feelings of anxiety, resentment, and fear. This swiftly led to a new authoritarianism and the persecution of all who thought differently, which, in the following months and years, triggered a breakdown of the system and a deterioration of the values and already acquired freedoms that had given Titoism a reputation as a one-party system more open and more humane than the Soviet model.

However, one more thing *must* be added. On June 9, 1968, immediately after the protests, the party adopted a set of guidelines portraying the country as a "self-governing democracy," developing unprecedented "human freedoms" and an "abundance of democratic forms" greater than any "democratic system in the history of mankind had ever been able to achieve." This façade was shattered by the tectonic shifts of August 1968—the occupation of Czechoslovakia "in the name of proletarian internationalism" by the Soviet Union and other Eastern Bloc countries.

The Yugoslav authorities and Tito reacted fiercely, rejecting the occupation and showing their solidarity with Czechoslovakian reformist leader Alexander Dubček and his government. Some of the harshest condemnations were leveled against the Soviet

Brezhnev regime and its hegemonism. These events left deep rifts in the structure of domestic and international socialism that would never be healed.

The Non-Aligned Movement

But what had led to this "torrid summer" of 1968? After being expelled from the Communist Information Bureau (Cominform) in 1948, an organization of communist parties dominated by the Soviets, Yugoslavia acquired a reputation as the leader of the Non-Aligned Movement. This was a federation of, primarily, dozens of newly liberated former colonies in Africa and Asia. Some of them were monarchies, some were republics or even picturesque and mystical military dictatorships whose leaders wore colorful togas and strange headwear and were accompanied by a retinue of tribal brethren.

Such leaders toured the Brioni Islands, where Tito's residence lay, in an ongoing pageant to "collect experiences" at factories and construction sites. Only when the state delegation began sailing from Alexandria or Calcutta to Indonesia and beyond—trips that would last three to four months—did this flood of visitors let up.

Due to the unique position and respect the Socialist Federative Republic of Yugoslavia (SFRY) enjoyed at the time, successful foreign trade was able to develop. Engineers, doctors, pilots, and even filmmakers traveled to far-off countries to provide "technical assistance." Meanwhile, thousands of "non-aligned students" studied at Yugoslavian universities.

Extreme unemployment after economic reform

The communication with the world at large and the brisk foreign trade required that the domestic economy abandon the bureaucratic Soviet-style planned economy. "Economic reforms" were launched that bred tension in the bureaucratic apparatus and the emerging working class, including downsizing, lay-offs, and performance-based remuneration.

In 1967, I was making two documentary films: *Pioniri maleni* [Little Pioneers], about juvenile delinquents, and *Nezaposleni ljudi* [The Unemployed], about the wave of unemployment. An idealist and party member at the time, I was surprised by the magnitude of social differences and the misery that my crew and I encountered. We filmed people living in dire poverty who blamed the government for its failure to adhere to socialist ideals. These two documentaries are still among the most poignantly critical projects we ever made.

At the time, the Yugoslavian employment office started promising jobs in West Germany, claiming that an official, bilateral agreement on this matter was imminent. It would be hard to imagine today the shock this news brought to working-class families at that time. Having only been dragged to the city from their villages as part of the industrialization drive a few years before, such families now had to deal with the difficult choice of whether to register to work and reside in a foreign country—and not just in any foreign country, but in the very country that had so often been at war with their own, as children learned day after day in school. Of the thousands of students living in dormitories—particularly in the biggest one, Studentski Grad, in Belgrade, where the 1968 protests had been ignited—many came from working-class families.

Doubts about the "Western Model"

In those years, doubts about the "Western Model" were prevalent. The United States was waging its war in Vietnam; the bombings and massacres sparked off mass demonstrations all around the world. The official Yugoslav line condemned the Vietnam War, but young people in Belgrade, Zagreb, and other cities still wanted to get personally involved. They wanted to show their solidarity and protest against "the opportunistic policy" of their country. The police (still called *milicija*, or militia, at that time) brutally suppressed several protests staged before the US Embassy in Belgrade in 1967 and in the spring of 1968.

This was the first time that the police stormed university buildings. Long discussions and party commissions dealing with those events brought professors and students closer together, as "the forums" at Belgrade and Serbian levels punished "undisciplined communists." In this heated atmosphere, in April 1968, news arrived from Poland that students and professors of Warsaw University had been punished for anti-bureaucratic demonstrations and for collaborating with the church. In May, as Belgrade students, we all listened and watched the developments in Berlin, Bonn, and Paris closely, and we engaged in street protests and petitions in support of the French National Student Union and extra-parliamentary opposition in the Federal Republic of Germany. We were just waiting for a "spark" to ignite the fire. The spark came in the night of June 2-3, precipitating the events of the Yugoslavian "1968" described above.

Strategies against criticism of the regime

In all of Yugoslavia, the most dangerous political volcano had erupted—that is, criticism of the regime inspired by Marxist ideas. It threatened to spread the solidarity of workers and intellectuals in confronting "the red bourgeoisie." The experienced Tito regime used every means at its disposal to crush its opponents and, in the process, sowed the seeds of the country's disintegration: it emphasized regional differences and sparked disputes between regional party leaders, who accused one another of displaying less caution toward "the enemy."

Communication between the students and workers was prohibited, and guards were posted at factory entrances. The state police scrutinized student publications and activists closely. The party cleansed its leadership of "anarchists" and filed the first criminal charges. University professors (particularly from the departments of philosophy and sociology), many of whom worked on the journal *Praxis*, experienced systematic persecution. Even Tito addressed this topic in a highly personal manner in a speech, somewhat inaccurately but harshly concluding, "Our enemies are some professors, 'Praxis' philosophers [*Praksisovci*] and other dogmatists ... We must stop such people, and we will stop them when we gain insight into their points of view and when we combat their negative activities with conviction. Finally, administrative measures must be taken at times. We must protect our socialist, self-governing system."

A call to restore socialism to its roots

The sudden occupation of Czechoslovakia in August added fuel to the fire in Yugoslavia. The party and the authorities feared that Yugoslavia might be the next country to experience such a "brotherly embrace." They churned out political condemnations of the Soviet decision and began preparing to defend themselves against a potential military attack. Disciplinary political measures were further increased. In the years that followed, the country would experience a period of re-Stalinization; many of the "anarcho-liberals, and pro-Western ultra-leftists" who had been denounced in 1968 would be labeled "anti-national elements" in the 1990s.

The revolts in Yugoslavia and Czechoslovakia in 1968, in essence, constituted a call to restore socialism to its roots. This call was not really heard. As a result, both Titoist and Soviet socialism became and remain a taboo topic, even for today's leaders. Only in recent years has the youngest generation of intellectuals in all the former

Yugoslav republics begun to analyze and reassess some aspects of this past.

* The author writes from the point of view of present-day Serbia. The title of the contribution, however, reflects the political alignment of the country in 1968.

Želimir Žilnik is the author of numerous short films, documentaries, and feature films that deal with contemporary problems and themes. His film *Rani radovi*, for instance, was banned under state censorship but was awarded the Golden Bear at the Berlin Film Festival.

WESTERN EUROPE

BELGIUM: THE END STARTED IN 1968

Paul Goossens

Since Belgium was the birthplace of surrealism, the practice of adding texts and explanations to existing images is never unnecessary here. Belgian surrealist René Magritte understood this very well, and—to avoid any misunderstanding—he added the words "Ceci n'est pas une pipe" to his one of his paintings. In this country, nothing is what it seems, and what you see is always ambiguous.

It was no different in 1968. Belgium was the only country in Western Europe where the student protest movement brought the government to its knees. That says something about the power of the Leuven student movement, but it also reveals something of the country itself. No matter how genuine the influence from the United States, the Netherlands (Provos) and Berlin on Belgian student leaders was, the "couleur locale" was just as important.

The intensification of the linguistic conflict

On Tuesday, February 7, 1968, after weeks of uproar and tumult at Leuven University, the Catholic-blue government of Paul Vanden Boeynants came tumbling down. At that point, *la contestation* in Nanterre and Paris had yet to begin. We had already had two years of sit-ins, public meetings, demonstrations, and occupations of university departments, for the Leuven question had been simmering on the Belgian burner for years. Since the early 1960s, Flemish parliamentary members had been insisting that the French-speaking section of the Catholic University of Leuven be moved to Wallonia, the French-speaking, southern part of Belgium. In this way, they hoped to halt the expansion of bilingual Brussels and to preserve the linguistic homogeneity of the Flemish region. Leuven is barely 30 kilometers from Brussels, and, as the Flemish rallying cry pointed out, it was in danger of being absorbed by the Brussels "oil slick." In this case, the French-speaking section played the role of the Trojan horse.

The Leuven controversy took place in a unitary, centralist Belgium that was divided along denominational lines. As yet there were no districts or municipalities with governments of their own, and even the political parties were still bilingual. The debate on splitting Leuven University was being carried out mainly in parliament and in the deadly dull debating clubs of what was then called the "Flemish Movement," an amalgam of language and culture lovers, teachers, and Flemish nationalists. Every now and then, there was a demonstration, usually in Leuven. The students were easily deployable foot soldiers and had no problem with the slogans and mottos being drummed into them.

The democratization of the universities

In 1965, this uncomplicated relationship began to cloud over, and a gap began to form between the Flemish Movement, mainly characterized by conservatism and nationalism, and the student movement, which was less and less willing to accept the patronizing stance of officials and started looking for new political horizons. Until the mid-1960s, the university recruited most of its students from the middle class. This was especially true for the Catholic University of Leuven, which always distanced itself from socialism and the social struggle and functioned as an elite breeding ground for the conservative and Catholic power structure.

With the democratization of higher education, however, a profound change began to take place in the student population. Workers' children started appearing in the lecture halls, which disturbed the established traditions, reflexes, and political dogmas. Homogeneous thinking came under fire, and the Alma Mater found existence in her ivory towers to be increasingly oppressive. The protest actions against the Vietnam War that were taking place at American universities triggered little reaction in Leuven, other than surprise at the impact that the students could have on university policy. That admiration increased when students at Berlin's universities began to revolt as well, and the Flemish press began to devote more and more ink to the "youth rebellion."

The Flemish student strike

May 13, 1966, was a turning point. That was when the Belgian bishops, Leuven University's organizing force, announced a position that was as tough as it was unambiguous: the French-speaking section would not be transferred. The content and particularly the tone of the pastoral letter did not go down well. A spontaneous strike broke out in the Flemish section, and every night the police had to set out with truncheons and water cannon to cool off the angry Flemish students. Suddenly, the Leuven question took on a decidedly anticlerical and anti-authoritarian tone, and the speeches and writings of the student leaders contained themes that had little or nothing to do with the traditional Flemish battle cries.

The democratization of universities, society, and the Belgian state was becoming an increasingly urgent point of discussion and more and more frequently resulted in conflicts with the various Flemish authorities. The 1966-67 academic year grew into an endless series of collisions between the students and the academic authorities, the police, Flemish political figureheads, and social commentators. These last were growing more concerned about Flemish students being derailed and Flemish demands going unheard ever more often. As many editorials insisted, it simply was not possible "that the Catholic character of the university was being tinkered with and that the Flemish front around Leuven was being weakened."

The Leuven time bomb explodes

The more the Leuven student movement became linked with international protest activity and began to show interest—in word and deed—in Vietnam, the writings of critical theorist Marcuse, and the critical university, the greater the gap between the radicals and the Flemish establishment grew. Although this establishment was entangled in a power struggle with the Belgian state, it was just as allergic to the student protesters over whom it had lost control, and who—God help us—had even started reading the writings of Karl Marx.

Although the Leuven student leaders distanced themselves further and further from the Flemish national discourse, they did continue to address the problem of the transfer of the French-speaking section of the university and constantly made fresh attempts to light the fuse on the Leuven time bomb (albeit now with left-wing arguments). It eventually worked. On January 15, 1968, when the French-language section of Leuven University publicized its plans to expand over the following years with no hint of a transfer, the students rose

Demonstrators march against NATO and the US during President Nixon's state visit to Brussels on Feb. 23, 1969.

up in revolt. For weeks, daily demonstrations were held, academic buildings occupied, and the protest spread to include all the institutions of higher learning in Flanders.

The end of unitary Belgium

The stalemate around Leuven had been broken for good, and, at the same time, a few important bulwarks of Belgian state and society had been shattered. On February 7, 1968, the government fell, then the Christian Democrats split into a Flemish and a French-speaking wing, and ten years later the move of the French-speaking section of the University of Leuven began. The country had undergone profound changes during those years. The state reform of 1970 put an end to Belgium as a unitary state and signaled the beginning of a federal structure. It can thus be said that the Leuven revolutionaries wrote history—Belgian history, to be sure—but most of them found this more than satisfactory.

Paul Goossens is a Belgian journalist.

DENMARK: PROTEST AND PRAGMATISM

Thomas Ekman Jørgensen

In 1968, Denmark experienced the mixture of protest and pragmatism that is typical of Scandinavian political culture. The country witnessed student actions and demonstrations that were on a par with other confrontations on the European continent, but at the same time there was a collective will to find a pragmatic solution to the conflict. This applied to both the students' demands for greater say and the young revolutionaries' desires for an alternative culture and lifestyle.

Reforms of higher education

The most important events of the year 1968 were the actions taken by students at the University of Copenhagen to have some say in university affairs. For many years, psychology students in particular had gone through official channels to be allowed a share in the decision-making. Inspired by an activist milieu, which had come into being especially in anarchist circles in Copenhagen, a little group gathered students in grass-roots assemblies to organize sit-ins at their department.

This action reverberated through the rest of the student population, which began organizing rallies and other protests. The rector stepped in and set up negotiations, and it was not long before an agreement was reached: psychology students were given greater say in the daily running of their department, but not in research. This resolution soon extended to the rest of the university. Shortly afterwards, the Danish government started to draw up a law based on the compromise reached in Copenhagen.

Christiania, the social experiment

History shows how protest movements have been able to combine their demands with a broader agenda. Danish politicians had long hoped to modernize the universities, and the rector of Copenhagen University had wanted to introduce reforms. Before 1968, politicians had met with resistance from the professors, but now they were able to make use of the student revolt to push their program through and break the professors' hold on power. In the 1960s, Danish authorities had launched a modernization program. They were resolved to break with old traditions to rationalize society, on the one hand, and to increase individual freedom as part of a cultural program, on the other.

In this spirit, countercultural projects often received direct financial and political support, or authorities sought to find compromises.

The clearest instance of such a compromise had to do with the "free city" of Christiania. In September 1971, several young people occupied a disused military barracks and declared it their home; it soon turned into an alternative "town within a town." Politicians decided not to clear the site; instead, an agreement was made to supply it with electricity and water, and Christiania fell into the category of "social experiment." Christiania stands as one of the very visible testimonies both to the countercultural scene of the 1960s as well as to Scandinavia's famous tolerance. It remains, however, an enclave with a largely symbolic value that should not overshadow the general development in education and social norms in society as a whole. The "free city" can and should first and foremost be seen as an example of the constructive interplay between the counterculture and the political authorities that generally characterized the Danish 1968.

Radicalization of the movement

The groups representing protest against established society—the rebellious students, the left-wing intellectuals, and the countercultural forces—worked together with the authorities at first. However, around 1970 the movement became more radical. Student thinking took on a more Marxist character, and many of the former student rebels began to discuss creating a genuine revolutionary party. From the universities, a political movement emerged that was unmistakably revolutionary. However, as primarily students were involved, the movement remained very theoretical.

The radical movement's aim was, first, to find the correct Marxist analysis of Danish society in order to formulate an objective revolutionary strategy afterwards. Hence, a large part of the activities consisted in studying Marxist classics; solidarity groups were much weaker than in neighboring Sweden and Norway. This was a left-wing parallel culture that appealed especially to the youth. The Danish student movement of the 1960s was small, shaped by just a few hard-working activists, but, in the 1970s, the movement gained enough support to return the old communist party, the DKP, and the new left-wing radical party, VS (Venstresocialister [Left Socialist]), to the Danish parliament [Folketing].

Nevertheless, around 1980, the former student rebels had grown disappointed that the revolution had failed to take place in Denmark or anywhere else in the world. Capitalism had gone through a tough crisis, but the working classes had not risen up. At the same time, many were disillusioned by the Cambodian-Vietnamese War (1975-1979). From the 1980s, a new generation of activists came on the scene, swapping the dream of revolution for the slogan "No Future."

When, in August 2007, *Der Spiegel* referred to Copenhagen as "cool, cultural and creative," the weekly German news magazine mentioned two phenomena that had contributed to the economic growth and the creative scene in the city: Christiania and the Roskilde Festival, an annual rock music festival begun in the early 1970s. To a large extent, both of these are products of the 1960s Copenhagen cultural scene with its emphasis on social experiments and direct participation. Christiania is still obviously indebted to the 1960s cultural scene and the early squatter movements. This is visible in the aesthetic identity of the area, as well as in its government, which is based on anarchist-inspired structures with authority in the common assembly [Fællesmødet] of all inhabitants. In the present (2009) process of "normalization" initiated by a liberal government supported by extreme-right nationalists, the fate of Christiania is an open question. The Roskilde Festival, too, has retained a large participatory element. It engages local volunteers in the organization and remains a non-profit event even though it is in the top league of international music festivals.

Two older ladies pass policemen before the US embassy in Copenhagen in 1970 in a protest against the US invasion of Cambodia.

The compromise between the state and the economy

The spectacular economic growth that has made Denmark a model for the early twenty-first century is connected to developments from around 1968. Many of the ideas from that time have been assimilated into society and have helped to develop the very capitalism the protests aimed to abolish. One obvious example is the reform of higher education. Overcoming the power of the professors meant that younger researchers had greater independence, and education came to serve a variety of ends. Pro-reform politicians worked with student rebels to create educational courses that were more problem-oriented and independent.

Nowhere is this more apparent than in the new experimental university RUC (Roskilde Universitets Center) in Roskilde outside Copenhagen. Students and politicians had different goals in founding the university, which generated conflict in the 1970s: students wanted the freedom to pursue Marxist studies, while the politicians wanted courses of study that catered to the labor market. In the end, though, the Marxist direction lost out and RUC became the darling of commerce. Like many of the reforms, this development carried forth the Scandinavian compromise between the state and the economy, with the state providing the structural framework for economic growth so that it could then finance a generous public welfare system.

Breaking down hierarchies

All of Danish society has experienced the breaking down of hierarchies and traditions since 1968. For example, the formal pronoun of address (De) has largely been abolished, replaced by the informal form (Du). Similarly, titles have fallen out of use: Hr. Direktør Jensen has become Hr. Jensen. The importance accorded to equality of the sexes is another very obvious example. Denmark was quick to say farewell to the traditional nuclear family as a foundation stone of society. Women were to be able to work, and the state was willing to provide the services, particularly child care, to make that possible. Both these views had a direct impact on the economic system.

The breakdown of hierarchies led to the typically Danish "flat enterprise," that is, a democratically organized business with close daily communication between management and workers. Women's entry into the labor market was the answer to the labor shortage and generated the potential for long-term economic growth. In summary, one may say that the revolutionaries lost. The reform of culture and society may have been radical, but it took place on the system's terms.

Thomas Ekman Jørgensen is a Danish historian specializing in comparative European history whose first book *Transformations and Crises* about the Left and the nation in Denmark and Sweden was published in 2008. He has published extensively on 1968 in Scandinavia and now works at the European University Association in doctoral education.

FRANCE: A JOURNEY TO FREEDOM*

Mohammad Bennis

Time and again, the wind of May 1968 wafts through my texts and my imagination, and it is always present in the events of our time—albeit in a different form. One word evokes May 1968 in me: freedom. Freedom is a word that May '68 gave me as a sign along the path I chose for myself.

Days that are still present for me: the defeat suffered by Arabs in the Six-Day War against Israel in June 1967, the defeat known as *Naksa* in Arab political and cultural discourse, was my first political and personal shock. I was about to launch into adolescence. The media also informed me daily about the Vietnam War and the vast damage done by American forces to a nation that wanted to be free. Occasional news items depicted the Vietnamese people's resistance to American colonization.

As a young man in my home country of Morocco, I recalled images of the French colonization throughout the nation, and especially in Fez. Then there was the Algerian liberation struggle. And Latin America was close to me, too, with its poets and Che Guevara. However, Arabs' *Naksa* in the 1967 war was something different. It profoundly shook my entire being and completely changed my feelings about the world as the victims of the isolated Palestinians multiplied like their pain and suffering. Then the revolution of May '68 suddenly occurred, coming from a place I never would have expected.

A cry of revolt from Paris

1968 was the year I graduated with my high school "baccalaureate." It was also the year I dreamed of leaving Morocco to continue my studies. At the beginning of May, something took place that could not remain hidden from view. I'm talking about the day I first heard of the University of Nanterre. The Sorbonne had been the reigning authority, the French university that had enchanted me, but now Nanterre ruled the streets of Paris, and the name of student leader Daniel Cohn-Bendit embodied a cry of revolt. Consequently, the month of May, when I should have devoted all my time to studying, was transformed into a feverish period whose developments reached me by way of French radio. I could tune in without difficulty and hear of the strikes, demonstrations, occupation of universities, mass meetings. And the heroes were young people—or, more accurately, university students.

Moroccan friends who had already started their studies in Paris also sent me their news and impressions of the student uprising. Directed against the dominant French values at the universities and in family and personal life, the uprising led me to dream of traveling to Paris as soon as my exam results had been announced. My grandmother promised to save a little money for me, and my friends in Paris encouraged the plan.

Freedom surrounded by tanks

Early one morning at the beginning of July, I descended from the train that had brought me, via Madrid, to the Gare d'Austerlitz in Paris. I made my way towards 5 rue des Écoles in the Latin Quarter, which housed the "Moroccan House," just a few steps from the Collège de France and the main entrance to the Sorbonne. This took me past remnants of the May events—proclamations and posters still on the walls. In the Moroccan House, I was welcomed by my friend Ahmad al-Alawi, who was writing his doctoral thesis. We didn't stay in his room for long since I longed to see the Latin Quarter. In front of the Collège de France, I experienced an everyday life that was unfamiliar to me.

Right in the heart of this area were tanks and soldiers, but to the right stood François Maspero's bookshop and beyond that the Seine. I felt joy and fury—joy because I was at long last in Paris, and fury over the military presence in the Latin Quarter. The remains of barricades stood in front of me. I wasn't aware that this was the end of the revolution. Instead, it seemed to me that I'd come to live for a month in two different epochs simultaneously: the time of the May revolution and the time of the "Enlightenment" in Paris, in the France of liberty and the French Revolution, now surrounded by tanks; it perfectly mirrored the style of French colonialism when Moroccans had demanded independence. But where is freedom to be found? And what does it signify?

Lessons from the French May

During this brief morning tour, I looked and I listened, making the acquaintance of the epochs Paris had endured: the monarchy, the French Revolution, the Paris Commune, and liberation from German forces. I only needed to take a few steps around the Latin Quarter to encounter young people from many different nations who had come to Paris to greet the sons and daughters of the May revolution and to learn from them. They dreamed of changing their lives—in the university and beyond. It seemed to be the day of resurrection.

I had a midday meal with my Moroccan friends at a restaurant in the university quarter of Sentier. The district bore the scent of revolutionary days. Posters. Slogans about freedom. Words and phrases nourishing my wish to write about the revolution with similar enthusiasm. In the restaurant, students' clothes testified to the rebellion against Parisian elegance despite the absence of any signs of chaos. My friends and I briefly discussed these traces of the May events and students' thirst for action, but these friends lacked clarity about what had happened or what was in front of them. They were still in shock. They could not understand why the French military and police had not shot at the demonstrators, as the Moroccan government would have done if people (or students) had openly rejected the state of things.

A policeman throws a tear gas grenade at a crowd of protesters on the Parisian Boulevard St. Michel on June 17, 1968.

On the streets, I saw the Parisian world and listened to the revolutionary thoughts that dominated the city. Sometimes I looked around and saw the remains of slogans about dreams, poetry, reality, desire, and hope. On these streets—and especially in the Latin Quarter—while I was looking at how the students had shaken the image of Gaullist France in May, I imagined that the surrealists had achieved their aims in that moment. Some of the slogans remain in my memory: "The dream is reality." "Ban prohibitions." "Anything is possible." "Poetry is in the streets." More than once, I stood before slogans calling for sexual freedom, which attracted me just as much as attacks on the state and family, or the anthem of praise for workers. There was also criticism of God.

Freedom of the body

I strolled under the sycamore trees along the Seine. I allowed my eyes to look and look. Beneath the bridges, I saw men and women embracing, which I found provocative. Embraces and long kisses and half-naked bodies stretched out on the grass. Soft skin almost touching. In these moments, I discovered physical freedom for the first time. Everywhere the body chose liberation from the constraints of decorum. The ecstasy of touch and the passion of love-making. Laughter or song. The body reveals pleasure without regard for what is forbidden. I watched from a distance and had no intention of disturbing these lovers—these disciples of psychiatrist Wilhelm Reich, who had promoted adolescent sexuality—writing new hymns of praise to love as if it were the very thing that the authorities did not dare understand, whose future they did not even want to imagine.

I usually went past the Place de la Bastille to a simple bar to drink to the health of the French Revolution. The days of that July I spent wandering the streets, nourished by proclamations of freedom and guided by the sight of other youth, were poems written deep within me. A month that quickly passed, and I could no longer imagine being separated from Paris. My memory and my imagination preserved it all. For me, Paris, with the different periods of its history, embodies the extended space of freedom I gained there.

Worlds of rebellion, desire, and craziness

I still remember the evening I left Paris. Around 10 p.m., I boarded a train that would take me toward Morocco via Madrid. I was fascinated by what I had seen, read, and heard. My innermost being was filled with worlds or rebellion, desire, and craziness. I left the Gare d'Austerlitz for the South. My South. Tangier, then Fez. I don't remember saying anything during this journey. I felt like a stranger to myself. Images of the city and of May mingled with images of the French Revolution and the Paris Commune, and with the names of poets and writers and artists and philosophers—or they mingled with the names of Arab and Moroccan writers and artists who were absolutely determined to learn the alphabet of modernity in Paris.

When I disembarked from the boat, moored in Tangier, I felt I was no longer the same person who had set off a month before. I had left something of myself in Paris and the May uprising. And something of Paris had become part of my feelings and thoughts. Those scenes simultaneously vanished and surrounded me on the way from Tangier to Fez. I yearned to return to Paris where the freedom of the body, of culture, of writing had broken through university walls and out onto the streets.

Liberated from any dogmatism

The revolution of May '68 was the rebirth of a critical attitude toward life and death. It was this critical attitude that I made my own when I adopted a leftist view of politics. My critical stand and freedom of expression carved out a gulf between me and any rigid adherence to norms or submission to trends that claimed to have a monopoly on the truth. Marxism led me to sympathize with the parties of the Palestinian and Moroccan Left, but it was the practical application to reality and new critical, philosophical texts that liberated me from any dogmatism.

Today, more than forty years after May '68, when I observe cultural or political life, I see that the feeling that predominates about what happened is regret. Many intellectuals (and politicians) in Morocco and the Arab world, just like many former May '68 activists in France (and other countries), regret what they once were. I, on the other hand, learned from May '68 that freedom is constantly in motion.

*An earlier version of this article appeared in the Goethe-Institut's cultural magazine *Fikrun wa Fann*.

Mohammad Bennis is one of today's most important Moroccan intellectuals and poets.

GREAT BRITAIN: "NO PLACE FOR A STREET FIGHTING MAN"

Hans Kundnani

In the summer of 1968, Mick Jagger looked with envy across the English Channel, where France had been brought to a standstill by the "événements" in Paris, and wrote the following lines: "Everywhere I hear the sound of marching, charging feet, boy / 'Cause summer's here and the time is right for fighting in the street, boy / But what can a poor boy do / Except to sing for a rock 'n' roll band / 'Cause in sleepy London town / There's just no place for a street fighting man."

The lyrics to the Rolling Stones' "Street Fighting Man," which was released that August on the album *Beggars Banquet*, pretty much says it all about 1968 in Britain. London may have been "swinging" in the 1960s, but in political terms, it was—compared to Prague, Paris, or West Berlin—relatively tranquil.

Frustration about British sleepiness

The previous March 17, Jagger had taken part in the famous London demonstration against the Vietnam War that was violently broken up by mounted police. The demonstration had begun peacefully in Trafalgar Square, where an estimated 10,000 people had assembled. The initial mood suddenly changed when the demonstration moved from Trafalgar Square to the American embassy in Grosvenor Square. The first frictions occurred when the mass of protesters came up against the police, who had created a blockade.

Deciding against retreat, the demonstrators broke through the blockade at isolated places with the aim of approaching the embassy building. The situation escalated and street fighting broke out between mounted police and demonstrators. The use of stones, firecrackers, and other objects as missiles left many injured on both sides. The violence of the British police toward the protesters led afterwards to controversy in the media.

Also among the protesters was John Scarlett, then an Oxford student and later head of MI6, the British foreign intelligence service. But this—a protest directed against the American, not the British, government—was about the closest Britain (though not the UK) came to fighting in the streets during the "year of the barricades." With the exception of Northern Ireland, where civil rights protests by the Catholic community began what became the "Troubles" that lasted for the next thirty years, there was little of the tremendous political upheaval that shook continental Europe.

A group of mothers in a women's organization that advocated medical assistance in the Vietnam conflict march with their children before the US embassy in London on Oct. 15, 1968.

Rudi Dutschke, the icon of the West German student movement, echoed Jagger's frustration about British sleepiness when he and his American wife Gretchen moved to London after he was shot in West Berlin in April 1968. He was disappointed to find that there was little enthusiasm for a full-scale revolution in the Britain of Prime Minister Harold Wilson and, using his usual Marxist jargon, complained in his diary of the "absolute lack of the subjective factor of revolutionary action in England." Dutschke would later be forced to leave the UK after he was denied a residency permit; he and his family finally settled in Denmark.

Differences in the generational conflict

The reasons behind this lack of revolutionary consciousness in Britain may have something to do with differences in the generational conflict that was everywhere at the heart of what became "1968." In West Germany, that conflict was sharpened by the postwar generation's consciousness of its parents' responsibility for Nazism and its sense of being "the children of mass murderers." Tariq Ali, one of the leaders of the British Vietnam Solidarity Campaign and probably the "Street Fighting Man" Jagger had in mind when he wrote the song, remembers meeting Ulrike Meinhof, then a columnist and later to become notorious as a member of the West German terrorist group, the Red Army Faction. "You don't understand the issue with our parents," she told him.

In Britain, the generational conflict had none of that intensity. Whereas the Federal Republic was a fragile, fledgling democracy, which the student movement saw as a continuation of Nazism, Britain was a relatively intact society that had prevailed against Nazism. In fact, although Britain had emerged from World War II financially bankrupt, it was, if anything, morally strengthened. Nor did British young people have a Vietnam War to fuel their rage at their own government as their American counterparts did (Prime Minister Wilson had refused to send British troops to Southeast Asia). Like their Utopian comrades everywhere else, young people in Britain dreamt of a better world in which, in Ali's words, "people should be measured not by success or material possessions but by the humanity of their aspirations," but they were simply not as tormented or angry as their fellow activists in Berlin or Berkeley.

Creative boom instead of a revolution

In 1968, there were sit-ins at universities like the London School of Economics and confrontations at art colleges that paralleled the student rebellions elsewhere. But in France and West Germany, protests about conditions in higher education (which had had to rapidly expand to accommodate the baby-boomer generation) quickly expanded into a critique of "authoritarian" society as a whole. In Britain, radical left-wing organizations like the International Marxist Group, to which Ali belonged, never had the influence that the German Socialist Student League [Sozialistischer Deutscher Studentenbund (SDS)] in West Germany did. Britain's postwar generation rebelled in different ways.

By and large, young people in Britain expressed themselves through culture, above all music and fashion, rather than politics—even the student movement in Britain, if you can call it that, was most vibrant in the art colleges. Instead of a revolution, an extraordinary creative boom took place in Britain in the 1960s. Whereas 1968 in Berlin was all about the Frankfurt School and fascism, in London it was all about Hendrix and hemlines.

Dramatic changes during the 1960s

The legacy of "1968" in Britain is therefore harder to pinpoint than in some other countries. Britain certainly went through dramatic social changes during the '60s—its class structure loosened, it became more individualistic, and old values like deference and decency gave way to new ones like self-expression and tolerance—but these were soft changes, manifested in attitudes and lifestyles, which happened gradually and beneath the surface rather than convulsively, as in France in 1968.

In Germany, the postmodern values that came out of the '60s came to be represented, above all, by the Green Party, where many of the "68ers," including future foreign minister Joschka Fischer, ultimately landed. But in Britain, with its majority voting system, no significant political party emerged from the protest movements of the 60s. Forty years on, our political landscape remains much the same as it was then. In the end, the most memorable thing to come out of Britain in 1968 was a song—albeit one about revolution.

Hans Kundnani is an author and freelance journalist in London.

GREECE: THE OTHER SIDE OF 1968

Petros Markaris

"Everyone will speak of this year / Everyone will be silent about this year," Brecht wrote in one of his poems entitled "Finland 1940." This is similar to how I feel about 1968. I am one of those who still want to speak. Most people prefer to remain silent. In any case, the younger generations know very little not only about what happened in 1968 in Europe, but also about what happened in Greece.

The year 1968 was the second year of the junta—the so-called Regime of the Colonels of 1967–1974—and it was a dark year. What made it even darker was the illusion of normality. In theaters, the curtain would rise every evening, cinemas would show new films, and bookstore windows were full of books. However, theaters staged harmless comedies, and national theaters staged only classical works selected by directors who had been appointed by the junta; cinemas showed films hacked up by censorship; and bookstore windows did not disclose the voluntary silence that Greek poets and writers had imposed on themselves, just as though it were a way of resisting the military dictatorship.

With an ear to the radio

The only cultural activity we could pursue relatively freely was auditory. And I am not just talking about music, or about our passion for singing forbidden songs. I am referring, primarily, to a radio culture focused on two foreign broadcasts: Deutsche Welle's Greek show and the BBC's Greek program. Unfortunately, there are no statistics about the number of Greeks who spent part of their day hanging on every word coming from their radios to find out what was really happening in their country, and to learn about the resistance activities of expatriate citizens and the attitude of other countries toward the junta.

These programs first informed us about the events of May 1968 in France and about the student movement in Germany and other European countries. Here, we first heard the names of the student leaders Rudi Dutschke and Daniel Cohn-Bendit. With our ear stuck to the radio, we found out about occupied universities and various states' inability to deal effectively with these revolts.

Quiet resistance

In the evenings, students, poets, writers, and intellectuals used to gather in someone's home or in out-of-the-way neighborhood taverns to exchange information and to comment on all they had heard during the day. To the Greek media, the May 1968 protests did not exist. Censorship not only prohibited comments on "anarchy" and the "disruption of the state" but banned news altogether. Nevertheless, the May 1968 events also inaugurated a new channel of communication. Every Greek who was not a junta supporter and could still travel abroad felt obliged to collect information from expatriates or foreign friends and carry it back home.

Initially, this silent resistance did not go beyond the limits of comfort. It provided the feeling of satisfaction and hope that comes from the idea that "something is happening," even though this "something," in this case, was happening somewhere else. Illegal underground activities proceeded for about two years and began to bear fruit in the early 1970s. The timing was not coincidental. The Greek colonels, unable to withstand the international outcry that had followed their hostile takeover in 1967 for more than two years, had gradually introduced a process of "liberalization," as they called it. Students, poets, writers, and artists eagerly seized this opportunity, thanks largely to the ideas they had gathered, piece by piece, from the May 1968 revolt in Europe.

Revolution in the arts

Theaters were the first to pluck up their courage. Cautiously, they began to use a new kind of discourse, often by means of plays that seemed harmless at first. A new generation of directors and actors, however, soon discovered Brecht's plays. In countries where political discourse is forbidden (this was one of the major differences between Greece and other countries that experienced the 1968 uprising), citizens always seek a substitute for it, and Brecht was the ideal substitute: a committed leftist, he embodied just what we were looking for. From 1970 to 1973, Brecht was ubiquitous: hardly a magazine in Greece failed to publish some text by Brecht, hardly a publisher failed to publish some book by him, and no theatrical company failed to stage at least one of his plays.

If there is a common feature between the 1968 uprising in West Germany and in Greece, it is the subversion that took place in the theater. In Greece, as in Germany, a new generation of writers, directors, and actors took center stage. These same directors and actors are still acknowledged today as the great (and now established) names of Greek theater.

In contrast, developments in poetry and literature were more predictable and less radical, perhaps because entire generations of poets and writers were practiced in the art of indirect discourse that is full of innuendoes and hidden meanings. They had been writing this way from the time of the Metaxas dictatorship (1936-1941) through the German occupation (1941-1944) to the end of the Greek Civil War (1946-1949).

Student resistance

Along with this resistance in the arts, a student resistance movement arose. Students began to occupy the universities in the early 1970s, culminating in the occupation of the National Technical University of Athens (Polytechneion) in November 1973. This is known in modern Greek history as the "Polytechneion Uprising." On November 17, 1973, the military dictatorship in Greece put a violent end to this pro-democratic demonstration with tanks and soldiers. More than twenty people were said to have been killed on the campus and hundreds more injured; no official number of victims was ever given. This student uprising is considered the climax of the resistance against the military government, having triggered the fall of the Regime of the Colonels in the summer of 1974.

Army tanks prepare to drive through the gates of the student-occupied Polytechneion in Athens, Nov. 17, 1973.

A Greek terrorist group formed in the wake of this tragic event, giving itself the name "17 November" in remembrance. Every year on this date, there are violent riots. The climax of the protests is usually a march past the American embassy. The demonstrators accuse the US of having supported the dictatorship in Athens and therefore making it possible for the student movement to be suppressed.

In essence, the generation of 1973 in Greece, the Polytechneion generation, is the counterpart to Europe's generation of 1968. Its members dominated Greece in the arts and especially in politics, where their influence is still omnipresent. However, just as with the German "68ers," people have now begun to view the Polytechneion generation in an increasingly critical light.

Petros Markaris is a Greek author who became internationally famous for his sociocritical crime novels about "Inspector Costas Haritos." His recent novel *Che Committed Suicide* was published in 2009.

IRELAND: BREAKING THE SHACKLES

Nell McCafferty

I was unemployed, in exile and in misery when 1968 opened. When 1968 closed, I was unemployed, back in my native land, and standing on a barricade, ecstatically engaged in the civil rights movement in Northern Ireland.

A Google search of that year, which saw changes around the globe, does not mention Ireland. This is astonishing. The "Celtic Tiger" Ireland did not arise overnight, becoming one of the most prosperous, best educated, and feminized countries in the whole world. It has taken nearly forty years, and the first step on that long march was taken on October 5, 1968, in Derry City, when people stepped out to rebel in the working-class ghetto of the Bogside, where I was born.

Members of two tribes

I was reared for exile, because the North of Ireland was under British rule and I was not welcome in my own place. The British had quit the South of the island—the Republic—in 1922, but maintained their strategic interest by leaving a surrogate provincial parliament in the North: Stormont, which had a built-in permanent Unionist Party majority, designed to guarantee one-party rule. Unionists traditionally subscribed to union with Britain, to the Queen of England, and to the Protestant Church. The minority nationalists traditionally subscribed to the end of British occupation, to a united Ireland, and to the pope.

I was in the minority, though I cared not a whit for nationalism and had long since abandoned the Catholic Church. Still, I looked suspicious—I looked like a Catholic. Do not ask how—we members of the two tribes could spot each other's identity a mile off. Anyway, I was on the dole and that proved it. (A university graduate on the dole? Yes, Your Honor, but that's because the Protestants thought I was a Catholic and would not give me a teaching job, and the Catholics thought I was an atheist and would not give me a teaching job.)

Because I did not care, I got out of the place in 1965. That was just as the rulers intended—exile—but I had not thought about that. I went on the road, as Kerouac suggested, lived in France, traveled through Europe and the Middle East, smoked dope in Turkey, and worked on a kibbutz in Israel. I was there for the 1967 expansionist war, which changed my perspective somewhat, and I ended up in London as 1968 opened.

"Destined for menial work"

It was a hard landing. I was politely turned down for professional jobs on the grounds that I was too old—a 25-year-old graduate already past her sell-by date. What the British meant was that I was Irish and therefore destined for menial work. There used to be notices in lodging houses that read "No Irish or blacks need apply." Sure enough, I ended up in the basement of a Wimpy Bar, ladling red tomato sauce from a barrel into bottles. My coworker, a black woman, ignored me, and her attitude was confirmed when this white woman was promoted upstairs to a job waiting tables. Had anyone known I was also gay, I suppose I would have been expelled back to the North, had there been such a legal mechanism available. Decades later, the British devised one, refusing entry to British-passport-holding nationalists from the North on the suspicion that they were terrorists.

Though the Jack Kerouac ideal was kicked out of me in those ten months of trying to earn a living in London, I was jealously, keenly aware of events and people elsewhere: "Danny the Red" in Paris, men circling the moon, Billy Jean King winning Wimbledon (you can spot one a mile off), the assassinations of Martin Luther King Jr. and Robert Kennedy, the Black Power salute in the Olympics in Mexico, the Prague Spring that brought on the Russian invasion.

Civil rights marchers baton-charged

I cannot remember the American feminist invasion of the Miss America beauty pageant in Atlantic City in 1968. Inasmuch as I identified with women's affairs, I could not understand why the beautiful Jackie Kennedy married Aristoteles Onassis. I did understand perfectly the student protests in the Republic of Ireland against the papal encyclical "Humanae Vitae," which reaffirmed traditional Catholic positions on birth control and abortion: it gave male student virgins an excuse to play cheeky chappy and shout the dirty word "contraception" in public. In a fleeting moment of desperation, I considered marriage—a man, and children, because, hey, it would mean money and a home. Swinging '60s, my sad and sorry female arse.

I left my efficiency in Kensington, London, and caught the boat home to Derry a broken, lonely woman. I arrived on October 6, 1968, and immediately joined in the riot that had begun the day before after the Royal Ulster Constabulary baton-charged civil rights marchers. The marchers had been trying to enter the walled city, which had withstood a siege by Catholic King James in 1698, and had maintained maiden Protestant purity ever since: the riot police spotted the Catholic identity underneath the civil rights person. The experience of rioting was wonderful. I never felt better in my life. Take that, bastards—a stone—for keeping me unemployed; take that, bastards—a petrol bomb—for refusing proper housing to my Catholic relatives who were wasting away in slums.

"You are now entering Free Derry"

Within weeks, I again felt lonely and excluded. An all-male assembly had elected an all-male Citizens' Association, which even included Protestant males. (The mantra of "One man, one vote" obviously included women, we were superciliously told.) The plan was to undermine Unionism by demanding full British rights, and if that undermined the union with Britain—actually, no, we hadn't thought of that. We just wanted a fair share of jobs and houses and votes. Our heady, unfocused aspirations were painted on a gable wall in the Bogside that famously declared "You are now entering Free Derry." (The slogan was borrowed from Berkeley, where protesting students had proclaimed, "You are now entering Free Berkeley.")

The conundrum and its solution—a power-sharing nationalist and unionist coalition at Stormont—took a while to solve, caused more than three thousand deaths, and involved fighting the British Army. The solution was achieved in the context of the European Union, membership of which allowed all sides to leapfrog metaphorically onto the continental mainland, where "Danny the Red," now a German member of the European Parliament, welcomed us home. It has to be noted that, although the power-sharing European Community model of integration after World War II provided the basis for our solution, the EC stood aside while the battle was fought within the sovereign United Kingdom of Great Britain and Northern Ireland, and it was America that came to our aid in the form of Bill Clinton.

The '60s ended with me working in exile once more as a journalist in Dublin, in what still is officially a separate and foreign country: the Republic of Ireland. Luckily, I was hired to report on the North, so I kept going back to Derry, which is one hundred and fifty miles up the road. I was still lonely. The whiff of Northern sulfur rendered me suspect in the South, as did the Northern accent—you can hear us a mile off, never mind spot us.

The Irish Women's Liberation Movement

In September 1970, I truly came home. The Irish Women's Liberation Movement was formed in Dublin. There were twelve of us, mainly journalists. Our main demand was simple: we wanted to legalize contraception. The pursuit of this demand aimed to rend asunder the Gordian knot of Catholic Church and state that was the Republic, where contraception was deemed both illegal and immoral; where female teachers and bank staff and civil servants were obliged to resign themselves to marriage; where single mothers were denied welfare and their babies were given up for adoption; where homosexuality was criminalized.

We decided not to mention the war then engulfing the North, lest the issue split the sisterhood in the South. Also, we thought that the best thing we feminists could do for the island of Ireland was to change the Catholic nature of the South so as to make Protestants on the island feel more at home. The situation suited me just fine. In the South, I could be a feminist; in the North, I could be a fighter. Few noticed my dual (split?) personality because the North knew and cared little about the South, and vice versa. People in the North read British newspapers and watched British television, because, among other things, their livelihoods depended on Britain. People in the South read Irish papers and watched Irish television because, among other things, their livelihoods depended on the Republic.

Publicity coup with aspirin

Then, one Saturday in April 1971, which had been designated "World Media Day," we pulled off a publicity coup that changed the entire social landscape. The event has entered history books as "The Contraceptive Train." Forty-nine women boarded a train in Dublin, where contraception was illegal, and crossed the border into Belfast, where contraception was legally available though restricted, its use frowned on by the patriarchy of both the Protestant and Catholic Church, and the patriarchy of all Northern political parties.

We went into a pharmacy, accompanied by television crews from America, Japan, and Ireland, and bought such of the mysterious contraband as we could without a prescription—contraceptive jelly and condoms. We had intended to buy the pill, but we hadn't realized that a doctor's prescription was needed. So we bought hundreds of aspirin on the reasonable assumption that Irish customs officers wouldn't know the difference (which they didn't).

That evening, back in Dublin, we declared our purchases to customs, refused to hand them over, swallowed some of the pills, declared the law obsolete, surged through the barrier and down to the local police station where we repeated the exercise, all in front of the world's media. We were never charged or arrested. The patriarchy turned a resolutely blind eye and hoped the whole thing would die by Monday.

Restricted right to abortion

Most people in the South hadn't seen a contraceptive. Most people in the North hadn't either. They recognized a good thing when they saw it, though. After our protest, the taboo against discussing contraceptive practice was smashed, and the legalization of contraception gradually followed. This led ultimately to the collapse of the authority of the churches North and South, Protestant and Catholic, and the rest is history. It took another twenty years to get full contraceptive rights in the Republic, the right to divorce came in 1995, and the right to abortion is so restricted that it is virtually unobtainable (even in the nominally British North).

Members of the Irish Women's Liberation Movement leave a pharmacy in Belfast after purchasing contraceptives to protest Ireland's ban on them, May 22, 1971.

Under European legislation, though, women on the island are free to travel elsewhere, without fear of prosecution, for abortion, and the now friendly relationship with Britain makes that wretched journey easier than it was. Some hold, mistakenly, that availability of divorce and abortion is the benchmark of feminist success. It is not. Recourse to either, though necessary, is a sign of failure. Who terminates pregnancy, puts a partner out of the house, and shouts "Success!"?

Success is the recognition in law of same-sex partnership; freedom to work for money, regardless of gender; welfare for single parents; the ending of conflict in the North; the joy that greeted the election of President Mary Robinson. Much has been done; there is more to do—all over the world. The Irish Women's Liberation Movement launched in Dublin in 1970 broke the shackles that bound women and men in sullen bondage beneath the amazing surface freedom of 1968.

Nell McCafferty is a journalist, playwright, civil rights campaigner, and feminist in Ireland. Her autobiography *Nell* was published by Penguin in November 2004.

ITALY: "WE DEMAND THE IMPOSSIBLE"

Giuseppe Carlo Marino

The student protest movement of 1968 in Italy was a long-lasting phenomenon. After its explosive reawakening in 1977, it gradually degenerated, tragically, into terrorist forms. This "extended" 1968 movement came to an end in the early 1980s, fading out amidst a social phase of "retreat" marked by the return to the reassuring world of "private" interest.

The later, more reality-oriented generations were more susceptible to market-driven needs and eschewed the ideas of their parents, who had cried "We demand the impossible!" The end result was that they compliantly adapted to the objective conditions of triumphant capitalism, which appeared to promise widespread prosperity and assured the most ambitious in society a certain social status (it was the era of Bettino Craxi, the long-serving socialist prime minister of Italy).

In a sense, the 1968 movement developed into its opposite. The rise of many of its activists to positions of power—in realms from politics to economics, from the academic world to public administration—is striking. Only a few years before, the "68ers" had hoisted the flag against the "system," that is, against capitalism, which they denounced as an oppressive and perverse form of power.

Did the 1968 movement fail?

Might it not be fair to say that the Italian movement of the 1960s plotted against itself? That its fate, paradoxically, was to convert the revolutionary momentum of its golden yet fatal year, 1968, into a counterrevolution? Can we say that, generally speaking, it failed? Although there is some truth to this argument, it is, on the whole, flawed because 1968 brought lasting changes to Italy. It permanently transformed old rural Italy and its urban counterpart, where great strides towards industrialization had been made (the so-called economic miracle). It brought about decisive and irreversible changes not unlike the great social revolutions in history.

Fight against the "bourgeois" model

Students played the leading role in this movement, though in Italy, it was the youth of working-class or even peasant background—who had been denied access to higher education for centuries—that drove the protest. Now they burst through traditional class barriers, making use of the very same channels of modernization that so-called neo-capitalism had opened. What was taking place was a shift from elitist university education, in which the "keepers of knowledge" enjoyed unlimited power, to higher education for the masses. The student forces took up the fight against the old bourgeois model, challenging the authoritarianism of the academic "establishment." Along the way, the whole "system" came under attack.

Through the conflict-laden dynamic of "father-son" relationships, the movement spread from campuses to the whole of society, reinforced by the utopian vision of collective freedom from all oppression. In this, Italy was no different from the rest of the world. Yet the Italian situation did highlight some specific kinds of "oppression" that the youth felt could be traced to "unfinished" democracy, the dominance of the clergy, and the "betrayal" of the anti-fascist values of the Italian resistance movement of World War II.

Criticism of present and past

The student movement in Italy was actually ahead of its time. It arose in 1964, at about the same time as movements in the United States and prior—if only by a few years—to the "French May" of 1968. Along with the students, young professors, lecturers (often with temporary positions), and assistants played a decisive role.

At the same time, a consciousness for equality of the sexes was developing. With access to higher education, women effectively reinvented feminism by abstracting it from a historical tradition that, in Italy, had been an elitist, middle- and upper-middle-class privilege. In lively exchanges with the older generation, the younger generation radically called every aspect of society into question with public trials and extreme revisionism. Young people pounded every facet of life with a wave of delegitimization; they directed fierce criticism at the present (the detested "system") and the past (the hypocritical certainties and assurances that the "bearers of consensus" had prescribed and dispensed).

Protests from left-wing and right-wing camps

The protests were guided by both left- and right-wing factions. On the left, the attack on the "system" did not spare the Italian Communist Party (PCI), which was accused of Stalinism and blind obedience to the Soviet Union. This gave rise to anti-Soviet movements that looked "beyond the PCI" and turned admiringly to the experiences of the Cultural Revolution in China and to Fidel Castro and Che Guevara, who came to be regarded as legends. On the right, an anarchic youth movement accused the official neo-fascist party, the Italian Social Movement (MSI), of adopting a pro-American and "anti-national" line. Against this backdrop, it is not surprising that violent clashes in universities, schools, and on the streets also ensued between the young leftists and anti-fascists, on the one hand, and between the right-wing and fascist forces, on the other.

Thus, it was really two different youth movements that participated in the protests. The left-wing activists (who had broken away from the PCI and the Italian Socialist Party (PSI)) far outnumbered those on the right and thus dominated at universities. They comprised a variety of groups such as Potere operaio [Power to the Workers], Manifesto, Servire il popolo [Serve the People], Cristiani per il socialismo [Christians for Socialism] and Lotta continua [Ongoing Struggle], which is to say they were Maoists, Trotskyists, Guevarists, "Third Worldists," and so on.

Part of a global youth movement

One peculiarity of the '68 movement in Italy was its infiltration by undemocratic forces directed by shady members of the intelligence services. Seeking to destabilize Italy, these forces schemed within the anonymous seats of hidden power (which were arranged parallel to, and often overlapping, the official power centers of the republic), preparing the ground for "coups d'état" in the fashion of the Greek colonels of the junta (1967–1974) with the goal of averting a communist takeover. But, of course, the student protesters were unaware of this. As in the rest

Student protest in Rome, May 1968.

of Europe, they were busy constructing a new collective mentality based in the values of authentic and natural living that they set against the authoritarianism, philistinism, hypocrisy, bigotry, and the "betrayal" of their elders and mentors.

The protesters, in effect, had joined into a sort of "youth globalization" that spread from Berkeley, California, and the civil rights movement of Martin Luther King Jr. and Malcolm X to the protests in Paris in May 1968. In the spirit of the Beat Generation, they had developed new styles and new languages of their own. They had become actors in a collective campaign of "cultural revolution," and it was on this terrain that they achieved success, securing certain civil rights (divorce, abortion, equal opportunities, sexual freedom, and so on) that impacted all of Italian society.

Failure of the anti-capitalist revolution

They failed completely, however, on the terrain of the anti-capitalist political revolution. Conditions at the time were not favorable to this cause. The working class itself was already feeling the effects of the epochal transformation sweeping through Western society, moving it towards "postmodernism" and deindustrialization. While the radicals of the youth movements in Italy were pressing for an anti-capitalist rebirth, the workers themselves—as Max Horkheimer noted with regard to Germany—sought merely to gain higher wages and access to the "opulent society" of consumerism. Among succeeding generations, the progress of postmodernism—spurred by the "electronic-information revolution" that had already arrived, interrupting the centuries-old course of the "industrial revolution"—precipitated a drastic break with the past.

The few radical activists, on the left and on the right, were not aware of all this. They were entrenched in the utopia of the "revolution" (communist) or the "revolt" (fascist), falling onto the tragic path of terrorism—one group against the other—with both sides being manipulated in various ways.

Unusable material from an old world

"Real" history left little room for utopias, however. Soon, the "68ers" had no "values" they could convey to the next generation with any credibility. Overwhelmed by the myth of the "new" and of the "future," subsequent generations tended to regard the past in general, and even the history that had produced their ideologies, as unusable material from an old world that could be discarded without regret.

Even the traditional passage of values from the older to the younger generation was interrupted as the youth became increasingly reluctant to accept the values of their elders. Gradually, the tendency to criticize or question those values diminished as well. Elders simply ceased to be important! Rather than rising up against them, the young generation preferred to ignore them. From then on, they sought "values" as commodities in the virtual marketplace of the future.

Giuseppe Carlo Marino is a Professor of Contemporary History at the University of Palermo. His many books include *Biografia del Sessantotto* (2005) and *Le generazioni italiane dall'Unità alla Repubblica* (2006).

NETHERLANDS: THE SECOND LIBERATION

Roel van Duijn

The Hague, 1960. During recess, my school friends and I happened to see a photograph of an old philosopher, Bertrand Russell, being picked up by the police in Trafalgar Square. He was taking part in a sit-in against the atomic bomb. Not long afterward, we blockaded traffic during the morning rush hour, sitting on the asphalt at the intersection of Javastraat and Anna Pavlonastraat—it was on the way to our Montessori Lyceum—and chanting: "Ban the bomb!"

I can still see us sitting on the asphalt that morning and blocking cars with our banners, and one hour later being literally dragged to court by the police to account for our defiant act. I felt a shock of rebellion when I read that atomic bombs were going to be stored in the Netherlands, too. We were war children, raised in the conviction that now, after fascism and violence, an age of peace must dawn.

My friend Peter Schröder and I made our first pamphlet. "Don't turn the world into Hiroshima" it read in orange letters. We pasted the pamphlets on bus shelters in fashionable neighborhoods using wallpaper paste. We were seventeen. The police carried us off in trucks. In my defense, I appealed to the unwritten laws of conscience borrowed from Cicero, but this did not make much of an impression on the judges.

Becoming a professional revolutionary

On a fiercely cold winter day, my friend Hans Korteweg and I sputtered to Amsterdam on his moped to organize the next demonstration. We skipped out of school to do this; I sat behind him and got very cold. I called my father from a houseboat. "You get back here, young man!" his voice cracked. "I've got just four hundred guilders left in the bank, and I'm sick. The principal of your school just called and told me that I had a choice between sending you to a psychiatrist or taking you out of school. So if you don't get back here right now, they're going to throw you out." "No," I replied resolutely, "I have an important political mission."

When I finally did come home, my father did not say a word. I felt his despair and anger, but also his concealed admiration. It did not break my heart that Hans and I had been thrown out of the gymnasium, even though it was only a couple of months before final exams. I carried on unflinchingly, agitating against the A-bomb mentality. My father did not know what to do, but I did: I got my hands on some yellowed books by the anarchist Mikhail Bakunin and Ferdinand Domela Nieuwenhuis, the savior of the working class, and I set out to become a professional revolutionary.

On the first day at my new school, the Dalton Lyceum, I noticed with pride that our opponents had scribbled "Van Duijn go home!" to greet me on the outside wall. After that the man in the wood veneer double bed in the bedroom next to mine kicked the bucket. At his graveside I said, "Bye, Dad."

"Provotariat" instead of proletariat

In 1963, when finals were over, I moved to Amsterdam. There I became a creature of my own making: a "Provo." I started working on the assembly line at the Amstel Brewery, screwing caps on bottles to earn money for a typewriter. I had learned from the anarchists that the revolution would start with the working class, but when I asked my new coworkers what they thought of having their money sent home without having to work for it, their answer disappointed me. They said they would miss their work, the purpose of their lives. I concluded that we were not going to get any revolution from the proletariat. We would need something else: the "provotariat" —the masses of rebellious youth, the idle riffraff, who were not afraid of a little rough-and-tumble.

Once I had my typewriter, the pamphlets and manifestos simply flew out of the house. We organized nightly happenings against "the addicted consumer" of tomorrow and brought new life to anarchism. I pasted a percussion cap in all three hundred copies of the first issue of *Provo*. "Grab a hammer and start the revolution in your own life with a bang!" I wrote underneath. In no time, the police were at the door. All of my materials, including the mimeograph machine, were confiscated. From then on, we could no longer keep up with the demand for our new magazine.

The white bicycle plan

Then we launched the white bicycle plan to put thousands of rental bikes on the street, free for anyone to use. We believed it was the city's job to maintain them. But when we publicly painted the first bicycles white near the Lieverdje statue on the Spui square, the police confiscated them. Professional revolutionary—can you still aspire to such a thing? Not that it was all that common back then, but in leftist circles it was something that exuded excitement, and that is why I wanted to be one so badly.

A professional revolutionary derived his prestige from more than giving incendiary speeches, writing subversive articles, and convening demonstrations and happenings. Part of it involved going to jail from time to time for organizing illegal gatherings or inciting subversive behavior—maybe for handing out currants, symbols of love, in public; or for walking down the street with a blank banner, even though demonstrations of any kind had been forbidden there; or for throwing a smoke bomb at the carriage of a just-married princess.

The Provo Movement's "White Bicycle Plan" in 1966 sought to provide thousands of white bicycles to the public in Amsterdam free of charge.

Solidarity in the House of Detention

I once spent five weeks in the House of Detention on the Leidseplein. There I could do a little extra reading (I did not have to work because the authorities feared that I would incite others to protest against the Vietnam War). Late Saturday evenings there was always a happening, and I could hear people chanting for my liberation outside: "Free Roel! Free Roel!" All the prisoners beat out the rhythm of the chant on the heating pipes so that the building shook. Once a week we were allowed to write a censored letter, and once a week we could have a visit from a girlfriend in the presence of a guard. The advantage of all this was that when we were back on the street, we could stare at the pedestrians and the Number 10 tram line with the happy feeling of freedom.

A professional revolutionary would go right back to work, however. The next issue of *Provo* had to come out; currants had to be distributed next to the Lieverdje statue, the little street urchin who symbolized, for us, the Addicted Consumer of Tomorrow, or a council of the international provotariat had to be convened. As professional revolutionaries, we were full-time Provos, full-time *Kabouters* [Dutch leprechauns, mischief-makers], and we made a living from it by giving interviews and lectures and by writing articles. In principle, we shared everything. At any given moment, our comrades could burst into our house and open the bread box or sleep in our bed. We could not get jealous because jealousy in love killed creativity. Or maybe not? My good relationship with my girlfriend grew free and ever freer.

Provo in the city council

I became a writer, councilman, alderman, and farmer. As a councilman, I did have to come up with a theory, of course: the two-hand doctrine. That meant working in the system with one hand and stirring up trouble via extra-parliamentary movements with the other. Naturally, we came up against authorities like Amsterdam mayor Gijs van Hall. "Van Hall ten val!" [Down with Van Hall] was our motto. And sure enough, the government dismissed him: they thought Van Hall was not coming down hard enough on the protesters. This was the wrong reason, we thought, and so we started a counteraction: "Don't dump Van Hall!"—which put an end to the last hopes of Van Hall's supporters that he would get another chance. The humiliated city council had no choice but to start allowing happenings and demonstrations.

It was late 1966, a year and a half before the revolutionary events of Berlin and Paris. That winter, sympathetic students and other kindred spirits from various foreign capitals occasionally visited us. Many of them had read our pamphlet, "Call to the International Provotariat," which we had distributed in several languages as far as Russia.

"Provo is dead"

When the movement disbanded in May 1967, six years after the death of my father, I became ill. "Provo is dead," I mourned, feverishly searching for the next thing. I crawled into bed. I thought about my farewell to my father. What had happened to Provo? What was to become of the revolution now? I fretted about the world after Provo. The doctor tried aspirin and penicillin, but after three months he came to the conclusion that nothing was wrong with me. "Go do something completely different, Van Duijn," he said with a stroke of genius. "Go work on a farm." Surprised, I set out on trembling legs. "Looverendale" organic whole wheat bread, which was produced on a farm on the island of Walcheren, was the only thing that occurred to me. The farmer agreed to allow me to be a volunteer apprentice—on the condition that I shave off my beard.

One evening, he and I walked through the fields, inspecting the weeds. In the neighboring field, a harvester was tearing at the potatoes. I asked him if we were going to get a monster like that to take care of our spuds. "No," he responded, sticking his chin into the evening glow. "Noisy machines chase away the kabouters, and we need them to keep our plants healthy."

Kabouter for the environment

I had found it! I shook hands with the farmer and left. In the train, I wrote a manifesto about the need for a Kabouter State. Human beings had to become cultural kabouters. As cultural kabouters, the new race would be able to restore balance with nature.

It was 1969, the end of a decade that had changed the Netherlands into a living democracy; a decade in which we, too, had exerted an unexpected but inspiring influence in Europe. For many people, the 1960s marked a second liberation. After having been freed from the Nazi occupation in 1945, we had now freed ourselves from the stuffy atmosphere of authority. Just recently, I read that the white bicycle plan is being introduced in Berlin, Paris, and Copenhagen.

Roel van Duijn founded the anarchistic Provo Movement in the '60s in Amsterdam. Now he is a member of the district council in Amsterdam Oud Zuid and an adviser to the lovelorn.

NORWAY: A POLITICAL AWAKENING

Dag Solstad

In January 1968, I married for the first time and moved into a flat in a student village attached to Oslo University, even though I was not a student myself. I just pretended to be one—I was really a writer, having written two works of prose, but my wife was certainly a student.

That Easter—it was actually Good Friday—I went to a party in a dormitory in the same student village where practically all the guests were left-wing students of various persuasions, from social democratic to the far left, many of whom were later to have careers as politicians or intellectuals. The atmosphere was agitated because the West German student leader Rudi Dutschke had just been shot.

Many at the party talked about going into town and demonstrating outside the West German embassy; others advised against this because too many had had too much to drink and were visibly under the influence on Good Friday. Perhaps because no agreement could be reached as to what was to be done, the agitated atmosphere subsided. Perhaps, too, because it was Good Friday and left-wing students felt it was provocation enough to be having a party, so even the most extreme of them felt it wisest to refrain from holding a political demonstration outside the West German embassy.

Emancipation instead of freedom

Then the spring of 1968 came, the Prague Spring, May 1968 in Paris. In June of that year, my first daughter was born. In July, I wrote a long essay about the exiled Polish writer Witold Gombrowicz, "The Necessity of Living Inauthentically," concluding it as follows:

> I have learned two very important things from reading Gombrowicz. 1) Instead of talking about freedom, I will talk about emancipation. 2) It is more important to be a good actor than a good human being. In addition, I have the satisfaction of knowing that this is a concept of freedom that those whom I have defined as my opponents are not pleased about my venerating. To talk about emancipation instead of freedom is something that suits a person

who, from within his inner depths, has realized that he is unfree.

The Paris revolt was put down—I cannot recall precisely when, but it was probably before I wrote those lines. On August 21, the Soviet troops moved into Czechoslovakia and occupied the country. I read about the French May of 1968 in the newspapers, but how much did that affect me? In May 1968, Czechoslovakia was more important to me than Paris, probably because no matter how radical I regarded myself as being, I was surrounded by and at the mercy of the language and field of vision of Western leaders.

Deep-seated hope

The Prague Spring and its vision of "socialism with a human face" seemed to offer hope and not merely to be an empty phrase, even for many a left-wing Norwegian. Indeed, it was a deep-seated hope. I'm not a "68er." I was young, 27 years old, and a radical. But I had also just become a father for the first time and was very much aware of my responsibilities as a provider. I was poor, had a strong wish to make a living from writing, and therefore was a concerned provider. That was my 1968.

But I was basically more radical than most, though not exactly in the sense of belonging to a particular political party. That is why I was able to register the political awakening that was taking place towards the end of the 1960s. I noticed that something was in the process of changing, also in Norway. But it was not in 1968 that I noticed this—it was in 1967. As mentioned, I was a radical, shaped by protests against nuclear weapons, the Vietnam War, and other classic left-wing causes.

Concerned for the future of the world

Something happened during the summer of 1967, not to me but to others. When I returned to Oslo University—where I did not actually study but pretended to—in the early autumn, I met students who had begun to talk in a manner completely different from just a few months earlier. They talked about something different, too. They were worried about the future of the world. They talked about us and the others, and that we lived on the sunny side of the world. People who had previously not thought about political dilemmas now did so; young people who had not been interested in justice for the peoples of the world now showed concern.

Maybe they had been thinking about this for some time but had hesitated to discuss it. It was as if a whole generation of young people had been walking around engaging in their own private thoughts and had suddenly decided to talk—and all at the same time. It almost seemed as if they had talked on command—and under considerable pressure. Something had influenced them, something obvious, but to me it was unclear how this had happened. Had it happened at the university colloquia, or in the seminar rooms during the spring term of 1967? During breaks at the seminars, during the lectures?

What is superficial has remained

It must have. In the space of a brief instant it surfaced, before slowly dying down over a period of ten to fifteen years. What is most superficial of the surface is all that has remained. I still wear the same type of trousers as back then. I always have two pair, always the same brand: Levi's. Everything else is gone. What I liked best, the reflectiveness of the youth, is gone. Our obvious disdain for advertising is gone.

What is left is rock music, which I have always found moving. Power rules, as it nearly always has, though now more proficiently and with more servants than ever before. I remember that it took more than ten years for me to realize that not all rich people are dim-witted—I truly had no respect for them. This is how one can be wrong.

Founding of the Newspaper *Klassekampen*

In March 1968, Rudi Dutschke gave a lecture in Oslo before the Norwegian Student Association [Det Norske Studentersamfund], the oldest association of students in Norway. He spoke out against the military and cultural imperialism of the United States and advocated that students reorganize into a "revolution from below."

In May 1968, the youth organization of the Socialist People's Party (SUF) [Sosialistisk Undomsforbund] realigned itself ideologically, calling itself "Marxist-Leninist" for the first time. Then, in 1969, it separated from the party organization for good. Thereafter, the student organization oriented itself entirely towards the Marxist-Leninist tradition, appending (ml) to its name to emphasize this fact and distinguish itself from the party organization SUF.

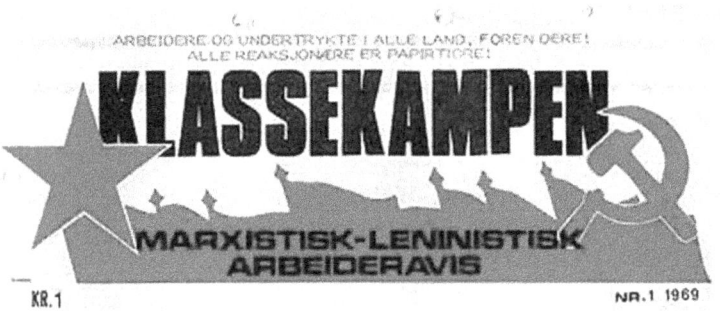

First edition of the Norwegian left-wing paper *Klassekampen* of 1969.

The objections that prompted the SUF (ml) to split from the Socialist People's Party concerned the party as such. It was said to be too old-fashioned, not sufficiently radical, and not in accord with the new ideas that were inspiring the youth organization. Further, the SUF (ml) also criticized the party's policy towards Israel in relation to the Six-Day War and argued that Israel could no longer continue to exist "in its present form."

Ensuing debates in the press and politics motivated the founding of the leftist newspaper *Klassekampen* [The Class Struggle] in 1969. The paper still exists today and is regarded as the main organ of the leftist movement.

Dag Solstad is a Norwegian author.

SWEDEN: WHAT HAPPENED TO 1968?

Svante Weyler

In autumn 2007, Swedish TV focused on a major TV event: *Into Battle!*—the history of 1968: politics, music, drugs, love. A young dramatist, a young director, and a young ensemble were to transform their parents' grand experiences into a TV spectacle. Advance interest was tremendous and the reviews effusive, from both left-wing and right-wing critics: "Yes, that's exactly how it was," they claimed. Then the public tuned out or continued to watch *Grey's Anatomy*.

The message was crystal clear: Stuff your 1968! And apart from a few exceptions in the jubilee years to date, the situation in literature and theater is similar. 1968 is a non-subject in Sweden. The children of 1968 aren't coming to terms with themselves, and their children aren't coming to terms with them. Is there, perhaps, nothing to come to terms with?

Student protests quickly ran their course

On the surface of things, 1968 in Sweden was by no means as dramatic as in countries such as Germany or France. Students in Stockholm did occupy their union building for a few days, but the effect of their threats was merely to prompt Education Minister Olof Palme to talk with them. There was a strong protest movement against the war in Vietnam, but it was characterized as much by classical Swedish moral traditions as by revolutionary fervor. The TV public of today recognizes this, having just as little interest in classical Swedish moral traditions as in 1968.

We switched to the informal mode of address, but that was not so much a result of '68 as a return to a prevalent Swedish custom. And radical Swedish policies on women and the family were actually the work of the liberals, which had started long before '68.

Changes in cultural organization

But even though '68 is not a common theme in novels and films today, the structure of Swedish cultural life on the whole is still a result of the events of that time. A social democratic idea developed by Olof Palme himself, namely, extending the welfare state to the field of culture, took root, and the structure is still working remarkably well today.

To be sure, nobody is called a "cultural worker" anymore, as was then the case, and dissatisfied artists and neo-liberals of staunch principles now and then question the subsidizing of culture, but the system can deal with this because wide swathes of the population recognize it as necessary. The balance between subsidy and the market works, and a modicum of funds has ensured a modicum of diversity. This may not be all that revolutionary, but it is still good.

No traces in politics

And what about 1968 in politics? It's just as hard to catch sight of it there. Our former prime minister Göran Persson could have been a "68er", but he comes from the countryside and seems to have missed it all. Whatever he spoke to former president Bill Clinton about, it wasn't the Rolling Stones. His successor as the leader of the Swedish Social Democratic Party Mona Sahlin proudly represents a number of the values that came to the fore in '68— "new" families, gay rights, feminism—

Minister of Education Olof Palme (2nd from right) and Ambassador of North Vietnam to Moscow, Nguyen Tho Chyan, in a torchlight procession against the Vietnam War in Stockholm, February 1968.

while at the same time firmly standing on reformist ground, which the "68ers" did everything in their power to undermine.

Her hero is Bruce Springsteen, not Bob Dylan. The present conservative prime minister, Frederick Reinfeldt, who spent 1968 in a nursery school, probably doesn't listen to any music at all, but when asked directly, he mentions ABBA as his favorite band.

Legacy of 1968 in the media

But there is one area in which the legacy of 1968 is very clearly visible, and that is in the media. This is not too surprising since the struggles of that era were largely carried out in and by the media, where many of the protesters gained their formative experiences. The concrete result has been free newspapers and magazines, spearheaded by *Metro*. The story behind this is interesting but a tad complicated.

Jan Stenbeck, a young man from a distinguished family that had taken some knocks, went to the US to study at Harvard Business School. He bore a grudge against Swedish big business for having been hard on his father. When he got back home, he inherited the big family fortune, which chiefly consisted of forests. Backed by this classical Swedish money, he wanted to transform Sweden, though by no means in a revolutionary way but rather in an ultra-liberal manner. After all, another consequence of '68 was the birth of the extreme Left's twin: neo-liberalism.

Invention of the free newspaper *Metro*

Stenbeck's main target was the media. They were to be "freed," both from the state and from big business. He first broke the Swedish ban on commercial television by broadcasting programs from London. He then tackled the press, creating the free newspaper *Metro*. In so doing, he reversed the traditional logic we know from the glorious nineteenth century, i.e., instead of starting off with content for which you try to get financing (advertising), he began with advertising for which he sought content (newspaper).

This is where '68 comes in. Stenbeck needed someone to pull this off in practice, and that needed to be someone who was not completely caught up in the classical "bourgeois" way of thinking and acting. Moreover, practically all the journalists Stenbeck gathered around him had their roots in the most extreme part of the '68 movement, Maoism.

Attack on the press

Just like Stenbeck, however, the Maoists were not very interested in the classical process of shaping opinion. Whoever is right has no need for discussion, and in this case, since the Maoists were categorically right, discussion could be replaced by propaganda. Stenbeck, on the other hand, replaced it with advertising. As it turned out, the two approaches could easily be combined once the Maoists tamed their political passions a bit. Stenbeck really enjoyed the collaboration, and the Maoists did, too, it has to be assumed, as it was far more lucrative than a previous collaboration with Beijing.

Metro became a success story, and even if it and the other free papers are now killing each other off, their effect will live on. They dealt a fatal blow to the traditional press—a far stronger blow than '68 ever managed to mete out.

Davis Cup Match Triggers Demonstrations

On May 3, 1968, various groups (church groups, youth associations, and extra-parliamentary groups) formed a united front to protest against the apartheid policy in Rhodesia during a Davis Cup match between Sweden and Rhodesia. Although the Swedish police were present to ensure that the tennis match could take place without incident, some of the demonstrators diverged from the specified route and marched on one of the gates of the stadium where the match was being held. Police attempted to dispel them with a baton charge and bombarded the sitting protesters with water cannon and tear gas. The sitting blockade made it impossible to shut the gate. The turmoil continued for several hours. The tennis match was finally called off and transferred to France.

On May 14, 1968, as a consequence of this and other clashes between protesters and police, the Swedish government under Prime Minister Tage Erlander invited 55 Swedish youth and student organizations to discuss the public order and the right to demonstrate with him. The government initiative was motivated by fear that conflict would escalate, which could trigger actions by the reactionary forces. The government sought to engage in dialogue with the demonstrators to avert further violence.

Svante Weyler is an editor, reviewer, and director of the publishing company Svante Weyler Bokförlag in Sweden.

WEST GERMANY: A RETURN FROM CULTURAL NOSTALGIA TO POLITICAL ANALYSIS

Claus Leggewie

One important and commonly known, though not decisive, trigger of the anti-authoritarian student revolts in West Germany was the police bullet that killed Benno Ohnesorg on June 2, 1967, in West Berlin. (In 2009, the perpetrator was unmasked as an informant of the GDR secret service.) The student Ohnesorg had been taking part in a demonstration against the state visit of Reza Pahlavi, the "Shah of Persia." Pahlavi (and his wife Soraya, especially) had captivated the German public via the tabloids, which treated them as a substitute for German monarchs, while the critical intelligentsia saw Pahlavi as a dictator and puppet of American imperialism in the Middle East. The writings of Iranian exile Bahman Nirumand and leftist columnist Ulrike Meinhof helped to educate students about the repressive forces of the Iranian state and stimulated outrage. The students staged an entirely peaceful demonstration against the state visit, just as they had previously done to protest the Vietnam War. This served as the catalyst for the international and transnational significance of the local student revolts.

Criticism of the US as a "protective power"

The people and politicians of Berlin reacted to these demonstrations with great irritation. The situation of this city divided by a wall since 1961 presented a peculiar irony in that it was precisely the students of the Free University (which had been established by the Americans) rising up in the "frontline city of the Cold War" against the "US as a protective power." The Springer press, which set the tone at the time, unequivocally supported the US in this role and sharply rebuked the student protesters. (Finally, in 2009, the Springer publishing house agreed to revise its former role under the scrutiny of neutral historians and observers.) The press claimed, accurately enough, that it was a "small radical minority" that was fouling its own nest, and that these students would be better off going "over there" (that is, to the part of Germany occupied by the Soviets, and to the "real existing socialism" of the GDR).

Nonetheless, attitudes were gradually beginning to shift, which garnered more popular support for the student protesters. In the German liberal middle class, people increasingly doubted the validity of the US-led war in Vietnam—then a minority opinion now shared by historians and the broader public in the US as well as worldwide. Moreover, relations with Israel grew more distant after the Six-Day War, which Israel launched three days after the Ohnesorg incident, on June 5, 1967. In the aftermath of this conflict, when Israel began the policy of settling in the occupied Arab regions—a policy still criticized today—the West's predominant support for Israel gave way to solidarity with the Palestinian Liberation Movement.

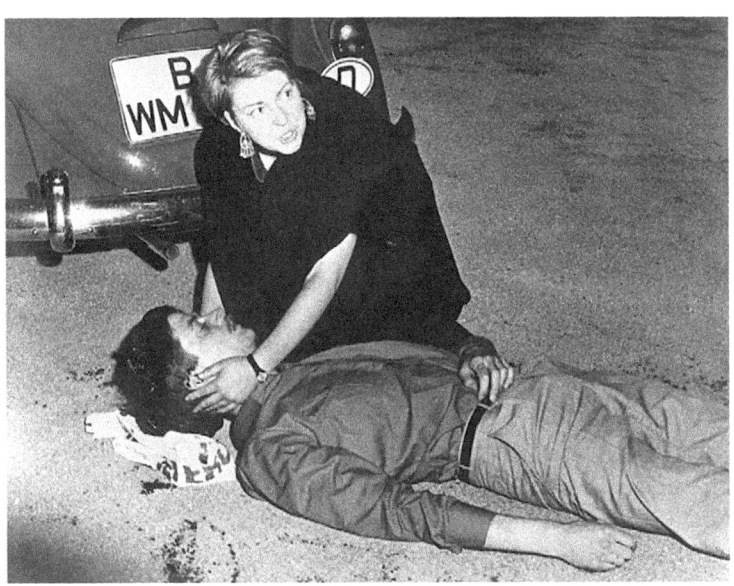

German student Benno Ohnesorg, dead in the arms of pedestrian Friederike Hausmann, after being shot by detective Kurras on June 2, 1967.

"Anti-Americanism" as a trademark of the radical Left

The various strands of development that merged in this dramatic week in June 1967 reconfigured the structure of world conflict in a way that can still be felt to this day. The East-West conflict and issues of decolonization diminished in importance as power struggles with Islamic states grew. In 1979, the Islamist Mullah regime ousted the Persian shah in Tehran; today it is in a bitter dispute with the United States. In turn, the US is fighting its "war on terror" in two of Iran's neighboring states, Iraq and Afghanistan, which in some respects carries forth the armed struggle conducted by social revolutionary guerrilla groups against "US imperialism" in the 1970s. Iranian president Mahmoud Ahmadinejad has rhetorically placed himself in the vanguard of an anti-American faction fighting against US hegemony, which is wavering—a front line which, if not for the Islamic fundamentalists, some former 1968 activists could probably join. "Anti-Americanism" was a trademark of the radical Left in the late 1960s. At the time, however, this was little more than a marginal stance that was unable to weaken the "soft power"—the cultural power of persuasion—or pose any sort of challenge to the military power, but now it has come to stand for a global shift in attitude. The reputation of the US is worse now than at any time since 1945, and the "last superpower" is unable to find any effective means to combat the asymmetrical manner in which its opponents conduct war.

Anti-authoritarian protest even in America

On the other hand, the sources of anti-authoritarian protest are to be found in the US itself: it is widely known that the protest wave started on the American West Coast (Berkeley) and took its lead, in terms of its content and form, from the homegrown dissent against the Vietnam War. European protesters adapted both outward symbols and philosophical foundations of this wave in their own revolts, including the American subculture of "sex, drugs, and rock 'n' roll," different forms of direct action (sit-ins, teach-ins, go-ins), and postindustrial and neo-spiritual ideas. On the European continent, this revolt was only quashed by Marxist-Leninist elements in an authoritarian backlash among the students themselves.

When people commemorate 1968 today, either semi-officially or privately, they can only focus on local and folkloric aspects of lifestyle and consciousness that they could easily integrate into the changed values of modernized, postindustrial societies. To understand the extent to which 1968—a year that characterized an era and broke with all that had gone before—was embedded in global developments that have continued to cause ripples right up to the present day, however, a detailed political analysis is needed. Such an analysis needs to take supposedly marginal aspects of the student revolt in the West into account. The Prague Spring marked the beginning of the end of Soviet rule over Central and Eastern Europe (though not of internal and external Russian authoritarianism); the Maoist "Three Worlds Theory", i.e., the battle of villages against cities, can be interpreted as the prelude to China's return to the world stage (still under communist leadership). At the same time, other members of the 1968 movement (among them the founders of the first global postmodern nongovernmental organization "Médecins Sans Frontières") took a stand in Biafra in Nigeria against a bloody ethnic civil war, and the dictators in the Latin American and Mediterranean regions of the world collapsed under the pressure of the "third wave of democratization."

Between 1965/68 and the next landmark year of 1979—the year of the Iranian Revolution, the disastrous invasion of Afghanistan by the Soviet Army, and the rise to power of Ronald Reagan—world politics changed radically, adopting a form to which the events of 1989 and 2001 hold the key: the disintegration of the Soviet Union and the Warsaw Pact merely postponed the dramatic loss of US hegemony in the world, which has now been displaced by a multi-polar global society. With the powerful influence of politicized religious movements and nongovernmental organizations, this global society is hardly likely to restore the sort of "world order" that the classical state system of international relations dictated.

Foreign policy and transnational dimensions

One recurring theme in this lengthy development is the increasingly critical attitude, even among Western nations, towards the US and Israel. Yet 1968 was by no means the kick-off of acerbic anti-Americanism; a good part of the anti-authoritarian Vietnam protest stemmed from the disappointment an entire generation of Americans and American supporters felt over America's betrayal of the republican values of its own constitution. Only then did the authoritarian wing of the student movement in West Germany fasten upon the more totalitarian traditions and excesses of the French and Russian Revolutions, coming to radically reject even the basic values of Western democracy and liberality. It is interesting to note the continuities and breaks in this process: while many former West German "68ers" remained faithful to a political-cultural anti-Americanism, which hates "America" across the board for all that it is and represents (rather than criticizing US decision-makers specifically for what they do or fail to do), many critics of America have returned to their disappointed love and affirm American values, even in cases where American policy contradicts them, such as in the Iraq War or in the unethical treatment of prisoners at the Guantanamo Bay detention camp in Cuba. In other words, the 1968 generation became both America haters and "anti-Germans"—forming a pool from which neo-conservatives and Third World activists alike are able to recruit support.

This circumstance has resulted in the development of two factions in international relations. On the one hand, America supporters, including militant opponents of "Islamo-fascism," which they perceive in Iran and al-Qaeda, have adopted a strange sort of "right or wrong, my America" philosophy. The anti-hegemony faction, on the other hand, has made strange bedfellows of America's opponents, including caudillos (militant leaders, like Venezuelan

President Hugo Chavez) and fundamentalists (like Iranian president Mahmoud Ahmadinejad).

In other words, any political analysis or review of the year 1968 should focus on the "foreign policy" and transnational dimension it had right from the start—as well as on the future of the West. Some observers claimed that the Iraq War was a founding moment that led to a Europe independent of the US, while others saw in it an opportunity to do away with the traditional European resistance to the American "empire." The fact that both of these interpretations proved to be overly hasty, especially now with the Obama administration, underscores the present need for the European Union to rethink, with deep historical insight, the role that it intends to assume as a global player in the political arena.

Claus Leggewie is a German political scientist. He has been a member of the German Advisory Council on Global Change for the German government since 2008 and director of the Essen Institute for Advanced Study in the Humanities (KWI) since 2007.

EPILOGUE

ONE, TWO, THREE, MANY 1968S? A PANEL DISCUSSION

Normal Birnbaum, Patty Lee Parmalee, and Tom Hayden

To commemorate the fortieth anniversary of the events of 1968, the German Historical Institute Washington, DC, organized a panel discussion with three activists and contemporary witnesses: Norman Birnbaum, Patty Lee Parmalee, and Tom Hayden. The event, moderated by Philipp Gassert and Martin Klimke (both GHI), took place on May 14, 2008. The opening statements of the panelists as well as their responses to the moderators' first questions are documented on the following pages. The GHI would like to thank the three panelists for making their contributions available for print.

Martin Klimke: Although the fires of the 1960s may have died down, the memory of that decade surely has not. The events of the metaphorical year 1968 and the decade in which it was embedded have long been overtaken by subsequent waves of historical and pop-cultural representations. This year in particular, the media attention, as well as the number of conferences, books, and lecture series dealing with '68 is at an all-time high.

Consequently, "1968" has, in fact, become a commodity that is on display in countless movies, musical references, and car commercials. As a veteran '68 activist in Uwe Timm's novel *Rot* [Red] proclaims, "If there were a revolution today, people would think it was an ad campaign."[1] The most recent wave of memorial fervor seems to fully adhere to this principle. In accordance with the insight of one of the protagonists in Hans Weingartner's movie *The Edukators* that "What used to be subversive is now for sale on the shelves," the 1960s and 1970s have experienced a renaissance across the cultural spectrum from Prada-Meinhof fashion to the use of neo-Marxist vocabulary in descriptions of today's globalization processes.

Of course, this renaissance has also engendered some '68 bashing among the protest movement's erstwhile opponents. In Germany, the end of the Red-Green coalition in 2005 and Joschka Fischer—the supposed symbol of the '68 generation—departing from active politics have turned into a swan song on this generation's failure to transform politics and culture with the "long march through the institutions." When drawing up a balance sheet on the political

[1] Uwe Timm, *Rot* (Munich, 2003), 283.

impact of this very generation, Edmund Stoiber, in 2005 the leader of the Bavarian branch of the conservative party, underscored that this cohort had successfully replaced values such as "decency, loyalty, and reliability with egotism" and destroyed the "we-feeling" of Germans. For Stoiber, they had given rise to the maxim "To each his own and to me the most," which after 1968, he claimed, became the governing principle in society.[2] At the beginning of 2008, this love-to-hate discourse received a further boost with the by now infamous publicity stunt of historian and public intellectual Götz Aly, who compared West German student activists of the 1960s to the National Socialists of the 1930s in his latest book.[3]

Anti-1968 sentiment has figured in public discourse in other nations, as well. French president Nicolas Sarkozy declared himself the representative of the silent majority in the last national election campaign, vowing to take on the legacy of May '68. In Poland, President Lech Kaczynski recently broached the subject of his country's anti-Semitic crackdown on its Jewish citizens in March 1968. Finally, in Britain, historian Michael Burleigh argued that "1968 was a narcissistic celebration of youth as opposed to such values as caution, responsibility, restraint and shame," and that although "Ronald Reagan and Margaret Thatcher may have won major economic battles with the unions or the Cold War with the Soviets ... they largely sold the pass in terms of 'culture', where the Left still exercises a compensatory 'hegemony'."[4]

Yet such critical remarks, often acts of political posturing, tend toward a narrow, sometimes national view of the protest movements and fail to see the broader context in which they occurred. Interestingly, German chancellor Angela Merkel recently pointed this out concerning the current debate about "1968" in the Federal Republic, which she characterized as marked by a distinct provincialism. Recalling her own East German perception of the "profound atmosphere of departure" triggered by the Prague Spring, Merkel argued, "This movement existed in America, in France, in Germany, but also in Eastern Europe. Therefore, what I miss in the current debate is the positioning [of 1968] in international developments .... Germans should please not consider themselves so important and imagine that they invented 1968."[5]

That such national debates continue to be so insular, even after forty years, is striking. Only slowly is it giving way this year to a more global perspective that historians, activists, and adversaries alike have long

2 "68er schuld an mieser Wirtschaft," *Die Tageszeitung*, August 31, 2005, 7.

3 Götz Aly, *Unser Kampf. 1968 – ein irritierter Blick zurück* (Frankfurt, 2008).

4 Michael Burleigh, "We Beat the 68ers Once. We Must Do It Again," *Telegraph*, May 4, 2008.

5 "Und es war Sommer: Interview mit Angela Merkel," *Süddeutsche Zeitung Magazin*, No. 9 (February 2008).

recognized. As former British student leader Tariq Ali phrased it, "A storm swept the world in 1968. It started in Vietnam, then blew across Asia, crossing the sea and the mountains to Europe and beyond."[6] Moreover, in the impressive array of memoirs, interviews, and opinion pieces that appeared during or leading up to this fortieth anniversary, a more reflective and balanced tone can be discerned in comparison to earlier anniversaries—next to the traditional defiant posture, of course. As the Scottish journalist Magnus Linklater observed,

> It is easy to deride the middle-class rebels who wore Che Guevara T-shirts or worshipped Malcolm X before going on to hold down executive positions or comfortable professorships in the bosom of the Establishment that they had sworn to destroy. But if, by the end of that momentous decade, it was no longer acceptable for a police force to beat dissenters to within an inch of their lives or a communist dictatorship to crush freedom of expression under its boot, then they deserve some of the credit.[7]

Even one of the most well-known representatives of the revolt, Daniel Cohn-Bendit, provocatively announced this year: "Forget it: 68 is over—buried under cobblestones, even if those cobblestones made history and triggered radical change in our societies! ... So, revisit 68? Yes, but only in order to understand it, grasp its scope, and retain what still makes sense today."[8]

And this is precisely what we have in mind for tonight. Our intention is not only to outline the battle lines and conflicts of the 1960s but talk about the lessons and legacies of this colorful decade. It is therefore a great honor to introduce three people who have agreed to share their memories and opinions with us tonight.

Our first panelist is Norman Birnbaum. He has been described as "one of the country's foremost public intellectuals." He has been active in progressive politics on both sides of the Atlantic, advising US trade unions, Robert and Edward Kennedy, as well as a number of organizations and political parties in Europe. From the late 1950s to the mid-1960s, he taught in England at the London School of Economics, at Oxford University, and at the University of Strasbourg in France. He is one of the founding editors of the *New Left Review*. He witnessed the creation of the British and European New Left first hand. Both during his time in Europe and after his return to the US, he played an important role as a link between the protest movements on both sides

6 Tariq Ali, "Where has all the rage gone?" *The Guardian*, March 22, 2008.

7 Magnus Linklater, "1968: We Made a Difference," *The Times*, March 19, 2008.

8 Daniel Cohn-Bendit, "An Elusive Legacy," *The Guardian*, May 6, 2008.

of the Atlantic. Norman Birnbaum currently is University Professor Emeritus at the Georgetown University Law Center. He is on the editorial board of the *Nation* and is a regular contributor to American and European newspapers. He is the author of numerous publications, most recently the monograph *After Progress: American Social Reform and European Socialism in the Twentieth Century*. He is currently writing a memoir entitled *From the Bronx to Oxford and Not Quite Back*.

Our second panelist is Patty Lee Parmalee. She was active in the student movements on both sides of the Atlantic. A cofounder of the University of California-Irvine Students for a Democratic Society (SDS) chapter, she traveled to Berlin in December of 1967 to write a dissertation on Bertolt Brecht. Before she could complete her dissertation, she was swept away by the German student movement and became an activist in the German Socialist Student League (Sozialistischer Deutscher Studentenbund, which shares the initials SDS with its American counterpart). Working with the American group "US Campaign to End the War in Vietnam," she took part in various activities: She helped organize dissident GIs in West Berlin, went to Cuba as part of a German SDS delegation, and cofounded the first expatriate chapter of the American SDS in West Berlin. As she told me, in Germany she learned that knowledge of Marx could be used to analyze contemporary relations of power and thus be a tool for organizing. Patty Lee Parmalee has also taught comparative literature and social relations at the California Institute of the Arts and Ramapo College in New Jersey. She was the LA bureau chief and labor editor for the *Guardian* and a member of the steering committee of the New American Movement and the Union for Radical Political Economics. She is currently an environmental activist in upstate New York and serves on the editorial board of *Capitalism Nature Socialism*.

Our third panelist is Tom Hayden. According to the *New York Times*, Tom Hayden was the single greatest figure of the '60s student movement. He was a Freedom Rider in southern Georgia in 1961. In 1962, he was involved in drafting what would later become the founding manifesto of the American SDS, the Port Huron Statement. From 1964 to 1968, he was a community organizer in Newark, New Jersey. He also participated in the strike at Columbia University in April 1968 and the demonstrations at the National Democratic Convention in Chicago in August of that same year. For this, he and seven others were indicted in what came to be known as the Chicago Eight conspiracy trial. As part of his opposition to the war in Vietnam, he made several trips to Cambodia and North Vietnam, including an especially controversial one in 1972 with his future wife Jane Fonda. After the war, he entered politics in California and served in the California State Assembly from 1982 to 1992 and in the California State Senate from 1992 to 2000. In recent years, he has taught at Pitzer College, Occidental College, and the Harvard Institute of Politics. He has written or edited fifteen books and hundreds of essays and op-ed pieces.

Now I will open the floor to the panelists. They will begin with a statement about their experiences of 1968, and then we will begin the question and answer session. Would you like to start, Norman?

Norman Birnbaum: I am very glad to be here with my old friends to participate in another one of those marvelous German Historical Institute activities that enrich the cultural life of our city. We are supposed to talk about experiences in '68. At least in Germany, and to some extent elsewhere, the phrase "68er" [*Achtundsechziger*] designates a common generational experience.

Patty Lee Parmalee: They call that the hippie generation here.

Norman Birnbaum: This is less the case here in the United States, where you can observe the precipitous flight of one of the presidential candidates from her own past. At any rate, I can't claim to be a "68er." I would rather claim to be a "38er." This made some difference for how I lived through '68 and the 1960s.

I was born in 1926. Once after talking at a major institute in a country that now lives on stronger than ever in memory, the German Democratic Republic (GDR), I was taken out to a (very mediocre) lunch at the Opera Café on Unter den Linden. My host (I think it was Otto Reinhold, then head of the institute, which dealt with ideological matters for party and state) said that he could not understand how an American knew so much about Marxism. I replied that I had had, for my period, a typical New York adolescence. I made the transition from Stalin to Trotsky at the age of twelve. I was at twelve in 1938, which was the year of the Munich Conference, the *Anschluss* of Austria, and of the winding-down of the Spanish Civil War. Also, it was the year of the final electoral defeat of the New Deal, when Franklin Roosevelt attempted to purge the Democratic Party.

It was quite a year to come to political consciousness. I think the long experience of that has shaped my perceptions and, indeed, shaped my actions over time. I later saw both the consolidation and end of the New Deal in the emergence of the American warfare-welfare state. I had a perfectly good place to observe this transformation from—Harvard (with its near total integration both in actual governance and its exquisite practice of apologetics) between 1947 and 1952. Afterwards I had my first encounter with Europe. When I got there, I met the German Left in the form of [the Marburg political science professor] Wolfgang Abendroth and some of the survivors of the plot against Hitler. Not all of them, by any means, were on the Left. That was an encounter with a very different kind of conservatism than the one I had known in the US. It paralleled my learning about German Catholicism and Protestantism—strikingly different at the time from many American churches with their national triumphalism.

I then settled in England to teach. I participated in the beginning of the British New Left. Great Britain was, for once, in the second half of the twentieth century, ahead of its time: the British '60s began in the '50s. The British New Left was attached to a large mass movement, namely, the first wave of protests against nuclear weapons in England, the Campaign for Nuclear Disarmament (CND). I think that experience of the British New Left, which had a troubled dialectical relationship with the Labour Party, had an effect on my later perceptions of things.

I also kept close contact with both Germany and France. From 1964 to 1966, I taught in France, where I had previously come to know the left Catholics, and, of course, a steady stream of intellectual migrants from the Communist Party. My colleague was the great senior, older French Marxist and philosopher Henri Lefebvre, who had long since broken with the sclerotic French Communist Party. Intellectually, the ex-communists were among the most interesting people in France. They covered an enormous spectrum. Furthermore, in the Soviet Bloc, I met dissidents and revisionists. In Eastern Europe, a great many people followed the activities that culminated in Western Europe in 1968 with great interest on television and in books, and eagerly and stringently questioned their Western friends about it.

Now, if you ask what lessons I drew from this, I think one of them was that even though these phenomena were international, they each had a particular national flavor and particular cultural accents. They each had a particular relationship to national histories, either long term or short term. The British New Left is inconceivable without the legacy of a certain kind of militant Puritanism in England. Obviously, the French New Left was inconceivable without the whole French revolutionary tradition. And, of course, the West German experience was shaped by the memory of the years 1933-1945 and the disaster of the German Left in the Weimar Republic.

Similarly, I would say that, in this country, our own student movement, or rather the movements of protest, which united several very different streams—black protest, the civil rights movement, anti-imperial protest—did draw on moral traditions, sometimes unconsciously, sometimes transmitted by intermediaries of an older age. It did draw upon both American notions of progressivism and the idea of an open future, as well as on American religious or Christian traditions wherein the nation was the Church. Here in the US, those on the Left believed that the nation had to become a church of redemption. Perhaps that is why they often reverted to sectarian models of behavior.

After the excitements of the '60s, I was convinced that the only path for reform in the foreseeable future was to join existing reformist structures and to begin working with trade unions, with Democrats like Ted Kennedy, and the Progressive Caucus in Congress.

What I took from this experience and particularly from the more exhilarating periods of the '60s was a sense of the possibility of groups and persons developing historical creativity. There are situations that are historically open, not predetermined. Things erupt at different times as the result of an overdetermined sequence of historical causes. This leads me to think that '68 can't be repeated. It's not a model for contemporary action—witness the utterly different tonalities of the present radical discussions in our country. On the other hand, the possibilities for openings should never be discounted. Those who seek a different society have to prepare themselves to be ready for those openings while doing the less exhilarating daily work of striving for reform in the unredeemed world. Well that's that.

Patty Lee Parmalee: Well, that's a hard act to follow. It's kind of liberating to be able to talk about the '60s because I'm forbidden to talk about this around my daughter. Every year, I go to an old New Lefties summer camp for a week with some friends and relatives. All the kids there always say, "Is that all? All you people want to talk about is the '60s." And every year we look for a theme and ultimately say: "Ah, why don't we just talk about the '60s again." I think people are pretty sick of hearing about it.

On the other hand, I think that the younger generation is envious in some ways. They feel left out because this happened before they had a chance to run around in the streets and act crazy. Yet sometimes they are a little embarrassed that their parents were that crazy. But they wish they would see something like that come around again.

What I can talk to you about is the experience of having been on the ground in a local SDS chapter. This was at the University of California-Irvine in the year that university started, 1965. I came from the University of Utah the previous year, where I had organized a teach-in against the war in Vietnam. This was really early and in a really unlikely place. It was very successful, however. It turned out that there were a lot of professors against the war, even back then. Knowing that I was going to go to this new university that was starting up, I thought there should be some kind of student movement there. Somebody was going to have to start it. So I started thinking about what it ought to be.

I read an editorial in the *Nation* about the various different student organizations CORE, SNCC, etc. It mentioned that SDS was the only one that was multi-issue. And I thought: "Well, if we are going to have a brand new organization at a brand new place, it better be multi-issue." That's how I came to join SDS, reading about it in the *Nation* and deciding that it needed to happen in Irvine. It was pretty early, when Carl Oglesby was president of the American SDS.

I have just finished reading Carl Oglesby's book *Ravens in the Storm*. He has worked on it for God knows how long. Looking back on what happened to SDS (it eventually killed itself), Oglesby seems to see the whole thing as a debate between himself and Bernadine Dohrn. There were a lot of other people involved, however, although you can see the different positions by looking at these two personalities. Essentially, Dohrn argued that all of our demonstrations, all our organizing on the ground, and all our community work had not stopped the war. She said that we needed to get serious. And to get serious meant being willing to participate in stuff like bombing.

I was of a different opinion. I always thought what was most important was to be able to reach as many people as you can. If you engage in scary tactics, then you scare off the public. And the public is who needs to be persuaded.

When I went to Berlin at the end of 1967, I immediately got swept up in the student movement. They were planning a big anti-Vietnam War demonstration. It was going to be preceded by what was essentially a giant teach-in. The German SDS called it the Vietnam Congress. They asked me to speak as a representative of US SDS. I called the talk "From Protest to Resistance," stealing a phrase Students for a Democratic Society had been using to analyze its own current phase. For some reason, little though I knew about the German movement, I thought I (or, rather, US SDS) had a lesson to teach about being serious and moving the masses.

Little did I realize how much I would learn from working with the Germans for over a year. It was my first acquaintance with the use of Marxist theory for understanding the forces in one's own society and developing a strategy. I was very impressed by the high level of debate in the endless, smoke-filled meetings. I was a little less impressed by the militancy of demonstrations, which, while exciting, ultimately seemed counterproductive. This was before Baader-Meinhof extremism arose, and also before the (quite different) Weathermen surfaced in the United States. Yet people everywhere were increasingly frustrated about being unable to stop this immoral war and were desperate to do something. Due probably to my wide-eyed curiosity and enthusiasm to attend every planning meeting I could, I was told at one point that I was suspected of being in the CIA. Back then (not so very long after World War II, after all), in the United States, Germans and Germany still represented evil, and I wondered who should be suspicious of whom. But I must say that the people I had the fortune to work with there were generally very accepting and helped me to find niches where I could be useful; it was, in fact, truly an international movement.

Tom Hayden: Thank you kindly for asking me to share. I've benefited very much from Martin Klimke's work in Heidelberg and at the LBJ Library in Texas. The ongoing declassification of documents, which he has helped in, is essential to getting the history out for everybody.

The question asked was: What were you doing then? Forty years ago now, I was just recovering from the murder of Martin Luther King Jr. His murderer had fled to Canada and to Portugal with passports and money. Yet, he was continually described as another lone assassin. I was, of course, unaware that the murder of Robert Kennedy was coming just a few days later.

I had deep feelings about these murders because I had gone to the South, to Georgia and Mississippi, at the beginning of the 1960s to participate in the civil rights movement, the direct action movement, the voter registration movement, the sit-ins, and the freedom rides. I also had become a friend of Robert Kennedy. We had an ongoing relationship, and I tried to urge him to step up and to oppose the war in Vietnam. I think if he and King had lived, the '60s would have been another story. We would now know what might have happened if a progressive majority had come to power. We would also be able to answer the question of what you can do with political power under a President Kennedy advised and pushed by a Dr. King. A friend of mine told me with those murders we became not has-beens—that's a phrase—but might-have-beens.

These murders killed off the possibility of this progressive majority, and history took a different course. That's part of the reason people often think of the '60s as chaos: Murders, riots, sex, drugs, rock 'n' roll. There is that kind of a kaleidoscopic image of the '60s that does not help us to understand what the essence was. Rather, it is important to make a list of achievements to lift the image of chaos. Let's make such a list before we go into the discussion:

Voting rights for Southern blacks and for 18 to 21-year-old Americans: that's 27 million people who previously could not vote or who were not registered to vote; the Indochina wars were ended; the military conscription system, that is the compulsory draft, was ended; congressional checks and balances were placed on the FBI and the CIA, at least temporarily for about a ten-year period; the growth of the imperial presidency was checked; President Carter granted amnesty to 50,000 young Americans who had gone to Canada as draft and war resisters; the Freedom of Information Act (FOIA) was passed—as a direct result, millions and millions of documents, certainly not all fully disclosed, revealing the secret operations of government have become available; the Roe v. Wade abortion or reproductive rights decision was made in 1973 as a direct result of the women's movements and the general liberalization that came with the '60s; I would even include the environmental laws signed by Nixon—the establishment of the Occupational Safety Health Administration (OSHE), the Endangered Species Act, and the Clean Air and the Clean Water Acts, which were the strongest environmental laws passed to this point. Those were direct outcomes of Earth Day, a typical '60s event, in which 20 million people went out on the streets on April 22, 1970, after a movement was started by a handful of people just a year before.

I also would include the invisible but fundamental reform of what kids are taught in school and college. It may not be adequate, but that's good. That's why we have a once and future SDS here in the room. Then there was nothing like [the progressive historian] Howard Zinn—you could not read these things in the classroom. You read the classics. Maybe if you were a sociology graduate student like me, you could get a little into Marx. But basically everything that you considered relevant in life was excluded by definition from the school curriculum. To get it required demonstrations: In Berkeley, for instance, I remember participating in demonstrations that caused the National Guard to be called out for weeks. Helicopters sprayed CS gas on people; demonstrators were constantly beaten; I was arrested; different people were all arrested. What was it all about? It was about including Black Studies in the curriculum, Women's Studies in the curriculum, Environmental Studies. All of these things that are now in today's curriculum were put there by the crudest of methods, by social movements that forced universities to come to terms with their emptiness.

The list could go on: Two presidents were thrown out of office. You might think of the '60s as not having accomplished all of these things. I am telling you, however, that until you think so, you won't be able to reclaim this era. I'll argue that the single most important reason that the '60s ended, besides the simple fact of the calendar, is not the counterintelligence programs, not the faction fighting within the SDS. Although that is important, it was the assimilation by the political system and the culture of the core demands of the '60s.

The '60s ended when the '60s won. Ever since there have been attempts to overcome and destroy the '60s—usually during Republican tenure, during the Reagan period, in particular, and by so-called neoconservatives who have been running things just off the road from then until now in Iraq. That contingent, that faction, is a direct result of their hostility and hatred toward the '60s; they're still at it, and they will be for some time.

If you think there is a lot of attention to '68 in 2008, just wait. Coming to your neighborhood culture center or historical institute: the fiftieth anniversary of everything that ever happened in the '60s is about to begin. It will begin on January 1, 2010. Things being what they are, the fiftieth anniversary will be celebrated with more intensity than the fortieth, and this will go on for 10 years.

I have two more points to make in conclusion. Here is a question I have asked my friend Martin and many others: I don't think we have come to terms with why the '60s happened as a global phenomenon. My brief comment is that it was not like 1848. 1848 I believe, was Eurocentric.

Norman Birnbaum: Absolutely.

Tom Hayden: The '60s were like nothing that had come before, which meant that it required some new means of communication, of course. I think it has to do with the institutions of the Cold War that organized the whole world into pro-US and pro-Soviet and China, Africa, Asia, Latin America. It excluded anti-colonial revolutionary countries or independence movements.

Even the beatniks in San Francisco complained about the stifling nature of the Cold War, which required repression, which required apathy, which required fear. I remember as a young boy I was constantly being sent under desks during the school day and being told by the school teachers that this would provide protection from an atomic bomb. This attracted my great interest: how would the desk prevent the blast, which we had all seen in movies and on television inflicted on Hiroshima and Nagasaki?

The question of why it happened is partly answered by the Cold War and partly, I think, by the peculiar nature of young people who came of age at a time when they dreaded the future being more of the past.

Everybody I knew in the 1960s had a problem with their parents: Their parents had not gone far enough; their parents had compromised. Where were the elders? It was not a youth crisis—it was an elder crisis. The absence of elders meant that people at my age—20-21—were thrust into leadership roles without knowing much about leadership, social movements, or history. It was because of the deficit caused by the elders, which I don't want to see repeated.

I want to make one other point to bring us up to date: [Republican presidential candidate] John McCain was bombing North Vietnam in 1967; his history is in the 1960s. [Democratic presidential candidate] Hillary Clinton had just got out of Wellesley, where she was a rising student leader, a defender of the Black Panther Party, and all sorts of things that are not well remembered. Her roots were in the pragmatic wing of the radical feminist, countercultural, civil rights, and peace movements. And that leaves [Democratic presidential candidate]

Barack Obama. I am going to disclose something for the first time: He may run but he can't hide from his '60s origins as he's learning more about his Hyde Park friends. There will be more to come about his associations with members of the Weather Underground, SDS, and Reverend Wright. Things that happened when he was five years old will come back to haunt him. They will, because it's open, contested space. In about 1979-80, he was a student at Occidental College in Los Angeles. Barack was drifting and discovering his African-American identity; he was going through this process of post-adolescent identity formation. He came upon a table where students were distributing leaflets about a divestment rally from South Africa. They were Students for Economic Democracy, which was the student branch of the Campaign for Economic Democracy I was chairing. We were organizing on campuses the divestment movement from South Africa, which was wildly successful—far beyond anything we could have imagined. This encounter led to Barack taking a leaflet and giving the first speech of his life from that platform on the need for students to get organized and the need to divest from South Africa and apartheid. I know this story because I recently received an e-mail from the student organizer back then who wrote, "He's transformational. I tell you this story: I saw Obama give his first speech, and it was spectacular. We began Barack Obama's speaking career, signed: 'Americans in Spain for Barack Obama: send money.'"

Philipp Gassert: Thank you for this excellent first round, which touched on many of the issues we would like to discuss tonight. Let me bring up an anecdote that was hotly debated in this recent presidential campaign. The remark that Hillary Clinton got so much criticism for: that it was Martin Luther King Jr. who moved ahead with the civil rights movement. But it also took a president to implement laws via Congress. That brings me to the question that I was hoping you would address and which Tom has already talked about in part: What was the relationship between the movement and the more established politics of the 1960s?

Norman Birnbaum: Despite the absurd reaction of some to her remark, Hillary Clinton was right that it took Lyndon Johnson as well as Martin Luther King Jr. to make progress in civil rights. We are sitting here in the GHI lecture hall under the portrait of Willy Brandt. In Germany, the nationally unique anti-imperial and anti-militarist and anti-revanchist themes and motives of 1968 flowed into the German version of détente, Ostpolitik. Ostpolitik not only stabilized the situation on the border between the blocs; it also was a major precondition of that sometimes gradual, sometimes sudden expansion of political discussion and open political conflict in the state socialist societies, which, in turn, made the events of 1989 possible.

Recall the not quite forgotten ideological discussions between the Social Democrats of the BRD and the Socialist Unity Party of the GDR, in which the Social Democrats were represented by movement thinkers like Erhard Eppler and Johanno Strasser. Social movements like those of 1968 do not necessarily end in immediate political changes. They can be understood as shaping the attitudes of the age cohorts who participated in the movements, indeed, who collectively created these. The cohorts move on, circumstances change, but possibilities ostensibly closed remain in their psyches as something other than memories, as a reservoir of responses which can be drawn on, reshaped, and reactivated.

Philipp Gassert: So how do you see the relationship between the movement and established politics? Was Tom right about Nixon?

Patty Lee Parmalee: That's a tough question. I was listening to an interview that Amy Goodwin did with Gore Vidal this morning on *Democracy Now*. He said at one point that the idea was that every major movement against capitalism has only strengthened it. I'm so glad that Tom gave that positive list. The same thing has been said about the New Deal frequently. When the people rise and demand that capitalism reform itself and it then does reform itself, it becomes stronger because it needed those reforms.

Norman Birnbaum: And it is no longer the original capitalism.

Patty Lee Parmalee: Yeah, capitalism is a chameleon for sure. This brings me to the point that we need to talk more about socialism. In other words, capitalism can only reform itself so far, but it still is the root problem.

Tom Hayden: Was Martin Luther King Jr. needed as well as Lyndon Johnson? Yes. The way I would put it theoretically is that social movements begin with outsiders at the margins in quite mysterious ways: four students sitting at a lunch counter in Greensboro, North Carolina. They didn't act alone; they had conversations; they remembered things that other people had told them. But at the end of the day, they did decide to go there. They had no idea if they would be entering oblivion or be thrown out of school. But they actually had even less of a concept that they would be entering history.

So it's a mysterious process, but if the core demand resonates with enough people and if they can survive the initial opprobrium and repression, they will enter the mainstream. At least the demand will enter the mainstream, and, at that point, politics becomes involved because politicians will oppose them, support them, or try to come up with a compromised version. It's inevitable because that's what politics is. They'll get to a point where their demand has majority support and, inevitably in our history, their demand wins. They then get disillusioned because they then think that capitalism has been strengthened. Capitalists are very unhappy because they've lost a lot of money and they've given people certain rights and protections that they didn't have before. A counter movement always starts to try to undermine the gains of the movement.

So the thing that was wrong with Clinton's formulation was that it was just a little too much of the "great man theory." Did it take a president? Of course. Did it take Martin Luther King? Of course. But they were leaders of processes that involved millions and millions of people giving their time, going to meetings, writing leaflets, marching, getting their heads bashed in; some of them died. The way to look at this is that social movements eventually succeed and demobilize. The reason this is not apparent to us (and this is pointed out by Dick Flax, my old friend from SDS) is because the benefits of the social movement become a part of everyday life. You don't even notice that the social movements have succeeded. As their activists retire back to everyday life to enjoy the benefits, the radicals are really frustrated: without them the movement never would have succeeded. But when it succeeds there is no justification for their radicalism any longer, not on a mass basis. Radicals become stranded, unless you believe more thoroughly in reform, and this is something we need to ponder.

Philipp Gassert: Is that something that you were aware of at the time, this dialectic between the movement, radicals, and the established political forces? Or is that more of a historical insight?

Tom Hayden: No, this was the early SDS view.

Norman Birnbaum: I first met Tom in September, I think of 1962. You were in Ann Arbor. I was then making a kind of pilgrimage, a visit, to the United States as the resident American of the British

New Left, which was much read about. I had the impression that the American New Left was very much aware of its organic connections to the union movement and to the possibilities of the Democratic Party. The latter had just been enlarged by the Kennedy presidency, and therefore this dialectic [of established politics and the movement] seemed to be present.

There is another dialectic, a historical one. Christopher Hill, the great British historian of the seventeenth century, wrote a book called *The Experience of Defeat*. What happened to the Fifth Monarchy, what happened to the left wing of the Cromwellian revolution after the Restoration, and how did that go into English and British culture? They were on the margins, yet they permeated the culture. They affected the emergence of the so-called Country Party in England, whose ideas directly influenced the American Revolution. Some of these processes take a long time; some can be grasped immediately.

Patty Lee Parmalee: I remember that we endlessly talked about reformist reforms versus revolutionary reforms. We tried to figure out which reforms to work on, and when to enact them so that they would lead to further attempts at reform rather than just be an end in themselves. I remember the eight-hour day was an example that was always given because workers would then have more time to talk about politics after they finished working.

Tom Hayden: Marx didn't create the Soviet Union, but he had a hand in the eight-hour day. Right, there is no question that that was one of his principle demands, in addition to his support of workers' strikes. It was a very revolutionary demand at the time, and it became the foundation for social democratic parties and labor unions. It was achieved, and it remained a consensus in certain countries for about fifty years. But then you notice a counter movement. The eight-hour day didn't really make workers want to be more radical; they were relieved that they didn't have to work sixteen hours per day. And now you see the countermovement—in the States you'll face this immediately, and in Europe. Few people remember the eight-hour day. They're all working more than eight hours. The demand has been slowly eroded. But nobody ever announces on behalf of the establishment, "We have ended the eight-hour day during my term in office." Though it's been gradual, they have. The eight-hour day is a memory now, and people are just trying to get back to ten or nine.

Martin Klimke: Two final comments before we open the floor: The three of you have all been very positive in terms of the establishment response and the way protest finds its way into society. As you know, Marcuse wrote about the phenomenon of "repressive tolerance." This is something I want to toss out here, that there is an alternative view about the "success of protest."

Furthermore, when we talk about the 1960s, we always seem to talk about the New Left and the protest movements on the Left. You mentioned the arrival of the neoconservative movement, which also had its roots in the 1960s, with Barry Goldwater and the New Right. It could be a question of discussion here: Are we leaving that particular story out? Because the New Right learned a lot from New Left tactics and grass-roots organizing. But now, I would like to thank the three panelists and invite people in the audience to react to our discussions and ask questions.

Norman Birnbaum, University Professor Emeritus of Georgetown University Law Center, witnessed the creation of the British and European New Left first hand and provided an important link between protest movements on both sides of the Atlantic.

Patty Lee Parmalee was a student activist in both the US and West Germany in the late 1960s. Currently, she is an environmental activist in upstate New York and serves on the editorial board of the international journal of theory and politics, Capitalism Nature Socialism.

Tom Hayden, very active in the US student movement in the '60s, was involved in founding the American SDS. Today, he continues to be a social and political activist, as well as a politician, educator, and author.

ACKNOWLEDGMENTS

We would like to express our sincerest gratitude to the Goethe-Institut, in particular Wenzel Bilger from the "Science and Society" division and Christoph Bartmann, head of the "Culture and Information" department, at the institute's head office in Munich, for the constant support and outstanding cooperation in making this volume possible.

Furthermore, we would like to thank the online office and all the individual Goethe-Institut branches around the globe that supported this project in innumerable ways, as well as the many translators who provided earlier English versions of these texts:

Helene Adjouri for Syria;
Don Bartlett for Denmark;
V. Brasanac for Yugoslavia;
Charlotte Collins for Lebanon;
Jennifer Cove for Turkey;
Greg Czarnecki for Poland;
Franco Filice and **Giovanna Pistillo** for Italy;
Nancy Forest-Flier for Belgium and the Netherlands;
Michal Ginter for Czechoslovakia;
John Irons for Norway;
Maria Koublanova for Russia;
Frida Lejonqvist for Sweden;
Tim Nevill for Egypt, Palestinian Territories, and France (from Arabic);
Antonio Seidemann for Argentina, Bolivia, Colombia, Mexico, Peru, and Venezuela;
Patricia C. Sutcliffe for Japan (from German);
Karolina Taktikou for Greece;
Jim Tucker for Hungary;
Jonathan Uhlaner for Thailand.

In addition, we owe a debt of appreciation to Bryan Hart for his tireless efforts in procuring the images and copyrights for their inclusion in this volume and, above all, to Patricia C. Sutcliffe for her thoughtful copy-editing, as well as for skillfully managing the communication with and coordination among the many contributors and Goethe-Institut branches worldwide.

Philipp Gassert and Martin Klimke, editors

PHOTO CREDITS

AP Photo, front cover and pp.

100 (Thailand), 140 (South Africa), 211 (Greece)

Bettmann/Corbis, pp.

44 (Canada), 68 (Venezuela), 80 (China)

Collection International Institute of Social History, Amsterdam, p. 227 (Netherlands)

The Granger Collection, pp. 113 (Israel), 240 (West Germany)

Robert Havemann Gesellschaft, p. 160 (East Germany)

Klassekampen/**Norwegian National Library**, p. 234 (Norway)

(With the help of the library at Volda University College)

Picture Alliance, pp.
30 (Argentina), 34 (Bolivia), 49 (Colombia), 53 (Mexico), 60 (Peru), 64 (USA), 74 (Australia), 85 (India), 90 (Japan), 96 (Pakistan), 106 (Egypt), 122 (Lebanon), 127 (Palestinian Territories), 149 (Syria), 156 (Czechoslovakia), 164 (Hungary), 168 (Poland), 172 (Russia), 177 (Turkey), 182 (Yugoslavia), 193 (Belgium), 197 (Denmark), 201 (France), 206 (Great Britain), 217 (Ireland), 236 (Sweden)

Rogers-Viollett/The Image Works, Inc., p. 133 (Senegal)

SV Bilderdienst, p. 221 (Italy)

Lightning Source UK Ltd.
Milton Keynes UK
UKHW03f1220290618
324952UK00005B/219/P